BURT FRANKLIN: BIBLIOGRAPHY & REFERENCE SERIES 302

INDEX

EXPURGATORIUS

ANGLICANUS:

INDEX

EXPURGATORIUS

ANGLICANUS:

OR

A Descriptive Catalogue of the principal Books

PRINTED OR PUBLISHED IN ENGLAND,

WHICH HAVE BEEN SUPPRESSED,

OR BURNT BY THE COMMON HANGMAN,

OR CENSURED,

OR FOR WHICH THE AUTHORS, PRINTERS, OR PUBLISHERS

HAVE BEEN PROSECUTED.

BY W. H. HART

BURT FRANKLIN
NEW YORK

Published by BURT FRANKLIN
235 East 44th St., New York, N.Y. 10017
Originally Published: 1872-1878
Reprinted: 1969
Printed in the U.S.A.
This book is complete in five parts ending
    at numbered page 290.

Library of Congress Card Catalog No.: 76-80250
Burt Franklin: Bibliography & Reference Series 302

INDEX

EXPURGATORIUS

ANGLICANUS:

OR

A DESCRIPTIVE CATALOGUE OF THE PRINCIPAL BOOKS

PRINTED OR PUBLISHED IN ENGLAND,

WHICH HAVE BEEN SUPPRESSED,

OR BURNT BY THE COMMON HANGMAN,

OR CENSURED,

OR FOR WHICH THE AUTHORS, PRINTERS, OR PUBLISHERS

HAVE BEEN PROSECUTED.

BY W. H. HART, F.S.A.

PRICE TWO SHILLINGS.

LONDON:

JOHN RUSSELL SMITH, 36, SOHO SQUARE.

1872.

The object of this work, which at present it is believed is sufficiently indicated by the title, will be more fully explained in the preface, which cannot as yet conveniently be printed. It is not possible to estimate the exact extent of the work, but it will be included in one moderately sized volume, published in parts of similar size and price to that now issued.

W. H. HART.

October, 1872.

INDEX EXPURGATORIUS ANGLICANUS.

1

A SUPPLICACYON for the Beggers. (Compiled by Simon Fyshe, ANNO MCCCCCXXIIII.)

This book gave considerable uneasiness to Cardinal Wolsey, who was personally attacked in it, and sought by every means to discover and punish its author. It was prohibited by a proclamation issued in June, 1530. An account of Simon Fish, "a zealous man for the reformation of abuses in the church" will be found in Wood's Athenæ Oxonienses and Tanner's Biblioth. Britan.

2

The Newe Testament, in Englysshe, (translated by William Tyndale.

Assumed to have been printed at Cologne in the Office of Peter Quentell and finished at Worms by Peter Schoeffer, 1525. It was inhibited by order of Bishop Tonstall and Archbishop Wareham and burnt. An imperfect copy is in the Grenville collection, British Museum.

3

The Parable of the wicked Mammon. (By William Tyndale), 1528.

The Obedyence of a Christen Man, and how Christen Rulers ought to governe. (By the same), 1528.

These books were prohibited by the before mentioned proclamation of June, 1530.

4

The Revelation of Antichrist.   No date.

This book was prohibited by the before mentioned proclamation of June, 1530.

5

The Summary of Scripture.   No date.

This book was prohibited by the before mentioned proclamation of June, 1530. . It is a translation by Simon Fish from the German.

6

An exposition upon the fifth, sixth, and seventh chapters of Matthew.   No publisher or date.

Printed for Tyndale while he was in Holland in 1537 by R. Grafton, for which he was thrown into the Fleet for six weeks.

7

The historie of Italie, a boke excedyng profitable to be redde ; because it intreateth of the astate of many and divers common weales, how thei have ben and now be governed, 1549.   London.

This book was suppressed and burnt by the Common Hangman, but a reprint was subsequently made in 1561. The original edition is very rare. "W. Thomas," says Holinshed, "who wrote the History of Italie and other thinges verie eloquentlie, was hanged and quartered at Tiburne, 18 May, 1554, for conspiring to murther Queen Mary." He had been Tutor to Edward VI, and some of his letters are preserved by Strype.

8

The Union of the two noble and illustre famelies of Lancastre and Yorke, beyng long in continuall discension for the Crowne of this noble realme, with all the actes done in both the tymes of the Princes, both of the one linage and of the other, beginnyng at the tyme of Kyng Henry the fowerth, the first aucthor of this devision, and so successively proceeding to ye

reigne of the high and prudent Prince, Kyng Henry the eyght, the indubitate flower and very heire of both the saied linages. Whereunto is added to every Kyng a severall table. (By Edward Halle), 1550.

This book was prohibited by a proclamation dated June 13, 1555. (Foxe's Acts and Monuments, vol. 7, p. 127, ed. 1847.)

9.

A declaration of the succession of the Crown Imperial of England. By John Hales. London, 1563.

This book was written in support of the marriage and the claims of Lord Hertford's children by the Lady Catherine Grey. The Queen was so angry at its appearance that the author was committed to the Tower, and Bacon himself, the Lord Keeper, who was suspected of having had a hand in its appearance, fell considerably in his mistress's favour.

10.

An admonition to Parliament. 1571.

The authors of this tract were most probably the Puritan divines John Field and Thomas Wilcox. It was frequently reprinted, and in 1572 Field and Wilcox presented a copy to the House of Commons, and were immediately committed to Newgate. By a proclamation dated June 11th, 1573, the admonition itself, and "one other also in defence of the sayde admonition" were commanded to be delivered up on pain of imprisonment, "and her highness further displeasure."

11.

A Treatise of Schisme shewing, that al Catholikes ought in any wise to abstaine altogether from heretical Conventicles, to witt, their prayers, sermons, &c., devided into foure chapters. By Gregorie Martin, Licenciate in Divinitie, Douay, 1578.

This book gave great offence to the Queen and her ministers, for it invites the ladies about the Queen's person to imitate the example of Judith in ridding the world of Holofernes. Though printed in 1578 it was not till 1584 that measures were taken concerning it.   A copy had been sent by Cardinal Allen to William Carter, the printer for a new edition.   That very copy, wanting the title page, is now in the Bodleian.   The impression was seized, and on January 10th, at a Sessions held in the Old Bailey, for the gaol delivery of Newgate, Cartar himself was there indicted, arraigned, and condemned of high treason for printing this book, and was for the same, on the next day drawn from Newgate to Tyburn, and there hanged, bowelled, and quartered. (Holinshed.)

12.

A Letter sent by F. A., touching the Proceedings in a private Quarell and Unkindnesse, between Arthur Hall and Melchisidech Mallerie, Gentlemen, to his very Friend L. B., being in Italy.   With an admonition by the Father of F. A. to him, being a Burgesse of the Parliament, for his better Behaviour therein.   London, by Henry Bynneman, 1579-80.

A book presenting a curious view of the habits and manners of the young men of family and fashion in the reign of Elizabeth. It is reprinted in the Miscellanea Antiqua Anglicana.   Upon a motion made by Mr. Norton in the House of Commons on February 4th, $15\frac{80}{81}$, stating that this book was "done and procured" by Mr. Arthur Hall, a member of that House : it was resolved that the Sergeant at Arms be forthwith sent to apprehend Mr. Hall, and the printer was also to be sent for; and accordingly on the 6th February Mr. Hall was brought to the bar and admitted the offence.   On the 14th February it was resolved that he should be committed to the Tower for six months, and so much longer as until he should willingly make a retractation ; that he be fined 500 marks, and be expelled the House of Commons. (Vide Commons' Journals, vol. 1, pp. 122, 124, 125, 126, 132, 136.)

13.

The Discoverie of a Gaping Gulf whereinto England is like to be swallowed by another French marriage, if the Lord forbid not the banes, by letting her Majestie see the sin and punishment thereof.   Mense Augusti Anno 1579.

According to Camden* the Queen was much incensed at this book, in which those of the Council who favoured the marriage are taxed as ungrateful to their Prince and Country; the Queen herself (in the midst of several flattering expressions) is glanced at as unlike herself; the Duke of Anjou slandered with unworthy reproaches; the French nation odiously defamed; and the marriage itself, in regard of the difference of religion, (as of the daughter of God with a son of Antichrist) with virulent words condemned, as profane, dangerous to the Church, and destructive to the Commonwealth; and this proved out of the Holy Scriptures, miserably wrested. Neither would the Queen be persuaded that the author of the book had any other intent but to procure the hatred of her subjects against her, (who had always no less regard of the love of her people than she had of her own authority, and as Princes use to do, made it her chief care to preserve her reputation) and privately to open a gap for some prodigious innovation; considering that the writer had not so much as mentioned the security of the Queen and realm, or prevention of dangers to either, and that the States of the Realm had before with all earnestness besought her to marry, as the most assured remedy against the threatening mischiefs. These things she declared by public proclamation,† wherein having condemned the author of the book as a publisher of sedition, she highly commended the Duke of Anjou's good affection towards her and the Protestant religion, and expressed her resentment that so great an injury should be offered to so noble a Prince, and one that had so well deserved, who had desired nothing to be altered either in the commonwealth or religion: and withal, she commended Simier, the Duke of Anjou's agent, for his wisdom and discretion, whom some had loaded with calumnies and slanders. She also advertised the people that the said book was nothing else but a fiction of some traitors, to raise envy abroad, and sedition at home; and commanded it to be burnt before the magistrate's face. From this time forward she began to be a little more incensed against the puritans, or innovators, from whom she easily believed these kind of things proceeded: and indeed, within a few days after, John Stubbs of Lincoln's Inn, a furious hot-headed professor of religion, (whose sister, Thomas Cartwright, a ringleader amongst the Puritans, had married) the author of this book, William Page, who dispersed the copies, and Singleton

* Life and Reign of Queen Elizabeth, p. 486.
† Strype's Annals, Vol. 2, p. 562.

the printer, were apprehended; against whom sentence was given, that their right hands should be cut off, according to an Act of Philip and Mary, against the authors and publishers of seditious writings. Though some lawyers muttered that the sentence was erroneous and void by reason of the false noting of the time wherein the law was made; and that that Act was only temporary, and died with Queen Mary. Of this number was Dalton, who often bawled it out openly, and was committed to the Tower; and Monson, a judge in the Court of Common Pleas, was so sharply reprehended, that he resigned his place, forasmuch as Wray, Lord Chief Justice of England, made it appear that there was no mistake in noting the time; and proved by the words of the Act, that the Act was made against those who should abuse the King by seditious writings, and that the King of England never dieth; yea that that Act was renewed Anno primo Elizabethæ, to be in force during the life of her and the heirs of her body. Hereupon Stubbs and Page had their right hands cut off with a cleaver, driven through the wrist by the force of a mallet, upon a scaffold in the market place at Westminster. The printer was pardoned. I remember (being there present) that Stubbs, after his right hand was cut off, put off his hat with his left, and said with a loud voice "God save the Queen." The multitude standing about was deeply silent; either out of an horror of this new and unwonted kind of punishment, or else out of commiseration towards the man, as being of an honest and unblamable repute; or else out of hatred of the marriage, which most men presaged would be the overthrow of religion.

On October 5th, 1579, a circular was prepared from the Council to the bishops, to give notice to the clergy and others that the seditious suggestions set forth in Stubbs's book were without foundation, and that special noted preachers should declare the same to the people.

Eleven copies of this circular are in the Public Record Office unfinished, some signed, others not fully signed, and some not signed at all; from which it would appear that none were sent, and that the matter dropped.

14.

Henry or Harry Nicholas, The works of.

These productions, which include a miscellaneous collection of books and tracts on the peculiar principles of the sect called

The Family of Love, were by royal proclamation dated October 13, 22 Elizabeth, ordered to be burnt, and all persons declared punishable for having them in their possession without the ordinary's permission.

This *Family of Love* or *House of Charity* as they styled themselves, were sectaries out of Holland who persuaded their followers "That those only were elected and should be saved, who were admitted into that Family, and all the rest Reprobates, and to be damned; and that it was lawful for them to deny upon their oath before a magistrate whatsoever they pleased, or before any other who was not of their family. Of this fanatical vanity they dispersed books amongst their followers, translated out of the Dutch tongue into the English, they were entitled The Gospel of the Kingdom, Documental Sentences, The Prophecy of the Spirit of Love, The publishing of Peace upon Earth. The author, H. N., they could by no means be persuaded to reveal; yet was it found afterwards to be Henry Nicholas of Leyden, who with a blasphemous mouth gave out, that he did partake of God, and God of his humanity. (Camden's Life and Reign of Queen Elizabeth, p. 477.)

15.

The confession and execution of John Slade. The confession and execution of John Bodye. (1583.)

A black letter tract dedicated to "Maister H. S., by R. B., from Winchester." Slade and Bodye were sufferers under the oppressive laws of the time against the adherents of the Catholic religion, and were executed in the autumn of 1583. (See Challoner's Memoirs of Missionary Priests.) This tract was suppressed and the author punished.

16.

A book without title or date, but plainly of Catholic tendency. (1584.)

This book was alleged to have been published or dispersed on January 22nd, 1584, by one Robert Sutton, a yeoman, and Charles Ratclyffe, gentleman, both of Aylsham in Norfolk, for which they were prosecuted; but the indictment was held to be insufficient. [1] It charges that "Robertus Sutton nuper de Aylesham in comitatu Norfolciæ yoman vicesimo secundo die Januarii anno

1　Judgment Roll, Queen's Bench, Mich., 26 & 27 Eliz., roll 37.

regni dominæ Elizabethæ Dei gratia Angliæ Franciæ et Hiberniæ Reginæ fidei defensoris &c., vicesimo sexto apud Aylesham prædictam in comitatu prædicto advisate *anglice advysedly* et voluntarie publicavit ut veritati consentaneum quendam librum continentem in se hæc anglicana verba sequentia videlicet *not to be wyth the Pope is to be wyth antecryste* Et sic prædictus Robertus Sutton tunc et ibidem assistebat *anglice stode wyth* ad extollendam jurisdictionem Pontificis Romani præantea usurpatam infra hoc regnum Angliæ contra formam statuti in hujusmodi casu nuper editi et provisi et contra pacem dictæ dominæ Reginæ nunc coronam et dignitatem suas &c. Item alias scilicet die et anno prædictis ad sessionem prædictam coram præfatis justiciariis per sacramentum juratorum prædictorum similiter extitit præsentatum quod Carolus Ratclyffe nuper de Aylesham in comitatu Norffolciæ generosus vicesimo secundo die Januarii anno regni dominæ Elizabethæ Dei gratia Angliæ Franciæ et Hiberniæ Reginæ Fidei Defensoris &c. vicesimo sexto apud Aylesham prædictam in comitatu Norffolciæ prædicto advisate *anglice advysedly* et voluntarie publicavit ut veritati consentaneum quendam librum continentem in se hæc anglicana verba sequentia videlicet *not to be wyth the Pope is to be wyth antechryste* Et sic prædictus Carolus Ratclyffe tunc et ibidem assistebat *anglice stode wyth* ad extollendam jurisdictionem Pontificis Romani præantea usurpatam infra hoc regnum Angliæ contra formam statuti in hujusmodi casu nuper editi et provisi et contra pacem dictæ dominæ Reginæ nunc coronam et dignitatem suas &c.

17.

Modest answer to the English Persecutors; or a defence of English Catholics against a slanderous libel intituled "The execution of justice in England." No publisher or date.

This book was published anonymously, but is known to be the production of Cardinal Allen. Thomas Allfield, a priest, who had (says Dr. Challoner) [1] found means to import into the realm some copies thereof, "and had dispersed them by the help of one Thomas Webley, a dyer; was called to an account, as was also the said Webley, and both the one and the other were most cruelly tortured in prison; I suppose in order to make them

[1]   Missionary Priests, p. 84.

discover the persons to whom they had distributed the said books.
They were afterwards brought to their trial and condemned on
the 5th of July, (1585), and suffered at Tyburn on the day
following; where both the one and the other had their life offered
them if they would renounce the pope, and acknowledge the
queen's church headship; which they refusing to do were both
executed."

The indictment against Allfield is as follows, (Lansdowne M.S.
British Museum 33, no. 58.

Londonia scilicet. Juratores pro domina Regina præsentant
quod cum per quendam actum in Parliamento dominæ Reginæ
nunc tento per prorogationem apud Westmonasterium sexto decimo
die Januarii anno regni sui vicesimo tertio editum et provisum
inter alia inactitatum et stabilitatum existit authoritate parliamenti
illius quod si aliqua persona sive personæ post finem quadraginta
dierum proximo sequentium post finem illius sessionis ejusdem
parliamenti infra hoc regnum Angliæ vel in aliquo alio dominiorum
dominæ Reginæ nunc vel in aliquo alio loco extra dominia dictæ
dominæ Reginæ advisate et cum maliciosa intentione versus
dictam dominam Reginam nunc devisarent et scriberent imprim-
erent vel exponerent devisaret et scriberet imprimeret vel exponeret
anglice sett forthe aliquem librum rythmum canticum vocatum *a
ballade* literam sive scriptum continentem aliquam falsam sediti-
osam et scandalosam materiam ad defamationem Regiæ Majestatis
vel ad animandam excitandam vel movendam aliquam insurrection-
em vel rebellionem infra hoc regnum aut aliquod dominiorum eidem
regno spectantium vel si aliqua persona seu personæ post finem
prædictorum quadraginta dierum sive infra hoc regnum aut alia
dominia ipsius Reginæ vel in aliquo alio loco extra dominia dictæ
dominæ Reginæ advisate et cum maliciosa intentione versus dictam
dominam nostram procurarent vel causarent procuraret vel causaret
aliquem talem librum rythmum canticum vocatum *a ballade* literam
sive scriptum scribi imprimi publicari sive exponi *anglice sett forthe*
et offensione illa non existente punibili per statutum factum in
anno vicesimo quinto regni nuper regis Edwardi tertii concernens
proditionem sive declarationem proditionis vel per aliquod aliud
statutum per quod aliqua offensio facta sive declarata fuit proditio
quod tunc quælibet talis offensio reputaretur et adjudicaretur felonia
et offensores in eodem inde convicti et attincti existentes paterentur
tales pœnas mortis et forisfacturas prout in casu feloniæ usitatum
fuit absque aliquo beneficio clericatus sive sanctuarii allocando

offensori in ea parte prout per statutum prædictum inter alia
plenius apparet.   Cumque hoc non obstante quidam Willielmus
Alleyn Theologiæ Professor desiderans dictam dominam Reginam
supremam dominam nostram in odium et malevolentiam apud omnes
subditos suos inducere et quantum in ipso fuit efficere ut omnes
subditi ipsius dominæ Reginæ existimarent quod dicta domina
Regina fuit heretica et elapsa a vera Christiana fide et quod fuit
apostata princeps advisate et cum maliciosa intentione versus
dictam dominam Reginam quendam librum in partibus transmari-
nis imprimi fecit continentem quamplurimas falsas seditiosas et
scandalosas materias ad defamationem dictæ dominæ Reginæ
nunc et ad excitationem insurrectionis et rebellionis infra hoc
regnum Angliæ et ad subvertionem veræ et sinceræ Dei religionis
in eodem regno recte et pie stabilitatæ videlicet in uno loco in
eodem libro hæc Anglicana verba sequentia.   *They* (innuendo
Edmundum Campion Radulphum Sherwin et alios falsos proditores
nuper de alta proditione attinctos) *might have spoken theire minde
boldely nowe at theyre passage and departure from this worlde as sythence
that tyme we understande a worshipfull laye gentleman* (innuendo
quendam Jacobum Leyborne nuper similiter de alta proditione
attinctum) *did, who protested both at his arraynement and at his death
that her Majestie* (innuendo dictam dominam Reginam nunc) *was not
his lawfull Queene for two respectes, the one for her byrthe, thother for
the excommunicacion ; her Highenes having sought neyther dispensacion
for the first nor absolucion for the seconde.*   Et in alio loco in eodem
libro hæc Anglicana verba sequentia.   *By the fall of the kinge from the
fayth the daunger is so evident and inevitable that God had not sufficiently
provided for our salvacion and the preservacion of his Churche and holy
lawes yf there were no waye to deprive or restrain apostate Princes* (falso
innuendo dictam dominam Reginam fore Principem apostatam.)
*We see howe the whole worlde did runne from Christe after Julian to
playne Paganisme, after Valens to Arrianisme, after Edward the Sixth
with us into Zwynglianisme, and would doe into Turcisme yf any powrable
Prince will leade his subjectes that waye.   Yf our fayth or perdicion shoulde
on this sorte passe by the pleasure of everie seculer prince and no remedie
for yt in the state of the Newe Testament, but men must hold and obey
him to what infidelitie soever he fall, then we were in worse case* (innuendo
cunctum populum hujus regni Angliæ) *then heathens and all other
humayne commonwealthes which both before Christe and after have had
meanes to deliver themselves from such tyrantes as were intollerable and
evidently pernicious to humaine societie* (falso prætendens per illud dic-

tam dominam Reginam fore intollerabilem et perniciosum tyrannum societati subditorum suorum.) *The bonde and obligacion we have entred into for the service of Christe and the Churche far exceedeth all other duety which we owe to any humaine Creature. And therefore where the obedience to the inferior hindereth the service of the other which is superior, we must by lawe and order discharge ourselves of the inferior. The wyfe yf she cannot live with her owne husband (beinge an infidell or an heretique) without injurie and dishonor to God, she maye departe from him or contrariwise he from her for the like cause, neyther oweth the innocent partie nor the other can lawfullie clayme any conjugall dutie or debt in this case. The verie bond slave which is in another kinde no lesse bounde to his Lorde and Maister then the subjecte to his Soveraigne, maye also by the auncient imperiall lawes departe and refuse to obey or serve him yf he become an heretique, yea ipso facto he is made free. Finally the parentes that become heretiques lose the superioritie and dominion they have by lawe or nature over their owne children. Therefore lett no man marveile that in case of heresie the Soveraigne looseth his superiority over his people and kingedome* (innuendo per illud quod dicta domina Regina nunc perderet superioritatem super subditos suos). Et in alio loco ejusdem libri hæc Anglicana verba sequentia. *And as for his holines accion in Ireland* (innuendo invasionem per medium Romani episcopi in Hibernia factam) *we that are neyther so wise as to be worthie nor so mallaparte as to challenge to knowe his intencions, councell, and disposicions of those matters, can nor will neyther defend nor condemne, onely this is evidente that these small succors which were given by him* (innuendo dictum Episcopum Romanum) *to the Irishe, or rather suffered at their owne adventure to goe into those warres came uppon the ymportunate sute of the sore afflicted Catholiques, and some of the chiefest nobilitie of that countrye, of whose continuall complaintes knowne calamities, and intollerable distresses of conscience and otherwyse yt maye be he was moved with compassion and did that in cause of religion against one* (innuendo dictam dominam Reginam nunc) *whome he toke in his owne judgement rightly by his predecessor's sentence to be deposed, and in a quarrell in his sight most just and godly. And perhaps he* (dictum episcopum Romanum innuendo) *was the rather readie to doe this for Irelande, for that the sea Apostolique hath an old clayme to the Soveraigntye of that countrie.* Et in alio loco in eodem libro hæc Anglicana verba sequentia. *And this our countrie's scourge* (innuendo hoc regnum Angliæ) *proceedinge wholye of our notorious forsakinge the Catholicke Churche and sea apostolique* (innuendo sedem Romani Episcopi) *began first in King Henrie the eight beinge Radex peccati of our dayes* ubi revera Domina Regina nunc non fuit nec est heretica nec elapsa a vera Christiana fide nec fuit nec est apostata princeps nec incidit in heresim nec perdidit superioritatem et jus super cunctum populum et regnum suum et in quibus regnis revera nullus episcopus Romanus habet potestatem deprivandi sive deponendi aliquem principem. Quidam tamen Thomas Allfild nuper de Londonia clericus statutum prædictum minime ponderans felonice ut felo dictæ dominæ Reginæ nunc decimo die Septembris anno regni dictæ dominæ Reginæ nunc vicesimo sexto apud Londoniam videlicet in parochia Omnium Sanctorum in Breadstreate in warda de Breadstreate Londoniæ advisate et cum maliciosa intentione versus dictam dominam Reginam nunc prædictum librum prædicti Willielmi Alleyne continentem prædictas falsas seditiosas et scandalosas materias in Anglicanis verbis superius recitatas et quamplurima alia ad defamationem dictæ dominæ Reginæ nunc et ad excitationem insurrectionis et rebellionis infra hoc regnum Angliæ diversis subditis dictæ dominæ Reginæ publicari et exponi causavit *anglice, did cause to be published and sette forthe* contra formam statuti prædicti in hoc casu provisi et contra pacem dictæ dominæ Reginæ nunc coronam et dignitatem suas.

The following account of the trial of Allfield, which took place on Monday, July 6th, 1585, is taken from Lansdowne M. S., (British Museum) 45, no. 74.

The effect and the substaunce of the matter that was done and spoken at the arraignement of Thomas Allfeild, a Jesuett Preiste, att Newgate, uppon Mondaie, the fifth Julie, 1585.

First he and his ffellowes were brought from Newgate and placed at the barre. My Lord Maior, My Lord Buckhurste, the Master of the Rolls, My Lord Anderson, Mr. Sackforth, Sir Rowland Hayward, Mr. Owen, Mr. Younge, and the Recorder, sett downe uppon the Benche. Mr. Towne Clarke redd the Commyssion of Oire and determiner; after this, a substaunciall jurie of the best commoners to the nosmber of twentie or thereabowtes, were sworne to enquire, &c.

Then the Recorder gave that speciall charge that belongeth to that commission; after that done, the enqueste of inquirie went upp into the Councell Chamber at the Sessions Hall : in which place Mr. Attorney and Mr. Solicitor did reade unto the enquest the three severall indictmentes, and there the offenders, uppon good evidence geven were indicted. Billa vera was sett uppon everye one of them. The enquest returned to the courte, and beinge called by name they presented the bylls to the courte; the Towne Clarke received them and delivered them to the Recorder, and he opened them and showed them to the rest of the Justices howe they were fownde. And thereuppon the Towne Clerke was willed to call them to the barr and soe to arraigne them, who begane first with Allfeilde, and the indictment redd, he was demaunded whether he were gyltie of the matter conteyned in that indictment, to the which he would make noe aunswere, and prayed that he might be hard speake, and thereuppon he used a certen ffrivolous speache conteyninge noe matter, the effect whereof was that the cause in question was such, that the same owght to be tryed before learned men in Divinitie, and not before layemen; and after with much adoe he pleded not gyltie. And being asked howe he would be tryed, and also beinge tolde that he owght to be tryed by God and the countrie, he made a longe staye, and saied that it was noe reason that xij ignorant men should trye a matter of religion, but that it owght to be tryed by learned men. And then was it told him, that a matter in ffact was laied to his charge, viz., for bringinge into the realme and utteringe of a certen slaunderous and lewed booke against her Majestie and the realme, devised by one Doctor Allen. To the which Allfeild aunswered and saied expresslie that the same booke was a loyall booke, a lawfull booke, a good and a true booke, and that the same was prynted in Parrys under the King's priviledge there; and was allowed for a good and a lawfull booke throwghowt all the universities in Christendome beyonde the seas, and that it towched nothing butt matters of religion. And beinge asked whether it were a matter of religion that the Pope had aucthoritie to depryve the Quene of England, and he aunswered that in generaltie it was a matter of Religion that the Pope had aucthoritie *to deprive any Kinge yf he sawe cause,* ffor that the Pope was a regall kinge and prince and that he might take armes in hand as well as other kinges might doe. Yt was aunswered him that the courte sate not to trye matters of religion, but a matter de facto, that whether he browght the said slaunderous bookes into the realme, and whether he had disparsed them. To the which he aunswered that he had brought ffyve or syx hundreth of the same bookes into the realme, and that he had disparced them as he sawe occasion. And further he affirmed expresslie, that the booke was a good booke and lawfull, and declared as he had before done, howe the same was allowed, &c.   And after he was urged to put himselffe uppon his tryall, and was put in remembraunce what the punishment of the lawe was, yf judgement were geven against him, de payne fort et dure.   And thereuppon yt was asked him howe he would be tryed, and he aunswered by God and the countrye; and then he was told by the courte, that uppon the evidence geven, he should be hard att large, and then was a jurye of verie sufficient commoners called, and he was especiallie warned by the Towne Clerke to take his challenges unto them as they should come to the booke to be sworne.   The jurye beinge sworne, the indictment was redd, the which conteyned divers faulse, lewed, and slaunderous partes of Doctor Allen's booke, tendinge playnlye by expresse wordes, not onelie to treason, but most manifest and shamefull slaunders against her Majestie.   Yet did Allfeild not sticke to saye, *that it towched not the Quene any moore then it did the Frenche Kinge or Spanish Kinge.*   He travelled verie much to make the Commissioners to beleve that they understood *not the slaunderous booke, addinge, this withall the same booke was especiallie devised and wrytten by Doctor Allen to aunswere him who had wrytten the booke of Justice of Englande, and not to slaunder the Quene.*   And after much speache used, and manye repeticions made all to one effecte, by Allfeilde, there was delivered to the jurye one of the bookes to compaire the wordes of the indictment with the booke and the examinacions, and they fyndinge them them to agree, and hearinge him soe stowtlie to justifie the same to be a loyall booke. They retourned after a competent tyme, and beinge called by name and the prysoner beinge called to the barre, they were asked first of Allfeild, whether he were gyltye of the offence that was conteyned in the indictment.   The fforeman sayed gyltie, &c.

And after beinge asked what he could saye whye judgment of deathe should not be geven against him, he aunswered that the offence was pardoned, the pardone was redd, and yt was told him that his offence was excepted out of the pardone.   And then did the Recorder call him fourthe, and recyted the effecte of the indictment and howe that he was fownd gyltie; and told him that he wondered that his ffather in Kinge Henrie's daies, beinge an usher of Eaton, and of a good religion, and had brought upp many learned devynes, and other that served the Quene in temporall causes, whereof hundrethes, the Recorder himselffe was one of the meanest, and that the same prisoner passed thorough the same Colledge, and so to the Kinges Colledge, beinge both of the

Quene's highnes foundacion : and nowe had he so unnaturallie and beastlie behaved himselffe that he was become the first that ever was arraigned of ffelonye of any that ever passed those Colledges by the space of these fiftie yeres and moore. And then saied the Recorder, ye knowe that Christ paied trybute to Cesor, and commaunded that Cesor should be obeyed, and that eche man should yeld to Cesor his dewties. And that St. Paule in the end of the Actes was accused for Religion by the Jewes, and it was told him that he should be sent to Jerusalem to be tryed before the Preist there. And he aunswered that he stoode before the Tribunall or Judgement seat of Cesor, and there he owght to be tryed. And soe he appeled to Cesor, where his cause was hard, and he dismissed. Here, quoth the Recorder, ye see that Christe commaunded that Cesor should be obeyed, he saied not deposed. And St. Paule did appeell to Cesor and not to Peter, because he tooke Cesor to be his lawfull kinge. And all men knowe that Cesor was not of the faith of Christ, nor yet did he beleve as St. Paule did ; and after a fewe wordes moore he gave judgement, and commaunded the Sheriffes to doe execucion. This Allfeild appered to have noe skill at all eyther in the old or newe Testament ; there appeared noe manner of learninge in him ; he was bolde, stowte, and arrogant,—he behaved himselffe more arrogantlie then any that ever the Commissioners had hard or seene in theire tymes ; his wordes were such against her Majestie, that all the people fell into a murmer ; he never used one worde of reverence towardes her highnes. And att his passage to execucion the people offered to praye with him and he refused theire offer, and saied that if there were any Catholickes there he would be glad to have theire assistaunce.

18.

The discoverie of witchcraft, wherein the lewde dealing of witches and witchmongers is notablie detected ; the knaverie of conjurors, the impietie of inchantors, the follie of soothsaiers, the impudent falshood of cousenors, the infidelitie of atheists, the pestilent practises of Pythonists, the curiositie of figure casters, the vanitie of dreamers, the beggerlie art of Alcumystrie, the abhomination of idolatrie, the horrible art of poisoning, the vertue and power of naturall magike, and all the conveiances of Legierdemaine and iuggling, are deciphered, and many other things opened which have long lien hidden, howbeit verie necessarie to be knowne.   Heereunto is added a treatise upon the nature and substance of spirits and divels, &c.; all latelie written by Reginald Scot, Esquire.   1584.

Many copies of this book were burnt by order of King James I.

19.

A Lamentable Complaint of the Commonalty, by way of Supplication to the High Court of Parliament for a learned ministry, 1585.

For printing this tract Robert Waldegrave was kept prisoner in the White Lion for twenty weeks, as asserted by Martin Marprelate in "Hay any worke for a cooper."

20.

Martin Marprelate Tracts.
1.—The Epitome, 1588.   2.—Hay any worke for Cooper; penned and compiled by Martin the Metropolitane, ; no date.   3.—Martyn Senior.   4.—Martyn Junior.

For printing and publishing these books, Sir Richard Knightly, Mr. Hales, and Sir —— Wickstone and his wife, were cited into the Court of Star Chamber on Friday, the 13th February, 31 Elizabeth, 1588.   Knightley was many times member of Parliament for the County of Northampton in the reign of Queen Elizabeth.   He was a great favourer of the Puritan party, and at the expence of printing these libels, as was reported, being influenced by Snape and some other leading ministers of this County.   These libels were printed by one Walgrave, who had a travelling press for this purpose, which was once brought down to Fawesley, and from thence by several stages removed to Manchester, where both the press and the workmen were seized by the Earl of Derby.

Sir Richard and his confederates were cited into the Star Chamber, and received the following sentences: himself for allowing *The Epitome* to be printed in his house, fined £2000; Mr. Hales for allowing *The Supplication to Parliament* and *Hay any worke for Cooper* to be printed in his house, 1000 marks; Sir —— Wickstone, for obeying his wife and not discovering it, 500 marks; Lady Wickstone for allowing *Martyn Senior* and *Martyn Junior* to be printed in their house, £1000; and all of them imprisonment at her Majesty's pleasure. Upon the intercession however of Whitgift, Archbishop of Canterbury, whom they had most insulted, they were set at liberty, and had their fines remitted.

21.

A Dialogue wherein is plainly laide open the tyrannicall dealing of L. Bishops against God's children; with certaine points of doctrine, wherein they approove themselves (according to D. Bridges his judgement) to be truely Bishops of the Divell. 1589.

This book was burnt by order of the Bishops, and is alluded to in Udall's Demonstration. It is in the form of a dialogue between four speakers,—"a Puritan, a Papist, a Jacke of both sides, and an Idoll Minister." It was reprinted in the year 1640.

22.

A demonstration of the trueth of that discipline which Christ hath prescribed in his worde for the government of his church, in all times and places, untill the end of the world. No publisher or date.

For writing and publishing this book John Udall, a Puritan minister, was brought before Lord Cobham and others on Tuesday, the 13th January, 15$\frac{89}{90}$, and examined as to the authorship; but on his refusing to be sworn he was committed to the Gate-house close prisoner. On the 24th July, 1590, he was arraigned at the assizes at Croydon and found guilty, and the next day was brought up for judgment, but after long arguing with the judges he was respited on condition of writing a humble submission or supplication to her Majesty for his offence. In February, 159$\frac{0}{1}$, he was again brought up at the assizes in Southwark, when he received sentence; soon afterwards her Majesty was moved to grant him a pardon, but it was never obtained. On March 3rd, 1593, he wrote a letter from the White Lion prison, Southwark, to Lord Burghley, beseeching release, having been in durance for three years. The Earl of Essex, he said, had the draft of a pardon ready for her Majesty to sign it, and he besought his lordship to solicit her to do so; but the appeal was of no avail, and he soon after died in prison quite heart-broken.

There is a copy of this book in the King's Library, Brit. Mus., and on one of the fly leaves the following note is written in an early hand. " Mr. Udall.—For this booke he was questioned, arraygned, and condemned, at which time he sayd, 'The blood of Udall (as Abell's against Cayne) shall cry out against you;" but he was saved by means of Sir Walter Rawleigh's mediation to Queen Elizabeth, but imprisoned all his time. The chiefest things they tooke advantage at was that passage towards the end of the epistle to the Bishops. *If it come in by that means that it will make all your hearts ake, blame yourselves.*

23.

Certain discourses written by Sir John Smythe, Knight, concerning the formes and effects of divers sorts of weapons, and other verie important matters militarie, greatlie mistaken by divers of our men of warre in these daies; and chiefly of the mosquet, the caliver, and the long bow; as also of the great sufficiencie, excellencie, and wonderful effects of archers: with many notable examples and other particularities, by him presented to the nobilitie of this Realme, and published for the benefite of this his native Countrie of England. London, 1590.

This work, according to Strype's Annals, 4, 46, was forbidden to be sold. In the Lansdowne M.S.S., Brit. Mus., (No. 64, art. 43) there is a letter from Sir T. Heneage to Lord Burghley, dated May 24th, 1590, concerning the suppression by the Queen's command, of this book.

24.

A Conference about the next succession to the Crowne of Ingland, divided into two partes. Whereof the first conteyneth the discourse of a civill lawyer, how and in what manner propinquity of blood is to be preferred. And the second, the speech of a temporall lawyer, about the particuler titles of all such as do or may pretende within Ingland or without, to be the next successior. Whereunto is also added a new and perfect arbor or genealogie of the discents of all the kinges and princes of Ingland, from the Conquest unto this day, whereby each man's pretence is made more plaine. Directed to the Right Honourable the earl of Essex, of her Majesties privy councell, and of the noble order of the Garter. Published by R. Doleman. Imprinted at N. with licence, MDXCIIII.

The intention of this book was to support the title of the Infanta against that of King James, after the death of Queen Elizabeth· The real authors were Robert Parsons the Jesuit, Cardinal Allen, and Sir Francis Englefield; and the printer is said to have been hung, drawn, and quartered.

It was rigorously suppressed, and by the Parliament of 35 Elizabeth it was enacted that "whosoever should be found to have it in his house should be guilty of high treason." It was also condemned by the University of Oxford on account of its dangerous positions, particularly that which says "Birthright and proximity of blood do give no title to rule or government;" and was burnt in the School Quadrangle there in July, 1683.

According to Camden, in his Life and Reign of Queen Elizabeth, (p. 576) the purport of this book, which quite laid aside the business of birthright, was : *That the ancient laws of the land relating to hereditary succession ought to be altered. That new laws ought to be made about the choice of a King, and that none but a Roma Catholick, how near akin soever to the Crown, ought to succeed to it.* Most of the Kings of England they traduced as mere usurpers,

and all of the blood-royal in England as illegitimate, and so
uncapable of succession. The King of Scots' title to the crown,
though most certain and indisputable, they attempted to invalidate;
and by sham tricks and devices endeavoured to set up the Infanta
Isabella, the King of Spain's daughter, purely for being a Roman
Catholic; a thing I am ashamed to mention, because *the Priest's
lips ought to preserve knowledge, and they should stand having their
loins girt about with truth.* Their first plea was, because, as this
book pretends, she fetches her pedigree from Constance, the
daughter of William the Conqueror, King of England, and wife
to Alan Fergant, Earl of Bretagne; whereas notwithstanding
Gulielmus Gemeticensis, who lived about that time, declares in
his last book, that she died without issue, and he is followed by
the consent of all the writers of the affairs of Bretagne. The next
pretence was, because she had her descent from Eleanor, the
eldest daughter of King Henry II, who was married to
Alphonsus IX, King of Castile, whereas Pope Innocent III makes
it out in Matthew Paris, (p. 381), that Maud, the wife of Henry
Leo, Duke of Saxony, and mother of the Emperor Otho IV was
his eldest daughter; and Robert, abbot of St. Michael's Mount,
who christened her affirms that she was born 1162. A third
argument was, because she was a descendant from Blanch, the
eldest daughter of the said Eleanor, which was proved to be false
both by Roderigo, Archbishop of Toledo, in his ninth book, and
Pope Innocent, a writer of better credit, and both of them living
in the same age. Another reason alleged was because she came
originally from Beatrice, the daughter of Henry III, King of
England, though 'twas forgot, in the mean time, that she had two
brethren, Edward I, King of England, and Edward, Earl of
Lancaster, from whom a great part of the nobility of England
were lineally descended, besides the Royal Family. Again they
asserted the Infanta's claim by the House of Portugal, and
maintained on the same bottom the title of the Dukes of Parma
and Braganza, from Philippa, the daughter of John of Gaunt,
Duke of Lancaster, whom they make to be his eldest daughter by
his wife Blanch; whereas Frosard, who was a courtier at that
time, proves (fol. 169 of the second part of his history) that his
eldest daughter was Elizabeth, wife to John Holland, afterwards
Duke of Exeter, from whose loins proceeded a large race of
nobility, all the kingdom over.

Among the Domestic State Papers of the reign of Queen Elizabeth there is extant a copy of a letter from Robert Parsons to an unknown recipient, dated June 15th, 1599, concerning the book now under description.   It is as follows:—

Doctour Gifforde hath a lettere to prove this discourse is of Parsons' doinge.	"The opinion and judgmente of "C. A. before his death, concerninge "the late printed booke of the Suc- "cessyon, and certayne pointes "therunto appertayninge.

"For that you are desirous my lovinge Frennd to understande
"of certayntie whether C. A. before his death had reade the late
"publyshed booke aboute the Successyon, and what his opinyon,
"judgment, and censure was of the same, and of all that
"affaires; and for that you shewe in your lettere, that greate
"difference and varyetie in judgmentes, discourses, reasons, and
"affectyons doe beginne to discover themselves ther, where you
"are about this matter, I shall answere your whole demaunde as
"truly and perticulerly as the compasse of a lettere will give me
"leave; havinge had (as you knowe) noe small meanes (by reason
"of my intrinsicall familliarrytie with C. A. and in his most
"secrette affaires) to knowe his meaninge fully in the cause.
"First, when I did assure you that C. A. reade over the booke
"more then once, and that with much attention, and liked the
"same excedinge well for the whole subjecte and argumente
"therof, esteminge yt very necessary for all sortes of English
"people that such a booke should be written, to give them lighte
"in a matter importinge them soe highlye as doth the successyon
"of the Crowne, wherof *all dependeth, that is to say, (as he was*
"*wonte to saye), both life, honor, goodes, and a greate peace of the*
"*soule;* and he woulde often affirme *that noe lawe in the worlde*
"could be more unjuste or more contrary to all reason or con-
"science then to forbide men to speake or treate of that which
"above all thinges concerneth them moste.   Secondly, I can tell
"you also that C. A. had studyed much this matter of successyon
"before his death, and had gathered divers notes and observa-
"tyons together with intention as yt seemeth *to have written*
"*a discourse* therof himselfe, if he had not bynne prevente by this
"other booke, which did soe much contente and satisfye him, as
"presently he lefte of that cogitation, and sente all his papers,
"or the most parte therof, unto Mr. Fra. Peter, with whome he

"had conferred largly not longe before his deathe, by letteres of
"this affayre, doubtinge somwhat whether the time for some cir-
"cumstances were fitte or noe to let the booke goe abroade,
"thoughe on the other side he were full of opinion that if it
"founde free passage it coulde not chose but doe infinite good.
"And as for the firste parte therof, which treateth of matter more
"in generall, and *sheweth that propinquity and ancetry* of bloude
"alone, althoughe it weare certaynely knowne, is not suffycyente
"to challenge admissyon to a crowne, excepte other conditions
"and circumstances requisite be founde alsoe in the person that
"doth pretende ; as namely, *witte, reason*, and above all other
"thinges true religion ; and that many nexte in bloude Royall
"have bynne justly barred and putt backe, and some alsoe
"deprived which were in posessyon, for these and lesser defectes,
"in all Christyan countryes throughout the worlde, and that this
"was allowed and ratifyed by God himselfe, and that all Christ-
"yan commonwealthes *had authoritye, yea obligation*, to doe and
"followe the same when just occasyon shoulde be offred.
"All these pointes, I say, which are largly handled in the firste
"parte of this booke, C. A. did greately like and allowe of, and
"sayde that they were pointes both true and evidente in them-
"selves, and substancyally proved by the auther of the booke ;
"and for the sayde author not to exasperate any parte, houldeth
"himselfe in these generall tearmes and propositions onely,
"without descendinge to perticulers.   C. A. was wonte to aply
"them to perticuler state and case of Englishe Catholiques
"in these our dayes, affirminge not onely they mighte use this
"libertye of admittinge or rejectinge the next pretender, what-
"soever his tytle were by meanes of bloud, in respecte of his false
"religion.   But moreover, that they *were bounde in conscynce* soe
"to doe, and that none mighte without committynge grevous
"synne, favour, further, ayde, or give consente to the admissyon
"of any Prince when the place should be voyde, that was knowne
"or justly suspected to be enimye to the Catholique Romayne
"faythe, or undoubtedly affected towards the same ; and whoso-
"ever for worldly or humayne respectes, as countryshippes, kin-
"dred, freindshippe, proper intereste, or the like, should beare a
"contrary minde to this, did greatly offende God therin, and
"oughte not to be accompted a true and zealous Catholique ;
"moreover, that all such as in our dayes or former tymes have
"**follow**ed the contrary courses in chosinge or admittinge ther

" princes, not respectinge God and his cause in the firste place,
" accordinge to goode conscyence, but followinge those humayne
" respectes above mentioned, have alwayes *lightly receaved theire*
" *distructyon by those selfe same Princes* whome soe corruptly they
" preferred; wherof C. A. would recounte often tymes more
" perticuler examples, and notable storyes both of our Country
" and of others round aboute us, and alwayes woulde conclude
" that whatsoever Englishman after soe longe a storme of heresye
" woulde not sticke onely and wholy to a knowne Catholique
" Prince for the next successyon, woulde adventure to followe
" other blinde, and broken hopes and respectes agayne was not
" worthy to have the name of opinion of a sounde Catholique,
" but either of a fonde or mallityous polliticke, and thus much
" for the firste parte of the booke.
" Touchinge the seconde parte, wherin the severall and perticuller
" titles of five royall houses or lyneages are discussed,—to witte,
" of the house of Scotland, Suffolke, Clarence, Britaigne, and
" Portugall; and they by the pretencions of all such perticuler
" persons as in our dayes doe or may pretende to the nexte suc-
" cessyon of Englande, by reason of the sayde houses; as namely
" the Kinge of Scottes, the lady Arbella in the house of Scotland,
" the Earle of Hertford's children, and the Earle of Darby in the
" house of Suffolke, and the Earle of Huntingdon and the Pooles
" in the house of Clarence, the lady Isabella, the Infanta of
" Spaine in the house of Bretaigne, and the Kinge of Spaine with
" the Dd of Parma and Braganza in the house of Portugall;
" of all these pointes, after dilligente readinge over and wayinge
" the booke, C. A., his opinyon was as followeth.—First, that
" ther was soe much sayde in this booke for and agaynst everye
" one of these five houses and the different pretenders that are in
" eache one therof, as in a very wise and learned man's judgment
" and conscyence was sufficyente to brede greate doubte which
" house hath the best tytle by neerenes and lawfulnes of bloud
" onely, all and every parte havinge probable reasons for itselfe
" and againste his adversarye, wherof he did inferre, that if the
" adversitye of religion where not in all these competitors such
" and soe greate as it is, yet might a good man for other lesser
" respectes and considerations of the whole publicke, make choise
" of any one of these house, or at the leastewise of the principall-
" este, with sufficyente reason to secure his conscyence for not
" doinge againste the right of successyon, the sayde righte beinge

" soe doubtfull and ambiguous as this auther doth prove it to be.
" Secondly, his judgmente was, that in respecte of restoringe or
" establishinge of the Catholique religion in our countrye, with
" other pointes therunto belonginge, much lesse doubte or scruple
" may there be, to choose, admitte, or refuse any one of these
" competitors which may be presumed *woulde best performe the*
" *sayde establishmente of religion*, and with lesse danger, trouble,
" warre, bloudshed, or dangers of our Countrye and common
" wealthe, wherunto princypally and onely, he would alwayes
" say, that good and wise oughte to have theire eye more then to
" other lesser respectes of fleshe and bloude.   And whether the
" partie was borne at home or abroade, weare of kindred or the
" like, for that the former points of religion, equitye, wisdome,
" couradge, and vertue in a Christian prince, maketh his people
" and common wealthe happye, and not whether he was borne
" amongst them or noe, and consequently are more to be respected
" in admissyon or conclusyon of any competytors.   And as for
" the severall tytles of these five houses, C. A. was wonte to saye
" that he would have wished with all his harte the like I have
" heard Mr. J. P. say alsoe, that seinge K. H. 7th was
" once placed in the Crowne, and had shewed himselffe a good
" Catholicke kinge, his yssue might have enjoyed the same for
" ever without any change or further examination of theire
" righte; but now forasmuch as through the haynous synnes as
" may be supposed of K. H. the 8, his ofspringe are fallen
" from the sayde Catholique religion, yt semeth God's most
" just judgmentes that ther tytles are called in questyon; and
" forasmuch as the tytle of Kinge H. 7th, of whome descended
" the twoe houses of Scotland and Suffolke, cometh but from
" John, Duke of Somersette, bastard sonne to John of Gaunte,
" Duke of Lancaster, by his thirde wife; and then the tytle of
" the house of Portugall cometh from Ladye Phillippe, eldest
" and lawfull daughter of the sayde John of Gaunte.   And that
" moreover C. A. had perticuler intelligence which the author of
" the booke seemeth not to have knowne when he wrotte yt, that
" yt apeareth to this daye by the recordes of England that when
" the aforesayde John, Duke of Somersett, (of whome Kinge
" Henry the Seventh and his line descendeth) was legittymate by
" parliamente, expresse exceptyon was made that noe pretention
" therby should be given to him or his posterytie for the Crowne
" of England; for these reasons and many others which the

"author aleadgeth in his booke, it semeth to C. A. that if the
"cause of Portugall should be put before equall judges, it
"woulde be very doubtfull which party woulde gette the better.
"And for the house of Clarence C. A. never made any accompte
"of the tytle in comparison of the yssue of Kinge Henry the
"Seventh, seinge that they of Clarence onely doe pretende by
"the daughter of George, Duke of Clarence, of the house of
"Yorke, yonger brother to King Edward the Fourth, and the
"house of Scotlande and other yssue of King Henry the Seventh,
"descended of Elyzabeth, eldest daughter of the same Kinge
"Edward the Fourth, whoe was eldeste brother to Duke George;
"soe as in the very house of Yorke the lynes of Scotland and
"Suffolke doe goe evydently before that of Clarence; and thus
"for the tytles of those foure houses. Touchinge the fifte house
"of Britagnye and Fraunce, whose heire is the lady Infanta of
"Spaine, C. A., his opinyon was that much was sayde and
"pithely in the booke, and that the quallitie and circumstance of
"the personne pretendente doe greatly comend the pretence, for
"that all thinges considered, he did see noe other person in the
"worlde soe fitte to ende all controversies, to breake all difficul-
"tyes, and to avoyde all dangers on every syde, as if this lady
"should be agreed on of all handes to have her title established.
"This C. A. would prove by manie arguments, utillityes, and
"commodyties which he sayde woulde ensue by this meanes more
"then by any other, as alsoe by the difficultyes and damages of
"all other wayes, whatsoever should be devised. For firste, he
"was wonte to saye, that if the house of Portugall should be
"preferred, many difficultyes would be aboute the admittinge of
"the Kinge of Spaine, both for that the English, of what stocke
"soever, would not willingly yelde to have ther Crowne subjected
"to any other, nor would other Christyan princes rounde aboute
"like of that increase of soe greate a monarchye, and conse-
"quently there woulde followe much warre and bloudshed; for
"the Dukes of Parma and Braganza, which alsoe are of this
"house of Portugall, though they be worthie Princes, yet greate
"difficultyes doe seeme woulde followe, both for that they wante
"forces sufficyently to gette and defende soe greate a Crowne;
"as alsoe for that theire tytles to the successyon of Englande
"may seeme in parte to be decyded against them alreadye in the
"controversye that is paste of the Crowne of Portugall, though
"some men will saye that there is a difference in the state of

" these twoe successyons. In the house of Suffolke, that con-
" teyneth the Earles of Hertforde and Darbye there are partely
" alsoe the same, and partly farre greater difficultyes; the same
" for that the powers are not like to be sufficyente for soe
" difficulte an enterprise, and farre greater, for that the tytles
" doe seeme evidently behinde that of Scotlande, which cometh
" of the eldeste daughter of King Henry the Seventh, and ther
" is onely of the yonger syde the impedimente of the religion,
" wherof I shall speake presentlye. There remayneth then onely
" the house of Scotland, and namely the Kinge's tytle, for of
" Arbellae's pretention C. A. never made any accompte at all,
" she beinge as is knowne of a seconde marryadge, and that
" intangled with many difficultyes and doubtes as the booke
" declareth; about which tytle of the Kinge of Scottes, C. A.
" was wonte to saye that albeyt for the causes above mentyoned
" of the quiet posessyon of Henry the Seventh, he was longe
" desirous that noe mutation should be made in this yssue,
" espetyally as longe as the Queene of Scottes lived, which was a
" knowne Catholique, and soe longe after her death as there was
" any hope of the reduction and conformitye of her sonne (nowe
" Kinge) to the Catholique faithe; upon which hope both C. A.
" and Mr. Fr. P. and other the freindes labored earnestly for
" his prefermente divers yeares together, yet afterwardes seinge
" the perseverance of the Kinge in his professyon of herysie, and
" consyderinge that havinge bin broughte up and nourished in
" the same from his tender yeares, though otherwise as it is
" thoughte of noe evill nature, it would be hard to expecte any
" sure or firme reduction in a prince of his yeares and libertye,
" and that of this one pointe notwithstandinge depended the
" whole good or distruction of our whole country and realme, C. A.
" beganne seriously to thinke better of the matter, and findinge by
" searche that the small obligation that he or other of the English
" nation have to this Kinge in respecte of his neernes of
" bloud above the reste as abondantly is shewed in this booke;
" and that on the other syde, conscyence did forbyd him to faver
" a pretendor of his religyon, what tytle or nerenes in bloud
" soever he had. For these causes and considerations C. A.
" changed his whole opinion in that behalfe; espetyally after
" divers learned and grave men of the Kinge's owne natyon
" which for many yeares had labored to doe him good every way,
" gave testymonye upon theire conscyences, they had noe hope

" or probabillitye lefte of his conversyon. And matters standinge
" thus, and beinge once brought within differency into this
" ballance of due consideration, ther offred themselves alsoe
" above and beyonde this, divers other pointes alsoe not unwor-
" thye to be wayed,—as for example, the hard and bricke com-
" bination or joyninge together of English and Scottes natures,
" customes, enclinations, and wills, under one Kinge, the dislike
" and repugnance that all other princes rounde aboute us would
" have that these kingdomes should be joyned in one, from which
" twoe fountaynes onely (if noe other difficultye were there)
" woulde never wante in matter both of endlesse strife from the
" firste of the twoe, neither helpe to encourage, continue, and
" maintayne the same from the second fountayne, which twoe
" ga.. inconveniences beinge joyned with the former, which is
" the greateste and chefeste of all others, that may be to witte,
" the King beinge soe hartely affected to heresye and drowned in
" the same, and soe allyed and entrapped every waye with
" heritiques that if he should for a shewe or for any temporall
" respecte, upon the perswasyons of some pollitique or Athiste,
" make countenance to be a Catholicke, ther could never be any
" true assurance had therof, nor hope of any sincere reformation
" by his meanes. All these considerations layde together in the
" brest of C. A., (that desired nothinge but the true honor and
" service of God, assurance of religion, and good of his Countrye),
" made him very pensive before his deathe, and to write many
" longe letteres of his owne hand to Mr. F. P. whoe then lay sicke,
" and finally after much musinge, and espetyally after he had
" much vewed and waighed well the reasons and discourses of
" this booke, he wholy thoughte to have changed his minde and
" to thinke of another surer course for the remedy of Englande.
" And it seemed that this cogitation was that if all other pretend-
" ers mighte be broughte to yelde to the tytle of the lady and
" Infanta of Spaine, noe waye nor meanes in the worlde coulde
" bee thoughte of, more sweete, agreable, and convenyente for all
" partyes and for all effects, for these reasons following. First,
" that she beinge the daughter and sister of whome she is, and
" of soe rare worthynes in her owne person as all the worlde
" talketh of, she could not be but indifferente and amyable unto
" all, neither coulde she wante sufficyente forces for her estab-
" lishment and defence afterwardes, and beinge maryed with
" some noble Catholique prince such as the Kinge her father

"should like before of, and England not mislike, albeit in theire
"owne personnes they woulde be strangers unto us for a tyme,
"yet would that quickly passe awaye, and then children would
"be Inglishe borne, and themselves entringe not by force, but
"by love and composition, would hould peace with all, and be in
"feare and jelosie of none, which in other pretendors cannot be
"soe effected; they would attende alsoe principally to the
"assurance of Catholique religion as the grounde of theire
"estate, wheras others must needes doe the contrarye for hould-
"inge ther freindes and partyes contented, and finally by this
"meanes all subjectyon to forrayne countryes or natyons should
"be avoyded, and England should gayne the power, ritches, and
"freindship of Spaine to asiste it in all needes, without perill of
"subjectyon to the same.   And if any would objecte that the
"lady Infanta or her ofspringe may come to live to inherite the
"kingdome of Spaine if the prince should have noe yssue, and
"consequently bringe England under that crowne, as alsoe the
"princypall, C. A. would saye that provisoe might be made alsoe
"thus,—to witte, that in such case the seconde childe or nexte
"of bloud might remayne with the Crowne of England, and soe
"avoyde that conjunctyon or subordination; moreover he sayde
"that noe composition could be soe profitable or sure as this, for
"our domesticall competitors, who otherwise of all liklyhood
"must needs extirpate and destroy the one the other, and all
"would joyne together to vex and weary the Scotts if they should
"come in, to which ende and effecte they should never want
"partyes, neither at home nor from abroade, as by reason is
"evidente, and soe our country therby would become a contin-
"uall feilde of warre and bloudshedde.   And wheras of all other
"pretenders the Kinge of Spaine is knowne to be most power-.
"able, and hath noe small title by the house of Lancaster as by
"this booke apeareth, noe way can be thought of, soe fytte and
"forceable to apease and ende that tytle, as if nowe by way of
"composytion he should be perswaded (as perhaps he might) to
"passe the same over to his daughter the lady Infanta, as by all
"likelyhood he might be induced to doe with good likinge alsoe
"of the Prince his sonne, for the affectyon that both of these
"must nedes beare to this lady, and for endinge of strife amonge
"our nation, and benefitinge our countrye, yf his Majestie by
"conveniente meanes were delte with herin, as C. A. greatly
"wisheth he mighte.

"These were the prudente and godly cogitations of C. A. in his
"latter dayes, wherof much he conferred with divers of his con-
"fidente freindes, and namely with Mr. F. P. by letteres as
"before I have sayde, and was privie to the same, and doubt not
"but many of those letteres and discourses are forthcominge
"when tyme shall serve, and for that he understoode that some
"of our nation that live out of Ingland did take other courses
"and made a devision from the reste, either upon passyon or
"other perticuler respectes or humaine infirmityes, not entringe
"soe deply and sincearly into the true consideration what is beste
"for God's service, and assurance of Catholique religion, and
"for the perfecte reductyon of our countrye to peace, justice, and
"pietye, he was much greved therwith, and toke it for a
"dangerous and evidente deceipte of the divell to bring all
"therby to devisyon and dissolation, as alreadye we prove by
"the divisyon that was broughte in Queen Marie's tyme to
"certayne pernityous heades amonge the principall concerninge
"the successyon which some good people desired and labored to
"have established then. But yet his hope was that upon the
"sighte of this booke, such of our nation as are wise and truly
"Catholique, seinge by the libertye and disunion all wilbe
"destroyed, would joyne together and with him and his freindes,
"if he had layde in some good meanes for savinge themselves
"and ther countrye, which was his owne; but a finall ende with
"often and most earnest protestations to such as dealte with him
"in these affayres that he was led by noe jotte at all of affectyon
"or disaffectyon towardes any prince or pretender livinge, about
"this matter of the Crowne, but that absolutely and onely he
"desired that pretender to be preferred without all respectes of
"country, kindred, bloud, freindshippe, or other such circum-
"stances, whoe mighte be presumed to be most fitte forr us, and
"by whome most assurance, hope, and probabillitye may be had
"of the former desired effectes of religion, justice, peace, good
"govermente, avoydinge of warre and bloudshed, sufficyente
"forces to defende us, union, love towardes the people of our
"nation, meanes to help them, contentmente of princes rounde
"about us, and the like.
"And this is all in effecte that I can write to you, ...
"mente and censure aboute the booke of successyon, and . . . . . .
". . . . . pious and prudente desires concerninge all that
"affayre. Our sinne permitted not to have such a man continue

"amongste us, for puttinge soe importante designments in "execution. And soe I cannot tell whether ever any of them "were broken by him to the Pope, Kinge of Spaine, or other "Prince to whome they mighte apertayne. And with this I "make an ende, biddinge you most hartely farewell, and besech- "inge our Saviour to preserve you, and directe all this greate "affayre of our next successyon to his greatest glorye, and most "good of our afflicted countrye.

"Yours to commaunde,

"R. P." [1]

25.

A New Discourse of a stale subject, called the Metamorphosis of Ajax. Written by *Misacmos* to his friend and cosin, *Philostilpnos*. Printed 1596.

This curious book was written by Sir John Harington, and for so doing he was forbidden the court by Queen Elizabeth, and a license was refused for printing the work. Watt, Lowndes, and all Bibliographers bear testimony to its great rarity. Dr. Johnson in his Lives of the Poets, devotes a page to a consideration and description of this curious work. He says, These tracts are perhaps the first specimens of the Rabelaisian satire our language has to boast. They are replete with that kind of humour which distinguishes the writings of the French Lucian, and partake of their grossness. The extreme rarity of these once popular trifles renders it doubtful whether Swift or Sterne were acquainted with them; yet there are passages in the works of both these eccentric writers so strongly resembling some of Harington's as almost to induce a suspicion that they had seen them; this resemblance however, may have arisen from the circumstance of their being, like our author, imitations of Rabelais and the other French writers of facetiæ.

Of the Metamorphosis of Ajax, the avowed purport is the description of a a species of watercloset which Sir John Harington had invented and erected at Kelston, his seat near Bath; but he has contrived to make it the vehicle of much diverting matter, evincing his extensive reading; he has also interspersed numer-ous satiric touches and allusions to contemporary persons and

1   Dom. Elizabeth, 1599, June, July, Bundle 271, No. 11.

events, many of which are now necessarily obscure, and which were no doubt one of the causes of its great popularity at the time of publication.

Elizabeth, however she might be diverted with the humour of this whimsical performance, is said to have conceived much disquiet on being told the author had aimed a shaft at Leicester. Its satiric tendency procured the writer many enemies; and it is supposed that he owed his good fortune in escaping a Star Chamber suit to the favour of the Queen, who yet affected to be much displeased, and forbade him the Court in consequence.

It was reprinted at the Chiswick press in 1814, from which edition some of the previous remarks are derived.

26.

Virgidemiarum, Sixe Bookes. First three Bookes, of Toothlesse Satyrs. 1.—Poeticall. 2.—Academicall 3.—Morall. London, printed by Thomas Creede for Robert Dexter, 1597. (By Bishop Hall.)

Virgidemiarum. The three last bookes, of byting Satyres. Imprinted at London by Richard Braddocke for Robert Dexter, at the signe of the Brasen Serpent in Paule's Church Yard, 1598.

These are among the earliest Satires written in the English language, and were much admired, but the publication was ordered to be stayed at the press by the Archbishop of Canterbury and the Bishop of London, and such copies as could be found were to "bee presentlye broughte to the Bishop of London to be burnte." They were reprinted in 1824, with the illustrations of Rev. Thomas Warton and additional notes by Samuel Weller Singer.

27.

A pithie exhortation to her Majestie for establishing her successor to the Crowne. Whereunto is added a discourse containing the author's opinion of the true and lawfull successor to her Majestie. Both compiled by Peter Wentworth.

Dolman's (i.e., Father Parsons) objections to the succession of James I were ably refuted in this volume, and the claims of the Scottish King set forth with sound argument; yet for daring to advise his sovereign the author was committed to the Tower, where he shortly after died, and his book was ordered to be burnt by the hangman.

28.

All Ovid's Elegies: 3 Bookes. By C(hristopher) M(arlow). Epigrams by J(ohn) D(avis). At Middlebourgh. (1598.)

This volume was condemned and burnt at Stationer's Hall by an order of the Archbishop of Canterbury and the Bishop of London, dated June 1st, 1599.

29.

The Metamorphosis of Pigmalion's Image. And certaine Satyres At London. Printed for Edmond Matts, and are to be sold at the signe of the Hand and Plough in Fleet street. 1598.

This book was written by John Marston. It is dedicated "To the World's mightie Monarch Good Opinion;" and the principal purpose of the author was to ridicule and to show the immorality and evil tendency of a class of poems then fashionable, and to which Shakespeare's "Venus and Adonis" belongs.

The main production consists of thirty nine six-line stanzas. The "certain Satires," four in number, and all written in couplets, follow, but the versification is sometimes harsh, and the rhyme frequently careless and defective.

Preceding the Satires is a Poem headed *Reactio*, wholly occupied by a vindication of the writers whom Hall had previously attacked in his "Virgidemiarum;" addressing that author, Marston exclaims:

> "Vaine envious detractor from the good,
> "What cynicke spirit stirreth in thy blood?
> "Cannot a poore mistaken title scape,
> "But thou must that unto thy Tumbrell scrape?"

and he subsequently adds fonr of the smoothest lines in his volume:

" So have I seene the March wind strive to fade
" The fairest hewe that art or nature made :
" So envy still doth barke at cleareste shine,
" And strives to staine heroyick acts devine."
The dedication to Good Opinion is subscribed W. K., the
initials of William Kinsayder, the name under which Marston
published his earlier productions.*

From the licentious character of this book the prelates Whitgift
and Bancroft ordered its suppression and destruction soon after
its appearance.

30.

The first part of the Life and Raigne of King Henry
the IIII. Extending to the end of the first yeare of
his raigne. Written by J. H. Imprinted at London
by John Wolfe, and are to be solde at his shop in
Pope's Head Alley, neere to the Exchange. 1599.

This book was written by Sir John Haywarde, L.L.D. It was
dedicated in very encomiastic terms to the Earl of Essex, but it
so highly irritated Queen Elizabeth, that proceedings were taken
against the author as appears from the following documents.

Among the Domestic State Papers of the year 1600 are interrogatories by Lord Chief Justice Popham, to be administered to
Dr. Hayward in these terms ;

" To examyn hym who made the preface to the Reader.
" Wherein he conceaveth or ment that booke might be not onely
" patterns for pryvat dyreccion and for matters of state, to
" instruct young men more shortly and old men more fully ?
" Where he hadd any warrant to sett down that Kyng H. the 2.
" never taxed the subject, or left 900000 li. in his coffers ?
" In what poynt were the othes unlawful taken by R. the 2. of
" his subjects ?
" When were any skattering forces sent in hys tyme into Ireland,
" and under whom, and what warrant hadd he to wryte so ?
" What moved hym to sett down that any were in dysgrace for
" their servys there ?
" What moved hym to sett down that the nobylyte were then
" hadd in contempt, or that they were but base that were culted
" about that Kyng ?

* Collier's Bibliographical Catalogue, vol. 1, p. 526.

"What moved hym to sett down that the subjects were bound
"for their servys to the state, and not to the person of the
"Kyng?

"What moved hym to maynteyn with arguments never men-
"cyoned in the history, that yt myght be laweful for the subjects
"to depose the Kyng for any cause?

"What moved hym to add unto yt so many presidentes off that
"kynd in alowans thereof?

"What moved hym to alowe that ys well for comen weal that
"the Kyng is dead?

"What was the true caws of settyng forth this symple story in
"this tyme, and thus fortefyed with arguments to the worst sens,
"omytt every princypal poynt that made agaynst the Traytors or
"Rebelles?

"Myght he thynke that thys hystory, sett forth in sort as yt ys,
"wold not be very dangerous to come amongst the comon sort
"of people?

"Whom he made prevy to hys purpos of wrytyng thys hystory,
"and what alowans gave they of it, where and when?

"Who were the anymatters of you to sett forth thys story, and
"to what end?

"When did you fyrst resolve to sett forth this hystory, and
"where and at what tyme did you begynne yt?

"By what meanes came you to the records of these thyngs
"which you have sett down to have been done in that tyme?*

Then follows an Epistle to the reader, vindicating the book
from intending any attack on the present times; thus,

"Gentle Reader, thy frendly acceptance of these loose labors,
"the accompt of my idle howres, from exercises of greater profit
"and use, hath moved me, before I proceede any further, to over-
"looke and overlicke them once againe, as the beare is said to
"doe her unformed whelpes, and thereby both in portion and
"proportion to amend the same. I *have purposely passed* over
"many imputations, and some secrete sences, which the deepe
"searchers of our time have rather framed then found: partly
"upon the science of myne owne conscience, and partly seeing
"no reason wherefore they should be more applied to this booke
"*then to the* originall authors out of which it hath bene gathered,
"onely one offence I thought meete to meete with, and that is,
"concerning the rehearsall *of certaine oppressions both unusuall*

* Dom. Eliz., vol. 274, no. 58.

" *and intollerable,* and to no profitable purpose and end; which I
" heare to be hardly thought of and taken, not in regard of any
" moderate judgment, which may easily perceive how full it
" lyeth in the plaine path of the history, but *for feare* of some
" quarrellous conceites, which may interpret it to be meant of an
" other tyme (although nothing like) then that whereof it was
" reported; which in one degree of melancholy further, would
" imagine the very belles to sound whatsoever hammereth within
" their heads. For my part *I am of opinion,* that no imposition
" at any time have bene either hurtfull to a prince or hatefull to
" the people, except two qualities do concurre : first, that it be
" excessive,—secondly, that it be wildly and wastfully expended :
" for if the one fayle, it never seemeth greevous; if the other,
" not odious. But if it be both moderate and also necessary; or
" great, joyned with greatnesse and importancy of neede : it
" standeth neither with reason nor with religion, for any subject
" to repine against it. *For the prince is a person of* authority and
" trust, *to imploy* the goods of the people, for their common good,
" *either* in maintayning order among themselves, or in repelling
" the enterprises of their enemies : neyther can they possibly be
" preserved by the prince, if they withdraw theire owne endeavour
" and supply. And this the ancient wise men have endeavoured
" by a fable to make familiare ; that all the parts of the body
" were once offended against the stomacke, for that they saw
" themselves vexed with perpetuall travayle and toyle, and the
" stomacke onely, not onely to be idle, but to consume all that
" they could provide. Hereupon they conspired together, that
" the hand should no more worke, nor the feete walke, nor the
" eye looke about, nor the mouth receyve, prepare, and send
" downe foode : so the stomacke not receyving nourishment,
" could not impart the same againe to every part of the body :
" whereby, first they languished and (being neere at the point to
" perish) at the last perceyved, that both their labour to get, and
" their liberality to geve, in appearance was for the stomacke,
" but in deede for themselves. This tale hath bene verified by
" many truthes, whereof I will rehearse one, and so not exceede
" the measure of an Epistle. When the Turke came against the
" city of Constantinople, the Emperour was not able to wage so
" many souldiers as might stand single upon the walles. Where-
" upon he often assembled the wealthy citizens, and sometymes

"went in person to their honses, leaving nothing undone or
"unsayd which might be of force to stirre in them either piety or
"pitty, both for the preservation of their country and frends, and for
"theire owne particuler safeties: but the miserable monymongers,
"being as loath to take benefit of their gold as if it had not bene
"their owne, buried it under the ground, and denyed that they
"were able to make contribution. So either for want or weake-
"nes of resistance, the Turkes soone became masters of the city :
"who in their first fury set all the streetes on streame with bloud,
"and afterwards, covetousnes succeeding cruelty, they left no
"closet nor corner unransacked and unrifled, wherein missing
"their expected pray, they ripped the bellies and searched the
"bowels of their wretched captives: lastly they turned up .the
"foundations of many thousand buildings, and there found such
"infinite masses of mony, as did strike them rather into a maze
"then into a merveylle, how so rich a city could possibly be taken.
"I would not wish the like mischance to our like dull and heavy
"conceyted repyners, which neyther see nor seeke any other thing
"but only the stuffing of their owne bags, because it cannot
"happen unto them without a greater and further mischiefe :
"but I could wish that they might be fitted as once were the
"Siracusans, upon whom when Dyonisius had imposed a contri-
"bution, they murmured and complayned, and denyed that they
"were able to beare that burthen ; whereupon he encreased the
"imposition and they likewise their complaints, but Dyonisius
"ceased not to levy it upon them, untill he perceyved them
"eyther content by being reduced to their duety, or quiete by
"being drawne drye.*

The folowing is the confession of Dr. Hayward, made July
the 11th, 1600.

11th July, 1600,   The confession of Doctor Heyward
at the Courte.   before the Lord Keper, the Lord
                        Admirall, Mr. Secretary, and Mr.
                        Chauncelor of the Eschequer.

" 1. He confessed that the stories mencioned in the Archbishop's
"oration, tendinge to prove that deposers of kings and princes
"have had good successe, were not taken out of any other cron-
"icle, but inserted by himselfe, but said that after in the history
"the Bishop of Carlile confuteth the same, but for the confutation
"the Bishop was committed to the Marshalsea, and the whole

* Dom. Elizabeth, vol. 274, no. 59.

"parlement concluded against the Bishop's opinion; and in troth
"in 1. H. 4. the Bishop of Carlile was attainted of treason.
"2. He confessed he had red of a Benevolence in the tyme of
"Richard 3. and not before, and yet that he inserted the same in
"the raigne of Richard 2.
"3. He said that as he toke it, the substaunce of the consultation
"for reducing the Irishe rebell, he had out of William of
"Malmesbury.
"4. He affirmed that presently after the booke was printed,
"Woolfe the printer thereof caried the same to the Erle of Essex,
"and about a moneth after the epistle was taken out.

Edw. Coke.*

On July 13th, 1600, Wolfe the stationer was examined before
Attorney General Coke respecting the printing of the book in
question. The examination is as follows:—

"The examynacion of John Wolfe, Stacionour, taken
"before me, Edward Coke, Esquire, Her Majestie's Attor-
"ney Generall, this 13 of July, 1600.

"He sayth that Docter Hayward beinge a meere strainger to this
"examynant, cam to hym and requested hym to printe the booke
"intytuled "Henry the Fourth," which he did in Februarye,
"1599. The booke havinge no epistell dedicatorye nor to the
"reader, when he brought yt firste unto hym, which this exam-
"ynat desiringe to have, he this examynate requested hym to
"dedicatt the booke to some man of honour and reputacion; and
"uppon some conference hadd between them, this examynat
"praid hym yt might be dedicated to the Earle of Essex, for that
"he was a marciall man and was for to goe into Ireland, and the
"booke treated of Irishe causes. And this examynat sayth that
"within a day or twoe after, Docter Hayward delivered to this
"examynate the Epistelles to the Earle and to the reader; and
"the booke beinge fynished, Docter Hayward then beinge sicke,
"this examynate carryed the booke to the Earle of Essex, then
"preparinge to goe into Ireland: which the Earle receved, and
"givinge noe aunsweire, carryed the booke with hym into his
"chamber, which he taketh to be at Whytehall; and abought a
"fortnight or three weekes after, the wardens of the company
"receved order from my Lord of Caunterbury that the Epistell
"dedicated to the Earle should be cutt out.

* Dom, Elizabeth, vol. 275, no. 25.

"And further sayth that fyve or sixe hundred of them weire sould
"before any suche comaundment was gyven; for he sayth that
"never any booke was better sould or more desired that ever he
"printed then this book was; and sayth that out of the residew,
"(beinge five or six hundred) this examynat cut out the said
"Epistell and sould them also within verry short tyme after.
"And aboughte Easter tearme followinge, the people callinge
"exsedinglie for yt, this examynate obtayned a new edition of
"the said Docter Hayward wherein many thinges weire altered
"from the former, and yet the vollume incresed.

"And sayth further that Docter Hayward understandinge that
"many hade spoken agaynst this former edition hadd made an
"epistell apologeticall to sett to the secoud edition, as this exam-
"ynate thinketh; and 15 hundred of these bookes beinge allmost
"fynished in the Whisson hollidayes, 1599, weire taken by the
"wardens of the Stacionours and delivered to the Lord Busshopp
"of London. And this examynate sayth that he dothe not
"remember the particuler allteracions which weire in the latter
"edition from the former, nor hathe not any of the said bookes,
"nor never finished nor sould any of the said bookes, nor cannot
"come by any of them.   And this examynate sayth that the said
"appologie, as he thincketh, did tend to no other end then to
"satisfie the people of the author's meaninge in wrytinge the
"booke, and that the author said he ment not as some interprit yt.
"And this examynate sayth that the said Mr. Docter Hayward
"when he was tould by this examynate that some did fynde faulte
"with the former edition, he desired this examynate to intreat them
"that he might speak with them to knowe what they did mislike,
"to the intent that he might express his meaninge therein.
"And this examynate sayth that the people havinge dyvers tymes
"sythence called uppon hym for to procure the continewation of
"the same history by the same author, he hathe likewise intreat-
"ed the same author to goe forward in wrytinge the said history,
"which he thincketh he hath don some parte of.

"This examynate sayth further that after the deliverye of the
"book to the Earle as aforesaid, he went three or four tymes
"within one fortnight after, by the Docter's consent, to the Earle,
"being at courte at Richmont, to lerne what the Earle would say
"to yt, but allwayes this examynat was putt of by some of the
"Earle's men with aunsweire the Earle was much busied aboute
"his voyage to Ireland. And so this examynate never spake

"with the Earle after the first deliverye of the bookes, and further
"sayth that all of the laste edditio̧n weire burnt in my Lord of
"London's house; and sayth that the coppie nowe delivered up-
"pon his examynacion is a trew coppie of the epistell appolegett-
"icall, the orygenall whereof this examynat delivered to my Lord
"of London under Docter Haywarde's owne hand. And sayth
"that the orygenall of the first edition beinge interlyned and
"altered accordinge to the second edition, for so much as was
"don this examynate delivered to Mr. Barker, Register of the
"Highe Commyssion. And sayth that sithence the last edition
"was supprest, a great number have beene with this examynate
"to have bought the same. And sayth that he hadd no recom-
"pence or composition at alle for the printinge of the said first
"and last edition, but of his owne free will he gave some halfe
"dosen of the said bookes, whereof one was to the Earle and the
"other to the author. And this examynate sayth further that he
"was commytted fourteen dayes for the printinge of the last
"edition, and lost all the books of that edition.
"Examinatur per
"Edw. Coke.   John Wolf." *

On July 20th, 1600, Samuel Harsnett, examiner of the press,
"afterwards Bishop of Chichester, sent the following letter and
"petition to the Attorney General to excuse himself for having
"approved Hayward's book, thus:—

"Right worshipfull, I have not yet received eny bookes from my
"Lord of London, and so am not able to performe my taske in
"comparing them according to my promise. This for griefe of
"hart and confusion of face I am skarce able to write, that I
"shold be behinde hand to your most graciouse divine kindnesse
"towards me. I have sent myne aunswer enclosed, the onlie
"part of my dutye that I cold performe, moste humblie beseeching
"your goodnes to accept it in good part, and to be a father unto
"me as you have begunne. The God of Heven sees and knowes
"I am innocent; at casus leso numine crimen habet, my poore
"estate, my credit, my selfe, and more then my selfe doe hang
"uppon your graisouse countenance, for I muste crave pardon
"to tell an unmannerlie secrett: I have a poore weake gentle-
"woman my wife in childbed, who since your messanger his be-
"ing at myne house did neither eat, nor drinke, nor sleape for
"fear, and yet I have twentie tymes reade over your most gra-

* Dom. Elizabeth, vol. 275, no. 28.

"ciouse lettars unto her. The Lord of Heven requite you, for
"I and my poore frends shall never be able, and so with teares
"I humblie take my leave. From my poore house at Chigwell,
"this XXti of July, 1600.
                "Your worship his bought
                "and bounden servaunt,
                            "Sa. Harsnett."
"In moste humble wise complaininge sheweth unto your Wor-
"ship your dailie Orator, Samuel Harsnett, that whereas the
"Author of a Pamphlet published in print in anno 1599, intituled
"the 'Raigne of King Henry the Fourth,' hath endevored to
"excuse his publishinge the sayd pamphlett, as being allowed
"and approved by your sayd Orator, it may please your worship
"in your grave wisdome to consider that this his allegation can
"be no colour of excuse unto him, in regard of these reasons en-
"suynge.
"Firste, for that it hath been custome and use for eny man that
"entended in good meaning to put a booke in print, the Author
"himselfe to present the booke unto the Examiner, and to
"acquaynt him with his scope and purpose in the same : the
"Author of this pamphlet concealed himselfe, and nether spake
"nor conferred with your Orator concerning this pamphlett, (not-
"withstanding we were both students togither in Pembroochall
"in Cambridge, and both of a tyme and standing in the colledge),
"but the Author delivered his pamphlet unto a gentleman in my
"Lord of London his house, who begged your Orator his appro-
"bation unto the same in the name of a cautel of our English
"chronicles phrased and flourished over onlie to shewe the Author
"his pretie witt.
"Secondlie, that whereas your Orator his approbation of eny
"booke whatsoever is but a leading and inducement to my Lord
"of London, my master, to passe his Lordship his further appro-
"bation to the same, without which his Lordship his further ap-
"probation your Orator his allowance is no sufficient warrant
"for the Author to prynt his booke : the Author of this pamphlett
"published his pamphlett without my Lord and master his ap-
"probation at all, contrarie to warrant in that behalfe.
"Thirdlie, the Author hath wronged your said Orator muche,
"and hath abused your Worship with false enformation, in
"alledging for himselfe that your Orator allowed his pamphlett
"as it was and is published in print ; for that the Author know-

" eth in his conscience this is true, that when his pamphlett had
" mine approbation it was heddlesse, without epistle, preface, or
" dedication at all, which moved me to thinke it was a meer rhe-
" torical exornation of a part of our Englishe historie to shewe
" the foyle of the Author his witt : and after myne approbation
" gotten thereunto, the Author foysted in an Epistle dedicatorie
" to the Earle of Essex, which I neither allowed nor sawe, and
" which if I had seen, I protest I shold never have allowed the
" rest of the pamphlett.

" Fourthlie, it may please your grave wisdome graciouslie to con-
" sider your Orator his mean condition and capacitie ; that your
" sayd Orator is a poore Divine, unacquainted with bookes and
" arguments of state, and with consequenceis of that nature; that
" your Orator for ten or twelve yeares past neither spake with
" nor saluted the Author of this pamphlett, and so is cleer from
" privitye with his entendementes and overtures in the same; that
" your Orator sett to his hand sodeinlie as mooved by his freind,
" never reading (uppon his salvation) more then one page of the
" hedlesse pamphlet; for which his unadvised negligence he
" humblie beggeth your moste graciouse milder censure, that it
" may be no imputation of bad meaninge unto him, who doth
" dailie in his poore calinge, moste hartelie and zealouslie pray
" for the happinesse of Her sacred Majestie and the state, and
" for the longe continuance of Her Highnes most graciouse,
" blessed, divine government over us, and doth from the bottom
" of his hart wishe shame and dreadfull confusion upon all calum-
" niators and underminers of the same.

    " Your worship's moste humblie
    " bounden Orator,
        " Sa. Harsnett." *

On January 22nd, 160⁹₀, Hayward was, while in confinement
in the Tower, further examined before Sir John Peyton and
the Attorney General, thus :—
    " The examination of John Heyward,
    " Doctor at lawe, taken at the tower,
    " this 22 of Jan., 1600.
" He confesseth that the preface to the reader was of his oune
" indightinge, and saith that he intitled the same under the
" letteres of A. P., as divers other wrighters had done in such
" like cases.

    * Dom. Elizabeth, vol. 275, no. 31 and 31 I.

" He saith that he spake in his preface generally of histories;
" and being demaunded, whether he intended not to applie the
" preface of his boke to his present historie, saith as before, he
" wrote his preface generally of all histories and intended no
" particular by itselfe.

" He saith that he read in Foxe's booke of Actes and monuments
" that King H. 2 never demaunded subsidie of his subjects,
" which he sett forth towards the end of the raigne of that Kinge,
" and there he found also that H. 2 after his death left in treasure
" nine hundred thousand poundes besides his jewels and plate,
" and being demaunded wherfore he inserted the same into the
" historie of H. 4, saith he taketh that to be lawfull for any
" historiographer to insert any historie of former tyme ynto that
" historie he wright, albeit no other historian of that matter
" have mencioned the same, and that libertie is allowed by
" Dionisius Hallicarnasseus.

" He sayth that the othe under hands and seales required and
" taken by R. 2, was to knowe what every particuler man was
" worthe, to thentent that they might be taxed thereafter; and
" no other othe was intended by this examinante.

" He sayth he found in Walsingham (as he remembreth) that the
" forces that were sent into Ireland by R. 2 were scattering and
" droppinge, &c., though not in those termes, yet to the like
" sence; and that those that did good service there were not
" rewarded with countenance, &c., : and sure he is that he had it
" there eyther in wordes or by actions; and also that he gathered
" out of the actions of that Kinge recorded by Walsingham, that
" matters of peace were managed by menne of weakest sufficiency,
" by whose councell eyther ignorant or corrupt, &c.

" He sayth the complaynt of Hereford to Mowbrey, reported in
" other cronicles, do imply in sence that the kinge's councell
" accounted auncient nobilitie a vaine jest,—wealth and vertue
" the ready meanes to bring to destruction : which complaint is
" extant in Hall and Polidore Virgill and many other wrighters.

" He sayth that he read in Bodine and other authors that the
" subject was rather bounde to the state then to the person of the
" kinge, which he inserted as a matter spoken by the Earle of
" Derby and Duke Hereford to serve his owne tourne, which is a
" libertie used by all good wrighters of historie, and to invent
" reasons and speaches according to the matter; and saith that

" Bodin's distinction is that where the government is democrat-
" icall or aristocraticall, there the subject is bound to the state
, ' rather then to the person that beare the title of a prince, but
" where it is monarchicall, as in England, there the allegiance is
" to the person of the prince ; and being demaunded wherfore he
" invented that the erle should speake so for that this government
" was monarchicall, sayth that he found but remembreth not
" where he spake to that purpose. And further saith that in the
" Bishops of Carlile's speache he hath sett down that distinction
" and confuted the error, and that he did of himselfe according
" to the example of the best historians ; and being reprehended
" for mencioning of that matter at all, speciallie because the Erle
" that held the error prevailed, and the Bishop that confuted it
" was punished, sayth that he did it after the example of the best
" historians, that applie spechis according to the matter. He
" sayth he sett forth the oration of the B. of Caunterburie accord-
" ing to the matter he found in other authorities, but remember
" them not, and cannot affirme that he found those eight stories
" in any oration the archbishop made in any other cronicle, but
" saith as before that it is lawfull for an historian so to doe, and
" besides he confuteth the same, page 107 in the Bishop of
" Carlisle's speach, the last line of that page.
" He confesseth that he bringeth in as his own speach that it was
" not amisse in regard of the comonwelth that he (meaning King
" R. 2) was deade, yet they who caused his death, &c., which he
' sayed of himselfe for preventing of civil warres in respect of 2
' concurrents or competitors. Being demanded what was the
" reason why he sett forth the orations of the B. of Caunterbury
" and the erle of Derby, seing that they tend to greate ill and to
" thinges most unlawfull, sayth that there can be nothing done,
" be it never so ill or unlawfull, but must have a shadowe, and
" every councell must be according to the action. He sayth that
" he selected out this single historie for that Hall beginneth there,
" and Ascham his scoolemaster commende that historie if it were
" well penned, before any other ; and being demanded wherfore
" then he followed not Hall in his historie, sayth that he followed
" him but suplied it out of other histories, and had an intention
" as he saith to have continued the historie.
" And for the words spoken by King R. 2, that princes must not
" rule without limitation, &c., he affirmeth that to be a true
" opinion so it be rightlie understood, and that he intended that

"the same was not to be taken generally, but that princes were
"to be limitted by the lawe divine and the lawe of nature onlie;
"and being demaunded where he had the same, saith that it is
"about 3 yeres since the booke was written, and cannot remem-
"bere out of what author he toke it, but saith he fynd it in Bod.
"...... and in the body of the civill lawes, &c.

"And being asked where he had this sentence, that othes are
"comonlie spurned aside when they ly in the way to honur or
"reveng, saith that the speach is of his own, as thinges done de
"facto et non de jure.   Being demaunded wherfore he added
"that King Richard II borowed money by privy seales, sayth
"that he thinketh he had it out of Walsingham.

"For benevolences he found the matter but doth not defende
"the woord.

"Being asked where he found the description of the erle to be
"not negligent to uncover the heode, to bowe the body, to stretch
"forth the necke and arme, &c., he saith that he found in Hall
"and others that he was of popular behavior, but for the parti-
"culars he tooke the libertie of the best wrighters of histories
"of that kynd.

"Also the descriptions of the erle in divers places of his historie
"he gathered out of his actions, and found the matter, not the
"verie forme of woordes, in any other, as farre as he can call to
"remembrance.*

"Being demanded, seing he wrote of matters of state and histo-
"rie, what menne of state or others he acquainted with his
"historie before he published it, aunswereth that he wrote of an
"historie about 300 yeres past, and therfore he acquainted no
"person therwith before he brought it to the printer.

"He sayth he began to wright this historie about a yere before
"it was published, as he remembreth, but had the intent above
"a dussen yeres before, but acquainted no man therewith.   He
"sayth that he had the articles and causes of deposition, the in-
"strument of resignation, the deposition, and other wordes out
"Hall and Walsingham; and sayth that he had nothing of the
"printer for printing of the booke.†
"   John Hayward.‡
"John Peyton.   Edw. Coke.

    * Pag. 4, 5, 6, 11, 39, 41, 43, 53, 75, description of the councel!.   Pag. 4,
25, 75, he describeth the erle.
    † Pag. 54 of his owne.
    ‡ Dom. Elizabeth, vol. 278, no. 17.

31.

The Letting Humor's Blood in the Head-vaine; with a new Morissco daunced by Seven Satyres upon the bottome of Diogenes' Tubbe. (1600.)
The Knave of Clubbs. 'Tis merry when Knaves meete. (1600.)

The author of these tracts was Samuel Rówlands, a prolific writer of the end of the sixteenth and early part of the succeeding century. He appears to have commenced his literary career in the year 1598 by the publication of a collection of sacred poems entitled "The Betraying of Christ, Judas in Despaire, the Seven Words of our Saviour on the Crosse, &c.," but soon found that humorous pieces were more saleable, and these being perhaps more suited to the bent of his mind, he changed his style accordingly.

The Knave of Clubbs upon its appearance in the year 1600 gave such offence, on account of the severity of its satire and the obviousness of its allusions, that an order was made that it should be burnt, first publicly, and afterwards in the Hall Kitchen of the Stationers Company. The order is dated October 26, 1600, and is worded as follows : " Yt is ordered that the next court-day two bookes lately printed, th'one called *The Letting of Humor's Blood in the Head Vayne*, th'other *A Mery Metinge*, or *'tis mery when Knaves mete*, shal be publiquely burnt, for that they conteyne matters unfytt to be published ; then to be burnd in the Hall Kytchen, with other Popish bookes and thinges that were lately taken."

The first tract mentioned in the order as containing matters unfit to be published was one of the most popular of Rowlands' productions. It was originally printed under the title given above, but upon its condemnation by the Stationers' Company, the bookseller changed its title to "Humour's Ordinarie, where a man may be verie merrie and exceeding well used for his sixepence," and published an edition of it without date ; but after the feeling had subsided in 1611, it again appeared with its original title, although the printer thought it prudent not to put his name on the title page. The Knave of Clubbs was reprinted and edited for the Percy Society in 1843 by Dr. Rimbault, and I am indebted to that gentleman's introduction for the preceding account of this curious book.

The Letting of Humor's Blood was reprinted in 1815 with an introduction and notes by Sir Walter Scott, who says of Rowland, "It has been remarked, that his muse is seldom found in the best "company; and to have become so well acquainted with the "bullies, drunkards, gamesters, and cheats, whom he describes, "he must have frequented the haunts of dissipation in which " such characters are to be found. But the humorous descriptions "of low life exhibited in his satires are more precious to anti-"quaries than more grave works, and those who make the "manners of Shakespeare's age the subject of their study may "better spare a better author than Samuel Rowlands.

32.

A discourse plainely proving the evident utilitie and urgent necessitie of the desired happie union of the two famous kingdomes of England and Scotland: by way of answer to certaine objections against the same. (By John Thornborough, Bishop of Bristol.) London, 1604.

The joiefull and blessed reuniting the two mighty and famous kingdomes, England and Scotland into their ancient name of Great Brittaine. By John Bristoll. Printed at Oxford. N. d.

On May 26th, 1604, the attention of the House of Commons was called to these books as tending to the derogation and scandal of the proceedings of that House in the matter of the Union, and a Committee was appointed to consider the heads of a message to be sent to the Lords touching the same, and on June 1st the Committee was named.

Shortly after this an inhibition from the Convocation House issued, and on June 21st, 1604, it was resolved " to pray confer-ence touching the instrument read by the bishops at the late conference, taxing the intermeddling of this house in matters of religion." Also "to desire the submission of the Bishop in writing, to be delivered unto them publicly in the House, before the Lords; and that the books might be prohibited and suppressed.[1]

These books were both reprinted in one volume in the year 1641.

1 Commons' Journals, Vol. 1, pp. 226 and 244.

33.

Eastward Hoe. As it was playd in the Black-friers by the children of her Maiestie's Revels. Made by Geo. Chapman, Ben. Jonson, Joh. Marston. London, 1605.

It is said that for writing this comedy, wherein the authors were accused of reflecting on the Scots, they were committed to prison, and were in danger of losing their ears and noses. They however received pardons, and Jonson, on his release from prison, gave an entertainment to his friends, amongst whom were Camden and Selden. In the midst of the entertainment his mother drank to him, and showed him a paper of poison, which she intended to have given him in his liquor, having first taken a portion of it herself, if the sentence for his punishment had been executed.

34.

A relation of the state of religion, and with what hopes and policies it hath beene framed and is maintained in the severall states of these westerne parts of the world. (By Sir Edwin Sandys.) London, 1605.

This book was printed without any author's name, and genererally passed as the production of Sir Edwin Sandys; but it appears from a subsequent edition published at the Hague in 1629, that the first impression of 1605 (at least so it is alleged) "was but a spurious stolne copy, in part epitomized, in part amplified, and throughout most shamefully falsified and false printed from the author's original, in so much, that the same knight was infinitely wronged thereby, and as soon as it came to his knowledge that such a thing was printed and passed under his name, he caused it (though somewhat late, when it seemes two impressions were for the most part vented) to be prohibited by authority, and as many as could be recovered to be deservedly burnt, with power also to punish the printers." This is referred to in a letter from Chamberlain to Carleton, of November 7th, 1605, preserved among the Domestic State Papers, where the writer says, "Sir Edwin Sandys' books burnt." There were subsequent editions in 1632, 1638, and 1687.

35.

The Interpreter, or Booke containing the signification of words : wherein is set foorth the true meaning of all, or the most part of such words and termes, as are mentioned in the lawe writers, or statutes of this victorious and renowned kingdome, requiring any exposition or interpretation. Collected by John Cowell, Doctor, and the King's Majestie's Professour of Civill Law in the Universitie of Cambridge. Cambridge, (1607.)

On February 24th, 1609, this book was referred to in the House of Commons by Sir Edwin Sandys, as "very unadvised and undiscreet; tending to the disreputation of the House, and power of the common laws ;" and on the 27th of the same month a Committee was formed to consider the book and to report thereon to the Lords.[1] On March 25th, 1610, a proclamation was issued prohibiting the buying, uttering, or reading of this book, in these terms :—

"This latter age and tymes of the world wherein wee are fallen,
"is soe much given to verball profession, as well of religion as
"of all comendable morall virtues, but wanting the actions and
"deedes agreable to soe specious a profession, as it hath bredd
"such an unsaciable curiosity in manye men's speritts, and such
"an itching in the tonges and penns of most men, as nothing is
"left unsearched to the bottome, both in talking and writing.
"For, from the verie highest misteries in the Godhead, and the
"most inscrutable councells in the Trinitye, to the verie lowest
"pitt of hell, and the confused actions of the divills there, there
"is nothing nowe unsearched into by the curiositie of men's
"braynes; men not being contented with the knowledg of soe
"much of the will of God as it hath pleased him to reveale, but
"they will needes sitt with him in his most privie closett, and
"become privye of his most inscrutable councells, and therefore
"it is noe wonder that men in theis our dayes doe not -spare to
"wade in all the depest misteries that belong to the persons or
"state of kinges or princes that are Gods upon earth, since wee

1. Commons' Journals, Vol. 1, pp. 399, 400, 404, 407, 408, 415, 416.

" see (as wee have alreadye saide) that they spare not God him-
" self; and this license that everie talker or writer nowe assumeth
" to himself is come to this abuse, that manye Phormios will give
" councell to Hanniball, and manye men that never went out of
" the compasse of cloysters or colleges will freelie wade by their
" writings in the depest misteries of monarchie and politique
" government. Whereuppon it cannot otherwise fale out but
" that when men goe out of their element and meddle with
" thinges above their capacitie, themselves shall not onlie goe
" astray and stumble in darknes, but will misleade alsoe divers
" others with themselves into manye mistakings and errors, the
" proofe whereof we have lately had by a booke written by Doctor
" Cowell, called the Interpreter. For he being onlie a civillian
" by profession, and uppon that large ground of a kynd of dic-
" tionarie as it were, following the alphabet, haveing all kynd of
" purposes belonging to goverment and monarchie in his waye,
" by meddleing in matters above his reach he hath fallen in
" manye thinges to mistake and deceave himself; in some thinges
" disputing soe nicely uppon the misteries of this our monarchie
" that it may receave dubtfull interpretations, yea in some poynts
" verie derogatorie to the supreame power of this crowne; in
" other cases mistakeing the true state of the parliament of this
" kingdome and the fundamentall constitutions and priviledges
" thereof, and in some other poynts speaking unreverently of the
" comon lawe of England and of the workes of some of the most
" famous and antient judges therein; yt being a thinge utterlie
" unlawfull to anye subject to speake or write against that lawe
" under which he liveth, and which wee are sworne and are re-
" solved to mayntayne. Wherefore uppon just considerations
" moveing us hereunto for preventing of the said errors and
" inconveniences in all tymes to come, wee doe hereby not onlie
" prohibitt the buying, uttering, or reading of the said bookes,
" but doe alsoe will and straightlie comaund all and singuler per-
" sons whatsoever whoe have or shall have anye of them in their
" handes or custodie, that uppon payne of our high displeasure and
" the consequence thereof, they doe deliver the same presentlie
" uppon this publication to the Lord Maior of London, yf they
" or anye of them be dwelling in or neere the said cittie, or other-
" wise to the Sheriff of the county where they or anye of them
" shall reside, and in the twoe universities to the Chauncellor our

"Vicechauncellor there, to the intent that further order maye be "given for the utter suppressing thereof. And because there "shalbe better oversight of bookes of all sortes before they come "to the presse, wee have resolved to make choice of commission- "ers that shall looke more narrowlie into the nature of all those "thinges that shalbe putt to the presse either concerning our "authoritie royall, or concerning our goverment or the lawes of "our kingdome, from whom a more strict accompt shalbe yelded "unto us then hath beene used heretofore. Witnes our selfe at "Westminster, the fyve and twentith daye of March.

"Per ipsum regem. [1] "

36.

The Lord Coke his speech and charge. With a discoverie of the abuses and corruption of officers. London, 1607.

This charge was given by Lord Coke at the Assizes held in Norwich on the fourth of August, 1606, and it was printed in the next year with an epistle dedicatory to the Earl of Exeter by R. P[ricket]. It was suppressed the day after publication, as appears from a letter of John Chamberlain to Dudley Carleton, dated Feb. 13, 1607. [2]

37.

The Argument of Master Nicholas Fuller, in the case of Thomas Lad and Richard Maunsell his clients. Wherein it is plainely proved that the Ecclesiasticall Commissioners have no power, by vertue of their commission, to imprison, to put to the oath ex officio, or to fine any of his Majestie's subjects. Imprinted 1607.

For writing this book, Nicholas Fuller, a barrister of Gray's Inn, was imprisoned by Archbishop Bancroft, and several notices of him appear in the Domestic State Papers.

1 Pat. Roll, 8 James I, part 30 dorso. A printed copy of this proclamation will be found among the Domestic State Papers, James I.
2 Domestic State Papers, James I, Vol. 26, no. 48.

In a letter from Carleton to Chamberlain of September 16th, 1607, the writer says, "The king went to Lambeth to encourage the Archbishop to proceed against Nicholas Fuller." Chamberlain writing to Carleton on December 30th, 1607, says that "Mr. Fuller has paid his fine, but submissions are expected which he cannot digest;" and again in a letter of January 5th, 1608, he says that "Fuller the puritan is freed." [1] This scarcely tallies with another account of Fuller, which says that on his imprisonment by Archbishop Bancroft, he remained in durance, and so died on February 23rd, 1619, aged 76 years.

38.

Conrad Vorst, The Works of.

Vorst was a celebrated Arminian divine. He was born at Cologne in 1569, and became Professor of Theology at Leyden in 1610; of which he was deprived in 1619 in consequence of a decision of the Synod of Dort. He died in 1622. In 1611 his books were publicly burnt in St. Paul's Churchyard and both the Universities by the King's order. [2]

39.

Francis Suarez, The Works of.

Suarez was a Spanish Jesuit. On Sunday, November 21st, 1613, some books of this author derogatory to princes were publicly burnt at Paul's Cross. [3]

40.

A book without title or date, but plainly of Catholic tendency. Written by John Cotton, 1613.

I have not been able to meet with a copy of this book, but the following extract from a letter from Rev. Thomas Lorkin to Sir Thomas Puckering, dated June 24th, 1613 [4] furnishes a brief notice of the author, and the proceedings against him for this publication.

1 Domestic, James I, Vol. 28, nos. 51 and 128, and Vol. 31, no. 2.

2 Wilson's Life and Reign of James I, contained in Kennet's History of England, vol. 2, p. 715, ed. 1706.

3 Court and Times of James I, vol. 1, pp. 279, 280. Also Domestic State Papers, James I, vol. 75, no. 28.

4 Court and Times of James I, vol. 1, p. 248.

"There hath lately come forth a proclamation against one Cotton,
"a west country gentleman and a great recusant, charging him
"with high treason against the King and state for having publish-
"ed a very scandalous and railing book against his Majesty; and
"promising a very large reward to whosoever could apprehend
"him and bring him in. At the very self same time, this Cotton
"being to cross the Thames and enquiring of the watermen what
"news, they not knowing the man told him what was newly
"happened concerning himself. Whereupon being landed, he
"muffled himself in his cloak, thinking thereby to pass unknown
"to any of his acquaintance that he might haply meet. But he
"had not passed thence many paces when one Maine, a follower
"sometimes of the late Lord of Devonshire, and a sure friend of
"his, meeting him in the street and discovering well what he
"was, warned him likewise of danger, with protestation never-
"theless not to make any benefit of the discovery of his friend,
"but wishing him to provide for his own safety. Thereupon
"Cotton demanding his opinion what he thought fittest to be
"done, he advised him to submit himself to the king's mercy:
"whose counsel he followed, and presently went and surrendered
"himself into my Lord of Southampton's hands, and so rests at
"his Majesty's mercy."

And in another letter from Lorkin to Sir Thomas Puckering,
"of June 30th, 1613,[1] the writer says "My last letters advertized
"you of what had lately happened concerning Cotton, who
"yielding himself to the king's clemency, doth nevertheless
"utterly disavow the book, and constantly denieth to be the
"author of it, Hereupon his study hath been searched, and
"there divers papers found, containing many several pieces of the
"said book, and (which renders the man more odious) certain
"relics of the late saints of the gunpowder treason, as one of
"Digby's fingers, Percy's toe, some other part either of Catesby
"or Rookwood (whether I well remember not) with the addition
"of a piece of one of Peter Lambert's ribs, to make up the full
"mess of them. If the proofs which are against him will not
"extend to the touching of his life, at least they will serve to
"work him either misery and affliction enough."

The following is a copy of the proclamation for the apprehension of Cotton :—

1   Court and Times of James I, vol. 1, page 251.

"By the King.

"A proclamation for the search and apprehension of John
"Cotton, Esquire.

"Whereas John Cotton of Warblington, otherwise of Subberton,
"in the Countie of Southhampton, Esquire, is by sundry strong
"and vehement presumptions, discovered to have committed
"matter full of very strange and execrable high treasons, against
"our person and state; and the same John Cotton (as it should
"appeare by all circumstances) hath, upon a guiltie conscience,
"and some privie intelligence of search intended for him, fled
"from his house and dwelling, and lurketh or wandreth in
"unknowen places; although it standeth not with the course of
"justice to condemne any man unheard, yet for that the
"presumptions and proofes appeare to be so forcible against him,
"as if after this publique notice, he shall not forthwith come in,
"and render himselfe, we shall have iust cause to conclude him
"guiltie; we have thought fit, (besides our more secret directions)
"to have recourse to the industrie and love of our people, which
"never failed us, in any case that concerned our safetie or honour,
"for his bringing forth or apprehension.

"Wherefore wee doe charge and command all our Justices,
"Mayors, Sheriffes, Bayliffes, Headboroughs, and Constables,
"and also all officers of our ports, to doe their best and utmost
"endeavours, to search for, and apprehend the said John Cotton;
"(of whom, for the better informing of those that know not his
"person, wee have caused a description to be hereunto annexed.)
"And doe neverthelesse require all our loving subiects, not only
"to be aiding and assisting to our said officers therein, but like-
"wise to use their owne particular diligence, care, and industrie,
"aswell for the finding out and apprehending of the said John
"Cotton, as for the giving intelligence and advertisement unto
"any of our justices or officers, where hee hath beene at any time
"lately seene or met, or otherwise where there is any likelyhood
"that he should harbour, repaire, or be received.

"And for the better encouragement of our loving subiects to doe
"their duety in this case (which wee take so much to heart) wee
"doe hereby declare, signifie and promise, that whosoever shall
"apprehend and bring into the hands of any our officers of
"justice, the person of the said John Cotton living, shall have
"for his reward the summe of one thousand crownes.

" And on the other side, if any of our subjects shall voluntarily
" receive, harbour, convey, favour, or conceale the said John
" Cotton, wee doe signifie unto them all, that we shall account
" them as partakers, and abettors of the said treasons: and if any
" of our officers, or others shall neglect or let passe any opportu-
" nitie, occasion, or meanes for the performance, or executing of
" their duety in this behalfe, we shall proceede against such per-
" sons to their condigne punishment with all severitie according
" to our lawes.

" Given at our Palace of Westminster the eleventh day of June,
" in the eleventh yeere of our reigne of Great Britaine, France,
" and Ireland.

                    " God save the King.

" John Cotton is of the age of fourtie eight yeeres, or thereabouts,
" of a reasonable tall stature, slender of body, the haire of his
" head and beard flaxen, but now inclining to white, well com-
" plexioned, with somewhat a long and leane visage.

" ¶   Imprinted at London by Robert Barker, Printer to the
" King's most excellent Maiestie.
                    " M.DC.XIII. [1]

41.

Abuses stript and whipt, or Satirical Essayes.   By George Wyther.   London, 1613.

For this publication Wyther was committed to the Marshalsea, where he remained several months.

42.

A book without title or date, written by Edmund Peacham, containing a libel on the Bishop of Bath and Wells, and other libels.   Circa 1614.

For writing this book Edmund Peacham, Rector of Hinton St. George, in the county of Somerset, was deprived of his living by the Ecclesiastical Commissioners on December 19th, 1614.[2] On the 18th January, 1615, Mr. Secretary Winwood, the Master of the Rolls, the Lieutenant of the Tower, and others, were direc-ted by the Council to examine Peacham, then imprisoned in the

1   Proclam. Collection, Dom. State Papers, James I, no. 23.
2   Domestic State Papers, James I, vol. 78, no. 78.

Tower, respecting his authorship of a treasonable book, and if he should be obstinate in refusing to give needful information, to use the manacles. In a letter from Chamberlain to Carleton of February 9th, 1615, Peacham was said to have been racked, but nothing could be got from him; and the king was much incensed against him. Most of the judges concurred in finding his case treason. He was tried and condemned for high treason in the course of the year 1615, and sentenced to be hanged, drawn, and quartered, but he died in Taunton gaol in the early part of the year 1616, as appears in a letter from Chamberlain to Carleton of March 27, 1616.[1]

43.

History of the World. By Sir Walter Raleigh, 1614.

This book was called in "for too free censuring of princes."[2]

44.

De Politia Ecclesiæ Anglicanæ. By Richard Mockett, D.D. London, 1616.

This publication fell under censure because it favoured the Calvinists. Dr. Mockett's intention was to give foreign churches a fair notion of the doctrines of the English church; and for that purpose he had translated the Prayer Book into Latin, adding Jewel's Apology and Nowell's Catechism. But in his translation of the Articles he had omitted the latter part, which sets forth ths power of the church in rites and ceremonies and in controversies of faith. Besides this, instead of printing the Homilies at length, he had given an abbreviation of them, not fairly representing the opinions of this church; and moreover, in a treatise of his own, he had not given the see of Winchester precedence over all others next to London, but only over those whose bishops were not privy councillors. Dr. Montagu, Bishop of Winchester, was at that time on bad terms with Archbishop Abbot, whose

1. Domestic State Papers, vol. 80, art. 6, 26, 38; vol. 81, art. 67; and vol. 86, art. 111.
2. Court and Times of James I, vol. 1, p. 291; also Domestic State Papers, James I, vol. 80, no. 1.

chaplain Dr. Mockett was; the king was appealed to; and the result was a public edict by which the book was ordered to be burnt. [1]

45.

A Bride Bush, or a Wedding Sermon, compendiously describing the duties of married persons. By the Rev. William Whately. London, 1617.

This sermon occasioned much controversy, and caused the preacher to be summoned before the Court of High Commission, but he finally submitted to the authority of the Court, and on May 4th, 1621, signed a formal recantation of the assertions in his book "that either adultery or long desertion dissolves marriage." This submission is preserved among the Domestic State Papers of the period, and is endorsed by Archbishop Laud. [2]

46.

A Book without title or date. By John Wraynham. Circa, 1618.

This book, of which I have not been able to meet with a copy, appears to contain an attack on the Lord Chancellor, accusing him of injustice in a chancery suit, and also slanderous words towards the king. For its publication Mr. Wraynham was cited into the Star Chamber, and received a severe sentence, which was however, through the instrumentality of the Chancellor himself, reversed, as appears from the following pardon preserved among the State Papers, and dated July 16th, 1619. "Grant to John "Wraynham, at intercession of the Lord Chancellor, of pardon "of the sentence of imprisonment for life, fine of £1000, standing "in the pillory, loss of his ears, &c., to which he was condemned "by the Star Chamber, for presenting a slanderous petition to "the King against the Lord Chancellor, who decided a cause "against him; also of pardon for putting his case and proofs "into a book, with an epistle to the King, and an epilogue, in "which were slanders and insolencies both against His Majesty "and the Chancellor.

1   See Edinburgh Review for July, 1871, page 179.
2   Domestic, James I, vol. 121, art. 7.

47.

Balaam's Ass.　Circa 1619.

Speculum Regale.　Circa 1619.

These two books were written by John Williams, Esquire, of Essex, barrister of the Middle Temple, who had been expelled the House of Commons on account of his being a Roman Catholic, and in them he affirmed that the king would die in the year 1621, grounded upon the prophecy of Daniel. These books Williams at his trial told the court were enclosed in a box sealed up, and thus secretly conveyed to the king; and were never printed or published. On May 3rd, 1619, he was arraigned at the King's Bench, Westminster, for this libel, and condemned to be hanged, drawn. and quartered, which sentence was carried out two days afterwards over against the Mews at Charing Cross.

Two manuscript copies of *Balaam's Ass* are extant, one in the University Library of Cambridge (Dd. III, 84, art. 2), and another in the Lansdowne M.S., No. 213, p. 59. It is entitled "Balaam's Asse, or a Free Discourse touching the Murmurs and "Feared Discontents of the Time, and directed to his then "Majestie King James, by way of Humble Advertisement."

Among the manuscripts in the Cambridge University Library is a duodecimo (class mark Ii, vi. 51), written in a hand of the seventeenth century, containing "Notes of cases in the Star "Chamber, 17-20 James I." On the last leaf is written the following, in the same hand:—

"A parcel of a pamphlett cast in the courte by Williams, bear-"inge the title of Balaam's Ass, for which he were after executed.

　　"4 letters doe the persoun shewe,
　　"The place, the tymes, the tymes of woe.

H. E. E. I.

　　"H. sheweth the churche's first deflection,
　　"E. brought the churche to large protection,
　　"E. gave a woman churche subjection,
　　"I. shewes sinn ripe and at perfectione.
　　"Now putt together, 3, they crie,
　　"Alas, 'twas hee,—the 4th, 'twas I.
　　"Thus these 4 letters shewe the fall
　　"Of them and of their generall.

"Advesperascit vita mea:
"Domine, suscipe vitam meam:
"Post has tenebas spero lucem.

These four letters evidently designate Henry, Edward, Elizabeth, and James.

The copy of Balaam's Ass in the Cambridge University Library consists of forty eight pages of small folio, neatly written in a hand of the seventeenth century.[1]

The following account of Williams's execution is taken from the State Papers of the period[2]

"Immediatly upon his comming to the gybbett, hee ascended
"up the ladder, where, turning his face to the people, hee first
"began with a hearty prayre for the longe lyfe and prosperous
"raigne of the King, and then hee proceeded to the acknowledg-
"ment of his fault, saying that hee had bin too buisy and sawcy
"with his majesty, and that hee was heartily sory for that hee
"had so much offended and distasted the King in wryteing that
"booke, which hee was ledd to doe out of an inconsiderate love
"to his contry; then hee told Mr. Dean and Mr. Fanshaw who
"told him that confession was not answerable to his offence that
"hee wold gladly speak and express him self in any thing they
"doubted of, wherupon Mr. Fanshaw demaunded of him if there
"were noe more of them bookes abroad; to which hee protested
"that there was not an other booke nor a peece of itt in the
"world besydes that. Hee questioned him further why hee wrote
"an Epistle to his Contrymen; he said, because it might come the
"sooner to his majestie's veiwe: and why he wrote a Propesy in
"his booke of the desolation of Whytehall, wherin he tooke upon
"him to tell so precyzely the year, the month, and the day, when
"the sayd howse shold be ruyened; to which hee aunswered,
"that hee hoped they wold not thinke him so fond as to conceave
"himself to be illuminated with any divine or propheticall spiritt,
"but that which hee wrote was Ironice. Then he fell to clear
"himself of an imputation . . . . upon him yesterday that hee was
"an Atheist, by reason of a passage in his booke, but hee pro-
"fessed himself to bee a right Romayne Catholicke, and that his

1 See Court and Times of James I, vol. 2, pp. 146, 157, 158, 160; also Howell's State Trials.
2 Domestic, James I, vol. 109, no. 14.

"fayth was, that he hoped to be saved cheifly and more effectu-
"ally by the blood of our Saviour shed for his sins; to which
"Mr. Dean answered that hee ought absolutely to relye upon the
"death and passion of our Saviour, and alleadged a place in
"Saint John that noe man cold come to the Father but by the
"Son only, wherupon hee demanded that if they wold have him
"make repetition of his fayth againe.... was the same as before
"hee wold. Mr. Dean told him that they wold willingly joyne
"with him in his prayres to God, hee said hee had done his de-
"votions ere he came to that place, and so gave the executioner
"a handkerchef, which hee tyed about his head, and whylst hee
"was so doeing hee prayed in Latin, and pulling the handker-
"cheif over his eyes hee said, 'Post tenebras spero lucem,' and
"so dyed."

48.
David Paræus, D.D., The Works of.

In June, 1622, the works of this writer were burnt at Paul's
Cross by order of the Privy Council. They were also burnt at
Oxford by order of the University, as seditious; and at a Senate
of the University of Cambridge they were "condemned to eter-
nal infamy," and forbidden to be read.* Paræus was a celebra-
ted Calvinistic divine of the Reformed Church. He was born in
Silesia in 1548, and died in 1622, having been Professor in the
University of Heidelberg.

49.
Mercurius Gallo Belgicus. 1623.

A set of this publication is in the Library of the British Museum, but the volume containing the year 1623 is unfortunately
missing. One of the numbers published in October, 1623, seems
to have contained objectionable matter concerning the King, for
on the 18th of that month the Lord Keeper addressed the following letter to Mr. Secretary Conway:

"Mr. Secretarie,
"Reading since supper this Mercurius Gallo Bellgicus
"which heere with all I send unto you, I finde a passage about
"the 35th page thereof soe full of falsehoodes and indignities

* Wood's History and Antiquities of the University of Oxford, ed. Gutch,
vol. 2, pp. 341-345; Cooper's Annals of Cambridge, vol. 3, pp. 143, 144;
Domestic State Papers, James I, vol. 132, nos. 47 and 48.

" towardes his Majestie, that (although I knowe what a despic-
" able esteeme this author hath borne for manie yeares together),
" yet doe I hold yt, in my poore discretion, verie unfitt that this
" discourse should be borne in the handes and tost in the mouthes
" of his Majestie's subjectes.

" I have therefore this night staied the further publishinge of
" this booke by my expresse warrant untill I shall receive your
" doome from thence, whether yt be to be contemned and past
" over or finallie to be suppressed ; I shall desire you to write
" unto me two wordes heerein. And soe I bidd you hartelie
" farewell, and rest

" Westminster Colledge,   " Your verie assured
" 18 October, 1623.   " Lovinge frend and servant,
                                          " Jo. Lincoln C(ustos) S(igilli)*

On the 25th October, Secretary Conway wrote in answer to the
Lord Keper to instruct him to restrain this publication. (See
Domestic State Papers of the period.)

50.

A demonstration of the unlawful succession of the
new Emperor, Ferdinand. 1623.

This was a tract sheet printed by William Stansby for Nathaniel Butter, bookseller, for which the Stationers' Company, by
warrant from the Council, nailed up Stansby's printing house,
and broke down his presses. He petitioned Secretary Calvert
for pardon and restoration to his business, but the result does
not appear.†

51.

Vox Cœli, or Newes from Heaven, of a Consultation
there held by the High and Mighty Princes, King
Henry 8, King Edward 6, Prince Henry, Queene
Mary, Queene Elizabeth, and Queene Anne ; wherein
Spaine's ambition and treacheries to most kingdomes
and free estates of Europe are unmask'd and truly rep-
esented, but more particularly towards England, and
now more especially under the pretended match of

* Dom. James I, vol. 153, no. 75.
† See Domestic State Papers, James I, vol. 157, nos. 40 and 41.

Prince Charles with the Infanta Dona Maria. Whereunto is annexed two letters written by Queene Mary
from Heaven, the one to Count Gondomar, the ambass-
adour of Spaine, the other to all the Roman Catholiques
of England. Written by S. R. N. I. Printed in
Elisium. 1624.

Votivæ Angliæ, or the desires and wishes of England. Contayned in a patheticall discourse, presented
to the Klng on New Yeares Day last. Wherein are
unfolded and represented manie strong reasons, and
true and solide motives, to perswade his Majestie to
drawe his royall sword, for the restoring of the
Pallatynat and Electorat to his sonne in lawe Prince
Fredericke, to his onlie daughter the Ladie Elizabeth,
and theyr Princelie Issue, against the treacherous
usurpation and formidable ambition and power of the
Emperour, the King of Spayne, and the Duke of
Bavaria, whoe unjustlie possesse and detayne the same.
Together with some aphorismes returned (with a large
interest) to the Pope, in answer of his. Written by
S. R. N. I. Printed at Utrecht, MDCXXIIII.

These books were written by Mr. Reynolds, Viscount Fielding's
tutor, and for so doing he was imprisoned. They displeased
the king much.[1]

In a letter from John Locke to Carleton, dated July 11th, 1624,
the writer says "A poor man is in trouble for printing a book
"called Votiva Angliæ; the Commission Court were about to
"liberate him, when the king ordered him to be remanded and
"to pay £1000 fine, as he was said to have gained £1000 by the
"book."

In or about the year 1626, Reynolds, who was then a prisoner
in the Fleet, addressed a petition to the Council in which he
stated that he was forced from France by order of the late king,
and on his arrival in England was committed to prison for being

1 Dom. James I, 1624, Aug. 14th.

the author of the "Votiva Angliæ," in which he deplored the loss of the Palatinate, and desired its restitution, which "every true hearted Englishman ought to wish and pray for;" and that he had been imprisoned full two years, during which time he incurred a debt of £300 for his maintenance; also that he owed sixty and odd pounds for which he was surety, and was threatened to be arrested for the same as soon as he was at liberty; and he concludes by praying for protection against arrest for one year. [1]

52.

A game at Chaess, as it was acted nine days together at the Globe on the Banks side. (By Thomas Middleton.) 1624.

The title is engraved, and contains figures of a fat bishop (the Bishop of Spalatro), a black knight (Count Gondomar), and a white knight (the Duke of Buckingham). For writing this play the author was committed to prison. In a letter written by Sir Francis Nethersole on August 14th, 1624, he refers to this play thus: "A new play, the plot of which is a game of chess, in which the whole Spanish business is taken up, and Gondomar brought on to the stage, is so popular that the players gain £100 a night. [2]

This play gave great offence to the king, for the players were very speedily called before the Council and forbidden to play until they had appeared before his majesty; [3] and on August 21st the Council sent the following letter to Secretary Conway.

"After our verie heartie comendacions according to his majesty's pleasure signified to this Board by your letter of the 12th of August, touching the suppressing of a scandalous comedie acted by the king's players, wee have called before us some of the principall Actors and demaunded of them by what lycence and authoritie they have presumed to act the same, in answer whereunto they produced a booke being an orriginall and perfect coppie thereof (as they affirmed) seene and allowed by Sir Henry Herbert, Knight, Master of the Revells, under his owne hand and subscribed in the last page of the said booke. We demaunding

1   Dom. Charles I, vol. 44, no. 78.
2   Dom. James I, vol. 171, no. 49.
3   Ibid, art. 60.

further whether there were no other partes or passages represented on the stage, then those expressely contained in the booke, they confidentlie protested they added or varied from the same nothing at all. The Poett they tell us is one Midleton, who shifting out of the way and not attending the Board with the rest as was expected, wee have given warrant to a messinger for the apprehending of him. To those that were before us, we gave a round and sharpe prooffe, making them sensible of his Majesty's high displeasure herein, giving them strict charge and commaund that they presume not to act the said commedie any more, nor that they suffer any other play or enterlude whatsoever to be acted by them or any of their company untill his Majesty's pleasure be further knowne. Wee have caused them likewise to enter into bond for their attendance upon the Board whensoever they shalbe called; as for our certifieing to his Majestie (as was intimated by your letter) what passages in the said comedie we should finde to be offensive and scandalous, wee have thought it our duties for his Majesty's clearer informacion to send herewithall the booke it self, subscribed as aforesaid by the Master of the Revells, that so either your self or some other whom his Majestie shall appoint to peruse the same, may see the passages themselves out of the orriginall, and call Sir Henry Herbert before you to know a reason of his lycenceing thereof, who (as we are given to understand) is now attending at court. So having done as much as we conceived agreable with our duties in conformitie to his Majestie's royall commaundementes and that which we hope shall give him full satisfaction, we shall continue our humble praiers to Almightie God for his health and safetie, and bid yow verie heartilie farewell. From Whitehall the 21st of August, 1624.

Your assured verie loving freindes,

G. Cant.
Th. Grandisone.

Arundell and Surrey.
Arthure Chichester.
Geo. Calvert.[1]

53.

Appello Cæsarem. A just Appeale from two unjust Informers. By Richard Mountagu. London. 1625.

1 Domestic, James I, vol. 171, art. 64.

For writing this book, Mr. Richard Mountagu, Canon of Windsor, Fellow of Eton, Rector of Stamford Rivers, and Chaplain in ordinary to his Majesty was brought to the bar of the House of Commons on July 7th, 1625, and articles were exhibited against him, but proceedings were dropped.[1] On January 17th, 1628, the book was called in and suppressed by a proclamation of which the following is a copy :—

A proclamation for the suppressing of a booke intituled *Appello Cæsarem,* or *An Appeale to Cæsar.*

" Whereas Wee out of our care to conserve and maintaine the church committed to our charge in the unity of true religion and the bond of peace, and not to suffer unnecessary disputes, which may trouble the quiet both of Church and State, have lately caused the Articles of Religion to bee reprinted, as a rule for avoyding of diversities of opinion, and for the establishing of consent in true religion ; we, continuing our desire to compasse this wished effect, and considering that the booke written by Richard Montague, now Bishop of Chichester, then but Batchelor of Divinitie, intituled (Appello Cæsarem or An Appeale to Cæsar) and published in the yeere (1625), was the first cause of those disputes and differences which have sithence much troubled the quiet of the church, have thought it fitting to take away the occasion by calling in the said booke ; and therfore we doe hereby will and straightly command all and singular persons whatsoever, who have or shall have any of them in their hands or custodie, that upon paine of our high displeasure and the consequence thereof, they doe deliver the same presently upon this publication to the Lord Bishop of the diocesse, or his chancellor, if it bee out of the Universities, or if it be in either of the two Universities, to the Chancellor or Vice-Chancellor there, whom wee straightly command to suppresse the same ; hoping thereby, that men will no more trouble themselves with these unnecessary questions, the first occasion being taken away.   But if wee shall bee deceived in this our expectation, and that by reading, preaching, or making bookes, either pro or contra, concerning these differences, men begin anew to dispute, wee shall take such order with them

1   Howell's State Trials; Commons' Journals, vol. 1, pp. 805, 806.

INDEX

EXPURGATORIUS

ANGLICANUS:

OR

A DESCRIPTIVE CATALOGUE OF THE PRINCIPAL BOOKS

PRINTED OR PUBLISHED IN ENGLAND,

WHICH HAVE BEEN SUPPRESSED,

OR BURNT BY THE COMMON HANGMAN,

OR CENSURED,

OR FOR WHICH THE AUTHORS, PRINTERS, OR PUBLISHERS

HAVE BEEN PROSECUTED.

BY W. H. HART, F.S.A.

PRICE TWO SHILLINGS.

LONDON:

JOHN RUSSELL SMITH, 36, SOHO SQUARE.

1873.

HART, PRINTER,]   [SAFFRON WALDEN.

and those bookes, that they shall wish they had never thought upon these needlesse controversies.

Given at our Court at White-Hall, the seventeenth day of January, in the fourth yeere of our reigne, of Great Britaine, France, and Ireland.

God save the King.

Imprinted at London by Bonham Norton and John Bill, printers to the King's most Excellent Majestie. MDCXXVIII.

54.

A short view of the long life and raigne of Henry the Third, King of England. Presented to King James. Printed 1627. 4to. Published anonymously. (By Sir Robert Cotton.)

This tract was reprinted in the first number of Morgan's Phœnix Britannicus, 1641, and also in the fourth volume of the Somers Collection of Tracts, 1651.

The printers were threatened with proceedings in the Court of High Commission for printing the same without licence, and Sir Robert Cotton, who admitted the authorship, also ran some risk, as appears from the following letter of the Bishop of London (dated February 15th, 1627) to Secretary Conway, and also the examinations of the stationers and printers.

My very honorable good Lord,

May it please your Lordship, I have found a booke intituled A view of ye long life and raigne of Henry ye third, King of England, which I send your Lordship with the examinations of all that I find guilty of ye setting of it forth under ye hand of ye Register by whom before me there examinacions were taken. The parties ar in custody and I meane to proceede against them by ye High Comission for printing ye booke without licence, leaving the matter of state to your Lordship's wisdome. Sir Robert Cotton acknowledgeth he writt the booke some 15 yeares agone, but denies that he hath any knowledg of or hand in ye now printing of it. Good my Lord, give me leave uppon such occasions as this to repayre to your Lordship, whose wisdome will mutch strenthen my poore endeavors to his Majestie's service in this kind, or any other that lies in my ability and power;

and so with my most humble acknowledgment of all your noble favours, I pray to God hartily to bless your Lordship, and remayne

Your Lordship's humble servant,

Geo. London.

From my House, February 15th, 1626.

Februarii 15to,
1626.

A briefe of the severall examinations taken before the Lord Bishop of London thes weeke, touching the booke entituled A veiwe of the long life and raigne of Henry the third, King of England.

Benjamin Fisher, a stationer of the City of London, acknowledgeth that he caused five hundred of those bookes to be printed, and no more; five sheets whereof were printed by one Okes a printer, and one other sheete whereof was printed by Breward Alsope and Thomas Fawcett, two other printers.

Of these books Fisher saith they have vented four hundred and twenty or thereabouts, and names some of the parties unto whom they have vented them: viz.—one hundred of them to one Peter Horson, the rest to severall stationers in the country, and that he bought the copy thereof of one Alsope a printer, and saith it was printed without licence.

This Alsope being examined where he had the copy saith he bought it of one Ferdinando Ely, a broker in bookes, and that the said Fisher sent Alsope to buy it of Ely, that he the said Alsope payd ·unto Ely xijd. for it, and having bought it delivered it presently unto Fisher, who caused it to be printed. Alsope he saith that he printed of that sheet delivered unto him as many as should make upp a thousand books of that sort, besides some waste sheets.

Ferdinando Ely being examined, denieth upon his oath that he ever had the copy of the said book, or that he sold it to Alsope, but afterwards uppon better remembrance saith that about two yeares since he sold a copy of a small book to the said Alsope, but what was the contents of it, or for how much money he sold it, he doth not remember.

Peter Horson being examined, confesseth that together with a letter he received an hundred of those books wanting two from the said Fisher, which letter importeth that they were printed at

Dort, and that the author of them was Sir Robert Cotton, and saith it is a book well penned; he hath dispersed divers of them and nameth some of the parties unto whom.

Okes the printer saith his sonn printed part of that book whilest he Okes the father was prisoner in the Compter, and saith that as his sonn told him he printed five hundred of them and no more, and saith they were printed for Benjamin Fisher aforesaid.[1]

Ita Testor { Thomas Mottinshed } deputatus Registrarii Regis.

55.

Religion and Allegiance. Two Sermons. By Roger Manwaring. 1627.

These two sermons were preached by Roger Manwaring, D.D., before his Majesty on the 4th July and 29th July, 1627, and were afterwards published under the before mentioned title, for which Manwaring was brought to the bar of the House of Lords. On the 14th June, 1628, that House gave judgment thus:—

1.—That Dr. Manwaring shall be imprisoned during the pleasure of the House. 2.—That he be fined £1000 to the King. 3.—That he shall make such submission and acknowledgment of his offences as shall be set down by a Committee in writing both at the bar and in the House of Commons. 4.—That he shall be suspended three years from the exercise of his ministry. 5.—That he shall hereafter be disabled from any ecclesiastical dignity. 6.—That he shall be for ever disabled to preach at the Court hereafter, and 7.—That his Majesty be moved to grant a proclamation for the calling in of his books, that they may be burnt in London and both Universities.

The following is the proclamation:—

A Proclamation for the calling in and suppressing of two Sermons, preached and printed by Roger Manwaring, Doctor in Divinity, intituled Religion and Allegiance.

Whereas Roger Manwaring, Doctor in Divinity, hath lately preached two Sermons, the one upon the fourth, the other on the nine and twentieth of July last, and after caused them to bee

1 Domestic State Papers; Charles I, vol. 54, nos. 4 and 5.

printed, and bound up into one volume, and intituled by him
Religion and Allegiance; in which sermons, although the grounds
thereof were rightly laid to perswade obedience from the subjects
to their sovereigne, and that for conscience sake; yet in divers
passages, inferences, and applications thereof trenching upon the
lawes of this land and proceedings of parliaments, whereof hee
was ignorant, hee so farre erred, that hee hath drawen upon
himselfe the just censure and sentence of the High Court of
Parliament, by whose judgement also that booke stands condemned. Wee, taking this into our serious consideration, and
beeing desirous to take away all occasions of scandall or offence,
have thought fit that those sermons, in respect of those inferences
and applications which hee made thereon, bee totally suppressed.

And to that purpose, wee doe hereby straitly charge and command all and every person and persons whatsoever, in whose
hands any of those bookes now are, or hereafter shall be, that
they foorthwith deliver, or cause the same to be delivered, to the
Bishop or other ordinary of that diocese or place where hee or
they at any time are, if it be not within either of our Universities; and if it bee in either of the Universities, that then he or
they deliver the same to the Vicechancellour of that Universitie,
to whom wee doe heereby give speciall charge and command to
cause them to be utterly suppressed.

And wee doe further charge and command, that no man hereafter presume to print the sayd sermons or either of them againe,
upon paine of our high displeasure, and of such further punishment, as for their presumption in that behalfe, may any way bee
inflicted upon them.

Given at our Court at Whitehall, the foure and twentieth day
of June, in the fourth yeere of our reigne of Great Britaine,
France, and Ireland.
God save the King.

Imprinted at London by Bonham Norton and John Bill,
Printers to the King's most excellent Majestie. MDCXXVIII.

On the 21st of June, Manwaring made a humble submission
to the House of Lords, and after the session was over, the fine
was remitted, the Doctor himself released from prison, two
livings given him, and in 1636 he became Bishop of St. Davids.

56.

An Appeal to the Parliament; or Sion's Plea against the Prelacie. Printed the year and moneth wherein Rochell was lost. (1628.)

This book was written by Alexander Leighton, a Scotch doctor of physic and divinity, father of the Archbishop. In this book the author calls bishops men of blood, ravens, and magpies; he declares the institution of episcopacy to be anti-christian and satanical; the Queen is a daughter of Heth, and the King is corrupted by bishops to the undoing of himself and people; and he approves of the murder of Buckingham. Language such as this could hardly have been passed over unnoticed. But it was not till June 4th, 1630, that the author was brought before the Star Chamber. There was no difficulty in pronouncing him guilty of seditious and scandalous writings; and he was sentenced to a terrible and barbarous punishment. Besides a fine of £10,000, and degradation from the ministry, he was publicly whipped in Palace Yard, made to stand two hours in the pillory, one ear was cut off, a nostril slit open, and one of his cheeks branded with the letters S.S. (Sower of Sedition.) After this he was sent off to the Fleet Prison. At the end of a week, "being not yet cured," he was brought out again, underwent a second whipping and repetition of the former atrocities, and was then consigned to prison to life, where he actually spent eleven years. In April, 1641, his sentence was reversed by the House of Commons, and he received such consolation as it could afford him, when it was decided that his former mutilation and imprisonment had been entirely illegal.

57.

A true relation of the unjust, cruel, and barbarous proceeding against the English at Amboyna in the East Indies, by the Neatherlandish Governour and Councel there. 1624.

This book was ordered to be suppressed by a warrant from the Council, dated September 7th, 1631; but the prohibition was revoked, and all restraint upon the sale of the book removed in the following month.[1]

1 Domestic State Papers, Charles I, vol. 205, no. 34.

58.

An examination of those things wherein the Author of the late Appeale holdeth the doctrines of the Pelagians and Arminians to be the doctrines of the Church of England. By George Carleton, Doctor of Divinitie and Bishop of Chichester. London, 1626.

This book was suppressed as appears from a letter from Sir Francis Nethersole to Elizabeth, Queen of Bohemia, dated February 14th, 1629, wherein the writer says, "The printers "have preferred a petition, alleging that of late books written "against Arminians have been suppressed, especially one written "by Bishop Carleton, but others written in their favour have "been licensed.[1]

59.

The Reconciler.

Babel no Bethel, that is, the Church of Rome no true visible Church of Christ. By H(enry) B(urton), Rector of St. Matthew's, Friday Street. 1629.

Maschil unmasked, in a treatise defending this sentence of our Church, viz., the present Romish Church hath not the nature of the true Church. By Thomas Spencer. London. N. d.

The Church of England's old antithesis to new Arminianisme. By William Prynne. London, 1629.

On April 20th, 1629, articles were exhibited by the Ecclesiastical Commissioners against the printers and publishers of these books, among whom was Michael Sparkes, stationer, who had been committed to the Fleet "for printing and publishing offensive books without license or warrant." In his answer to the articles objected against him by the Commissioners, Sparkes denies the present binding authority of the decree in the Star Chamber for regulating printing, as directly intrenching on the hereditary liberty of the subjects' persons and goods, and being contrary to Magna Charta, the Petition of Right, and other statutes. He presumed that Court would no way infringe the

1 Domestic State Papers, Charles I, vol. 135, no. 40.

liberties of his Majesty's subjects, which his Majesty professed in his late declaration that he would constantly maintain. He admits that he printed "Babel no Bethel," but conceives that there was nothing contrary to the established doctrine of the Church of England therein, and that he had endured a hard imprisonment already for the same, which he hopes will excuse his further answer. He says that some part of Mr. Prynne's book was printed by Augustine Matthewes, and other part elsewhere. He conceives the book itself to be a just and necessary defence of the Church of England against the Arminians. He refuses to confess the printer that printed part of the book, and thinks the Court will not desire it, in regard that he (the printer) has done all to the glory of God, the honour of the King, the good of the Church, and the welfare of the doctrine of the Church of England and the religion established.[1]

60.

Rome's Ruin. 1631.

Articles were exhibited by the Ecclesiastical Commissioners against Michael Sparke, James Bouler, Nicholas Bourne, and Henry Overton, servant of Mrs. Shefford, of London, stationers, charging them with having caused to be printed without license this "scandalous book," wherein are passages taxing not only the whole state, but also some particular bishops and persons of eminent place in the church.[2]

61.

De regno Hiberniæ Sanctorum Insula Commentarius, Authore Illustriss, ac Reverendiss. Domino D. *Petro Lombardo* Hiberno, Archiepiscopo Ardmachano, totius ejusdem Regni Primate, olim in Alma Universitate Lovaniensi S. Theol. Doctore, & quondam Præposito Ecclesiæ Cathedralis Camaracensis, &c. Lovanii, 1632.

This book was ordered to be suppressed and prosecuted by Lord Deputy Strafford, at the direction of the King.

1 Domestic State Papers, Charles I, vol. 142, no. 22.
2 Ibid, Charles I, vol. 205, no. 102.

62.

Histrio Mastix. The Player's Scourge, or Actor's Tragedie. By William Prynne. London, 1633.

In this remarkable book the author speaks in such unmeasured terms of "women actors" that it was considered to be a special attack on the Queen, who had herself taken part in the performance of a pastoral at Somerset House. Therefore on February 7th, 163$\frac{2}{3}$, Mr. William Prynne, utter barrister of Lincoln's Inn, was brought to the Court of Star Chamber on the information of the Attorney General for writing this book, and at the same time were brought up Michael Sparkes and William Buckner, the one for printing and the other for licensing the same book. The book was condemned to be burnt, and Mr. Prynne was adjudged to be put from the bar and to be for ever incapable of his profession, to be expelled from the Society of Lincoln's Inn, to stand in the pillory in Westminster and Cheapside, to lose both his ears, one in each place, and with a paper on his head denoting his offence; to pay a fine of £5000 to the King, and be perpetually imprisoned. Buckner was sentenced to imprisonment according to the course of the Court, and to pay a fine of £50 to the King. Sparkes was sentenced to pay a fine of £500 to the King, and to stand in the pillory in Cheapside without touching his ears, with a paper on his head to declare his offence. The sentence against Prynne was executed the 7th and 10th days of May following.

63.

A Defence of the most ancient and sacred Ordinance of God, the Saboath Day. Second edition, corrected and amended. By Theophilus Brabourne, Clerk. 1634, circa.

I have not been able to meet with a copy of this book, but there is at the British Museum a volume by the same author, which may be the first edition of the one now under consideration. It is entitled "A discourse upon the Sabbath Day, wherein are "handled these particulars ensuinge. 1.—That the Lord's Day "is not Sabbath Day by divine institution. 2.—An exposition "of the 4 commandement so farr forth as may give light unto "the ensueinge discourse; and particularly here it is showne, at "what time the Sabbath Day should begine and end, for the "satisfaction of those who are doubtfull in this point. 3.—That "the seaventh day Sabbath is not abolished. 4.—That the "seaventh day Sabbath is now still in force. 5.—The author's "exhortation and reasones, that nevertheless there be no rente "from our church as touchinge practise. Written by Theophilus "Brabourne. Printed the 23rd of Decemb., Anno Dom., 1628.

In 1634 Brabourne was cited before the Court of High Commission for writing this book, and in his answer he confessed to have composed and caused to be printed beyond sea five hundred copies of the same, in which he was alleged to have broached "erroneous heretical and judaical opinions." Being admonished to renounce his opinions, he acknowledged himself to be a Sabbatharian, and as much bound to keep the Saturday's Sabbath as the Jews were before the coming of Christ. The Court pronounced him a Jew, a heretic and schismatic, and adjudged him worthy to be severely punished. He was ordered to be deprived of all his ecclesiastical livings and dignities, and to be deposed and degraded from his holy orders and function in the university, pronounced excommunicate, fined £1000, condemned in expenses, ordered to make a public submission *conceptis verbis* at such times and places as the Court should appoint, and remanded back to prison until the Court advise on some other course for delivering him over to the secular power if he persisted in his opinions.

64.

Flagellum Pontificis et Episcoporum Latialium. Auctore Johanne Bastwick. 1635.

This book, "though professing to be directed against the "Church of Rome, 'tis more than manifest," Laud says, "that "it was purposely written and divulged against the Bishops and "Church of England." For this Bastwick was cited before the High Commission Court, when thirty seven articles were charged against him. He was acquitted of all the charges except one, and that was his maintaining bishops and priests to be the same order of ministers, or, as he expressed it himself, "Impingitur "horrendum crimen quod infulis et apicibus jus divinum nega-"verim, quod Episcopi et Presbyteri paritatem asseruerim." For this he was condemned to pay a fine of £1000, to be excommunicated, to be debarred from the practise of his profession, his book to be burnt, and he himself to pay the costs and remain in prison till he recanted; and "that is," he says, "till domesday in the afternoone."

65.

A divine tragedie lately acted: or a collection of sundry memorable examples of God's judgments upon Sabbath breakers. By William Prynne. London. 1636.

News from Ipswich, discovering certaine late detestable practises of some domineering lordly prelates. By the same. Ipswich. 1636.

The first mentioned book was directed against Noye, the Attorney General, who, it was made out, was visited with a judgment from heaven whilst laughing at Prynne as he stood in the pillory. For writing and publishing these books, the latter of which was styled "a pernicious damnable scurrilous invective and libel," an information was exhibited in the Star Chamber against the author, and on the 14th June, 1637, he was sentenced to lose his ears in the Palace Yard at Westminster, to be fined £5000 to the King, and to perpetual imprisonment. He was also condemned to be stigmatized in the cheeks with two letters, S. and L., for a seditious libeller; and on the 30th June, the sentence was carried out with barbarous cruelty, but at the beginning of the Long Parliament Prynne was liberated.

66.

The Lord's Day, the Sabbath Day, or a Brief Answer to some passages in a late Treatise of the (Lord's) Day: digested dialogue-wise betweene two Divines, A. and B. 1636.

In March, 1637, articles were objected by the Commissioners for Causes Ecclesiastical against James Hannum, of St. Clement Danes, London, wax chandler, for selling this book, as well as Bastwick's Apologeticus. He was required, by virtue of his oath, to set down how many of the said books he had uttered, vented, or sold, and of whom he had them and to whom he sold them. He was also charged with knowing that these books were never licensed to be printed or sold, but were printed by stealth by some friend of his. Also that one or more of the said books was lately taken in his house.[1]

67.

ΠΡΑΞΕΙΣ ΤΩΝ ΕΠΙΣΚΟΠΩΝ, sive Apologeticus ad Præsules Anglicanos criminum Ecclesiasticorum in Curia Celsæ Commissionis. Autore Johanne Bastwick, M.D. 1636.

This was written by Bastwick, while he was in confinement in the Gate House Prison, in answer to a book by Thomas Chowney, a Sussex gentleman, who maintained that the Church of Rome was a true church, and had not erred in fundamentals. For writing and publishing this book, as well as the Litany (presently described), an information was exhibited in the Star Chamber against Bastwick, and on June 14th, 1637, he was sentenced to lose his ears in the Palace Yard at Westminster, to be fined £5000 to his Majesty and to perpetual imprisonment. He was confined in the castle or fort of the Isles of Scilly, but was liberated by the Long Parliament.

68.

An Apology of an Appeale. Also an Epistle to the true-hearted Nobility. By Henry Burton, Pastor of St. Matthewe's, Friday Street. 1636.

For God and the King. The summe of two Sermons preached on the fifth of November last in St. Matthewe's, Friday Streete, 1636. By Henry Burton, Minister of God's word there and then.

Burton was born at Birsall in Yorkshire in 1579. He was educated at St. John's College, Cambridge, and became Rector of St. Matthew's, Friday Street about 1626. He had been Clerk of the Closet to Prince Henry, and afterwards to Prince Charles; a position in which he was not continued when Charles became King. In this bitter disappointment he produced the

---

1 **Domestic State Papers, Charles I, vol. 351, no. 101.**

books now under consideration, for which he was prosecuted in the Star Chamber, and sentenced to lose his ears in the Palace Yard at Westminster, to be fined £5000 to the King, and to perpetual imprisonment. He was confined in the Isle of Guernsey, but was liberated at the beginning of the Long Parliament.

69.

The Letany of John Bastwick, Doctor of Phisicke, being now full of devotion, as well in respect of the common calamities of plague and pestilence, as also of his owne particular miserie, lying at this instant in *Limbo Patrum.* Printed by the speciall procurement and for the especiall use of our English Prelats, in the yeare of remembrance, Anno 1637.

The answer of John Bastwick, *Doctor of Phisicke,* to the exceptions made against his Letany by a learned Gentleman, which is annexed to the Litany itselfe, as Articles superadditionall against the Prelats. This is to follow the Letany as a second part thereof. Printed in the yeare of remembrance, Anno 1637.

The Answer of John Bastwick, *Doctor of Phisicke,* to the information of Sir John Bancks, Knight, Atturney universall. Printed in the yeare 1637.

XVI New Quæres proposed to our Lord Prælates. Printed in the yeare M.DC.XXXVII.

The first mentioned book, the "Letany" was at first only shown to a few friends in manuscript, but afterwards it came to be printed in this way. John Lilburne, afterwards a Lieutenant Colonel in the Parliamentary army, and who behaved with such gallantry at Marston Moor, was introduced to Dr. Bastwick in 1637, and was so much pleased at hearing the Letany, that having a little ready money at command, he undertook to get it printed in Holland. Bastwick was at first averse to this, as he distrusted a friend of Lilburne's who would have to assist in disposing of the impression. His scruples however were overcome, and the Letany, together with the "Answer to the Information of Sir John Bancks, Kt., Atturney Universalle," committed to the press. The first edition realized a handsome profit; but Archbishop Laud got scent of the publication, laid hold upon the disperser, and made him confess who was the chief actor in the affair. Accordingly when Lilburne landed with another impression, he was seized along with his cargo, and the books burnt by the hands of the common hangman. Lilburne, and Wharton, (who dispersed the books) were further cited to the Star Chamber, and on February 13th, 1638, sentenced to be remanded to the Fleet, there to remain till they conformed themselves to the order of the Court, and to pay £500 apiece to his Majesty's use; and before their enlargements out of the Fleet, to become bound with good sureties for their good behaviour. Lilburne was to be whipped through the streets from the Fleet to the Pillory at Westminster, and together with Wharton to be set in the said Pillory, and from thence returned to the Fleet, there to remain. This sentence was carried into execution on April 18th, 1638, and the same day the Court passed the following further sentence upon Lilburne "for uttering sundry scandalous speeches, and scattering divers copies of seditious books among the people," while he was in the pillory, that he should be laid alone with irons on his hands and legs in the wards of the Fleet where the basest and meanest sort of prisoners were used to be put, and that the Warden of the Fleet take special care to hinder the resort of any persons whatsoever to him; and particularly that he be not supplied with money from any friend, and that all letters, writings, and books brought to him be seized and delivered to their Lordships; and all persons visiting him to be reported to the Board. However, in November, 1640, on petitioning Parliament he was liberated.

70.

Britannia Triumphans: a Masque presented at Whitehall by the King's Majestie and his Lords on the Sunday after Twelfth Night, 1637. By Inigo Jones, Surveyor of His Majestie's Workes, and William Davenant, Her Majestie's Servant. London, 1637.

This masque is said to have been suppressed from the statement on the title page of it being acted on a Sunday, and the clamour it excited.

71.

Sunday no Sabbath. A Sermon preached before the Lord Bishop of Lincolne at his Lordship's visitation at Ampthill in the County of Bedford, August 17th, 1635. By John Pocklington, Doctor of Divinitie, late Fellow and President both of Pembroke Hall and Sidney College in Cambridge, and Chaplaine to the Right Reverend Father in God the Lord Bishop of Lincolne. London, 1636.

Altare Christianum, or the Dead Vicar's Plea. Wherein the Vicar of Gr. being dead yet speaketh and pleadeth out of antiquity against him that hath broken downe his altar. Presented and humbly submitted to the consideration of his superiours, the governours of our Church. By John Pocklington, D.D. London, 1637.

For writing these books Pocklington was deprived of all his livings, dignities, and preferments, and prohibited the King's Court. These proceedings were instituted against him at the instigation of Archbishop Williams. On February 10th, 1641, the House of Lords ordered that these two books should be publicly burnt in the City of London and the two Universities by the common hangman; and on March 10th, the House ordered the Sheriffs of London and the Vice-Chancellors of both the Universities forthwith to take care and see the order of the house carried into execution.[1]

72.

An Introduction to a Devout Life, 1637.

This is a translation of the "Praxis Spiritualis, sive Introductio ad vitam devotam," by the celebrated Catholic divine, St. Francis de Sales. Archbishop Laud in writing to his Vice-Chancellor in

1 Lords' Journals, vol. 4, pp. 161, 180; Howell's State Trials, vol. 5, p. 765.

1637, speaks thus of the book, "There was an English trans-
"lation of a book of devotion, written by Sales, Bishop of Geneva,
"and intitled Praxis Spiritualis, &c., licensed by Dr. Haywood,
"then my chaplain, about the latter end of November last; but
"before it passed his hands, he first struck out divers things
"wherein it varied from the doctrine of our Church, and so passed
"it. But by the practice of one Burrowes (who is now found to
"be a Roman Catholic (those passages struck out by Dr. Hay-
"wood were interlined afterwards, and were printed according to
"Burrowes's falsifications. The book being thus printed, gave
"great and just offence, especially to myself, who upon the first
"hearing of it, gave present order to seize upon all the copies,
"and to burn them publicly in Smithfield. Eleven or twelve
"hundred copies were seized and burnt accordingly.[1]

The following is the proclamation for suppressing the book :—

"By the King.

"A proclamation for calling in a book entituled An Introduction
"to a Devout Life; and that the same be publikely burnt.

"Whereas a book entituled An Introduction to a Devout Life,
"was lately printed by Nicholas Oakes of London, and many of
"them published and dispersed throughout the realme, the copy
"of which book being brought to the Chaplaine of the Lord
"Archbishop of Canterbury for licence and allowance, was by
"him, upon diligent perusall, in sundry places expunged and
"purged of divers passages therein tending to Popery. Never-
"thelesse, the same book, after it was so amended and allowed
"to be printed, was corrupted and falsified by the translator and
"stationer, who between them inserted again the same Popish
"and unsound passages; and the stationer is now apprehended,
"and the translator sought for, to be proceeded against according
"to justice. His Majesty, out of his pious and constant care to
"uphold and maintain the religion professed in the Church of
"England in its purity, without error or corruption, doth there-
"fore hereby declare his royall will and pleasure to be, and doth
"straitly charge and command all persons, of what degree, qual-
"ity, or condition soever, to whose hands any of the said bookes
"are or shall come, that without delay they deliver or send them
"to the Bishop or Chancellor of the Diocesse, whom his Majestie
"requireth to cause the same to be publikely burnt, as such of

1 Laud's Chancellorship, fol. 1700, p. 129.

"them as have beene already seized on have been by His Majes-
"tie's expresse command; and to this His Majestie's royall
"pleasure, he requireth all his loving subjects to yeeld all due
"conformity and obedience, as they will avoid the censure of
"high contempt.

"Given at our Court at Whitehall, the fourteenth day of May
"in the thirteenth yeare of our reigne.

"God save the King.

"Imprinted at London by Robert Barker, Printer to the
"King's most excellent Majestie; and by the Assignes of John
"Bill. 1637.

73.

The Jubilee of Jesuits.   Circa, 1640.

In this book it was contained that the Papists should fish in
troubled waters while the King was at war with the Scots, with
prayers in it for the holy martyrs that suffered in the Fleet sent
against the heretics in England, 1639.   It is undoubtedly the
same work as is entitled "Jubileum sive speculum Jesuiticum
opera et studio I. L. W. O. P.," of which there is a reprint in the
British Museum dated 1643.   On the 14th November, 1640,
Thomas Chude and John Clay were called in before the House of
Commons to testify touching this book, when Chude declared he
had one in his custody; he had it from a woman at Redriffe, wife
to H. Goodwell, a cobbler, whose wife was a Papist; he delivered
the book the same day he had it to the Sheriff of London, Sheriff
Warner.[1]

74.

Information from the Estaits of the Kingdome of Scotland to the Kingdome of England.   1640.

By a proclamation of March 30th, 1640, "against libellous
"and seditious pamphlets and discourses sent from Scotland,"
this tract was prohibited on account of its containing "many
"most notorious falsehoods and scandals to the dishonour of His
"Majesty's proceedings with his subjects in Scotland."

1 Commons' Journals, vol. 2, p. 29.

75.

Mr. Maynard's Speech before both Houses in Parliament, upon Wednesday, the 24th of March, in reply upon the Earle of Strafford's Answer to his Articles at the Barre. 1641.

On April 6th, 1641, it was ordered by the House of Commons that enquiry should be made after the printer and venter of this speech, and that all diligence was to be used in suppressing the same.[1] A copy exists in the British Museum Library.

76.

The Anatomy of Et cætera. Or the unfolding of that dangerous Oath in the close of the Sixth Canon, As it was contrived by the Bishops and some of the Clergie in their late Oath Ex Officio, cunningly obliging the Consciences of His Majestie's Subjects to observe and obey whatsoever errours they would impose. Condemned and dissected in a passionate Conference betwixt the two zealous Brothers Roger and Ralph, penned at the first injunction of the new Canons, and now publisht since their abolishment. By an Oxfordshire gentleman. London, 1641.

On August 24th, 1641, it was resolved by the House of Commons that Richard Heren should be sent for as a delinquent by the Sergeant at Arms for printing this pamphlet; and also that Thomas Bray, an Oxon scholar, who turned the pamphlet out of poetry into prose should also be sent for as a delinquent.[2]

A copy is preserved in the British Museum Library. It commences thus :—

"Two of the zealous Tribe being inspired, as they tearmed it,
"and having a greater parcell of the spirit than at other times,
"after a great deal of chat, now concerning this thing, and now
"concerning that thing, at last drew themselves as far as the
"*New Canons*, where they read, but yet you must not thinke that

1. Commons' Journals, vol. 2, p. 116.
2. Commons' Journals, vol. 2, pp. 268, 269.

"it was without rubbes and jarres, but comming to the *Sixth*
" *Canon* that ended with *Et cætera*, at the very sight of which he
"swelled as much as *Goliah* with his weaver's beam, and thus
" began to break forth in these or the like tearmes.

" *Roger*. I that have behaved my selfe so well, that now I am
" in sincerity elected a Zealous Brother, I that having my worth
" seen am for it rewarded with twenty Nobles *per annum*, besides
" what I collect every year from our Female Charity, considering
" with myselfe what a vile and indiscreet thing these new Oathes
" and Canons are, I am even wrapt besides my selfe, and with
" this very word, or letter, or syllable, or whatsoever it is, I must
" and will dissect it.

" *Ralph*. Why brother *Roger?* Art thou of so shallow capacity
" as thou makest thyselfe to be? Have patience pray, and rather
"finde fault with the Printer than with the thing printed, or
" rather with him which set the Printer on worke than with the
" Printer himselfe, these times are corrupted, for why? corrupt
" men have ruled us here in this Land.

" Here could *Roger* hold no longer, but like to a Beardog, he
" yawnes, and barkes, and bawles, saying,

" *Roger*. In sincerity brother *Ralph*, thou doest not know what
" an urging this is to me, see what a vile mishapen monster it is,
" this *Et cætera*, God blesse us! is a Limbe of the Devill ;" &c., &c.

And it concludes thus :—

" Well, these two Zealous Brothers had dranke so long together
"that they played the beasts, like a couple of drunken rogues,
" &c., and then they must needs quarrell, and make themselves
" and Religion in them to be scoffed egregiously, and indeed it
" is an ancient proverbe, *When theeves fall out, true men come by*
" *their goods*.

" It chanced that Roger gave Ralph some words in his drinke,
" which did not very well please him, which made Ralph break
" out beyond the bounds of modesty, and told him that he was a
" dissembling knave, and that he could prove him so, for said
"Ralph, *Is it not the part of a knave to carry another man's wife so*
" *far as Banbury in Oxfordshire, and there to live with her, and keep*
" *her as your owne wife? fie, fie, for shame*.

" *Nay*, said Roger, *hic-up*, if you go to that, *hic-up*, you are as
" arrant a knave as my selfe, *hic-up*, for do you remember, you Slave
" you, how you wisht your wife in the *Low Countries*, to say, that you

" *were her brother, because she was fair, and that it might be said that*
" *you imitated Abraham, when he was a good man, whereas thou art a*
" *stinking Rogue.*

"Thus they brawled, and scolded, and scolded, and brawled,
" till they fell asleep, in which pickle I left them."

77.

The order and course of passing Bills in Parliament. 1641.

On June 3rd, 1641, the House of Commons referred to the
Committee concerning printing, the consideration of the printing
of this book, and they were to report to the House what they
thought fit to be done therein; and to send for the printer
thereof, and the parties who conceived themselves to be preju-
diced by that false copy.[1]

A copy is preserved in the British Museum Library.

78.

The true relation of the French Ambassage. 1641.

On July 12th, 1641, the House of Commons ordered that the
printing of this pamphlet be referred to the Committee for printing, where Sir Edward Dering had the chair; and on the 18th
November following, it was further ordered that Alsop the printer
should be summoned to attend and answer such matters as should
be objected against him concerning the printing of this pamphlet,
and that some course was to be considered for preventing
inordinate printing for the future.[2]

79.

The Copy of a Letter sent from the Earle of Holland to an Honourable Lord at the Parliament. 1641.

On August 20th, 1641, the House of Commons referred to the
Committee concerning printing to enquire who printed this letter,
and to take some course and propound it to the House for preventing the inordinate licence of printing. On enquiry it was
found that Thomas Symonds was the printer, and it was resolved

1. Commons' Journals, vol. 2, p. 166.
2. Ibid, pp. 206, 319, 324.

that he should be sent for as a delinquent for printing this letter
without any order of Parliament, after that he was acquainted
with the order of the House inhibiting the printing of anything
concerning the proceedings of that House.[1]

A copy is preserved in the British Museum Library.

80.

Sir Kenelme Digbye's Honour Maintained by a most
couragious Combat which he fought with the Lord
Mount le Ros, who by base and slanderous words
reviled our King.   Also the true relation how he went
to the King of France, who kindly intreated him, and
sent two hundred mēn to guard him so far as Flanders.
And now he is returned from Banishment, and to his
eternall honour lives in England.   Printed at London
for T. B., 1641.

A pamphlet of five pages, of which there is a copy in the
British Museum Library.   On the title page is a rough woodcut
representing two men fighting a duel.

On November 24th, 1641, the House of Commons ordered that
the Committee for printing should enquire after the printing of
this book.[2]

81.

A terrible outcry against the loytering exalted
prelates.   By H. Walker.   1641.

On December 20th, 1641, the House of Commons resolved
that Walker should be sent for as a delinquent by the Sergeant
at Arms for being author of this pamphlet; and the printing of
this and other books by the same author was referred to the
Committee for printing.[3]

82.

Noli me tangere is a thinge to be thovght on.   Or
Vox carnis sacræ clamantis ab Altari ad Aquilam
sacrilegam.   Noli me tangere ne te perdam.   1642.

1. Commons' Journals, vol. 2, pp. 266, 268, 269.
2. Ibid, vol. 2, p. 324.
3. Ibid, vol. 2, p. 349.

On January 31st, 164½, the House of Commons referred this book to the Committee for printing, to enquire out the author and the printer thereof.[1] It has an engraved frontispiece wherein is represented an *"Altare,"* upon which an offering is consuming in fire, *"Ignis sacer;"* above the offering is *"Sancto nomini caro sacra."* An eagle grasps at part of the offering, *"offam rapit Aquila carbone adhærente;"* another eagle hovers above, with a second portion, *"Portat ad pullos in nido,"* and flying towards a nest, *"Aquilæ nidus,"* which is in the branches of a tree. On the trunk of the tree is *"Ardet carbone nidus quo perit soboles impiæ genitricis."* An Eye is visible in clouds, inscribed *"Vidit offensus Oculus supremi;"* also a clenched fist, above which is *"Percutit extensa manus supremi."* Rays proceed from the eye downwards over the altar and its adjuncts, and are respectively inscribed *"Advertit peccatorem in progrediendo,"* *"Aspicit peccatorem in peccando,"* *"Acceptat sacrificia peccatorem condonando,"* and *"Accipit peccatorem sacrificia comburendo."* A ray is directed to the nest, and inscribed *"Animadvertit in peccatorem posteros plectendo."* The old British Museum Catalogue ascribes the authorship of this tract to Mr. Ephraim Udall.

83.

The Lord Digbies Speech in the House of Commons to the Bill of Attainder of the Earle of Strafford, the 21 of April, 1641. Printed in the yeare 1641.

On July 13th, 1641, the House of Commons resolved that this speech contained untrue and scandalous matters concerning the proceedings of the Committees of the Lords and Commons, and that the publishing and printing of that speech by Lord Digby, after a vote passed in that House, was scandalous to the proceedings of that House, and a crime; and it was also ordered that all the books so printed should be publicly burnt on the following Friday, in various parts of London by the Common Hangman.[2]

A copy exists in the British Museum Library.

84.

Master Glyn's Reply to the Earle of Strafford's defence of the severall Articles objected against him by the House of Commons. London. Printed for Lawrence Chapman, 1641.

1. Commons' Journals, vol. 2, p. 404.   2. Ibid, p. 208.

On May 11th, 1641, the House of Commons ordered that this speech, which was printed and went under Mr. Glynne's name, should be suppressed and the printer punished : and the Master and Wardens of the Stationers' Company were to attend the House to employ their best endeavours accordingly.[1]

A copy exists in the British Museum Library.   It is in quarto, and contains 56 pages.

85.

Verses lately written by Thomas, Earle of Strafford. 1641.   A folio broadside, containing nine seven-line stanzas.

On May 14th, 1641, the House of Commons ordered that the consideration of printing these verses be referred to the Committee for printing of books.[2]

A copy is preserved in the British Museum Library.   The verses are as follows :—

(I.)

"Go, Empty Joyes,
    With all your noyse,
      And leave me here alone,
   In sweet sad silence to bemoane
      Your vaine and fleet delight,
   Whose danger none can see aright,
   Whilest your false splendor dimmes his sight.

(II.)

Goe and insnare
    With your false ware,
      Some other easie Wight,
   And cheat him with your flattering Light;
      Raine on his head a shower
   Of Honours, favor, wealth, and power;
   Then snatch it from him in an houre.

1.   Commons' Journals, vol. 2, p. 142.
2.   Ibid, vol. 2, pp. 146, 148, 160.

(III.)

Fill his big minde
With gallant winde
  Of Insolent applause;
Let him not fear all-curbing Lawes,
  Nor King nor People's frowne,
But dreame of something like a Crowne,
And climing towards it, tumble downe.

(IV.)

Let him appeare
In his bright Sphere
  Like *Scynthia* in her pride,
With star-like troups on every side;
  Such for their number and their light,
As may at last orewhelme him quite,
And blend us both in one dead night.

(V.)

Welcome, sad Night,
Griefe's sole delight,
  Your mourning best agrees
With Honour's funerall Obsequies.
  In *Thetis'* lap he lies,
Mantled with soft securities,
Whose too much Sunshine blinds his eyes.

(VI.)

Was he too bold,
That needs would hold
  With curbing raines, the day,
And make *Sol's* fiery Steeds obay?
  Then sure as rash was I,
Who with ambitious wings did fly
In *Charles* his Waine too loftily.

(VII.)

I fall, I fall;
Whom shall I call?
  Alas, can he be heard,
Who now is neither lov'd nor fear'd.
  You, who were wont to kisse the ground,
Where e're my honor'd steps were found,
Come catch me at my last rebound.

(VIII.)

How each admires
Heav'n's twinkling fires,
    When from their glorious seat
Their influence gives life and heat.
    But O! how few there ar',
(Though danger from that act be far)
Will stoop and catch a falling star.

(IX.)

Now 'tis too late
To imitate
    Those Lights, whose pallidnesse
Argues no inward guiltinesse:
    Their course one way is bent.
The reason is, there's no dissent
In Heaven's high Court of Parliament.

London, printed 1641.

86.

The Saint's Beliefe. By John Turner. 1641. A folio broadside.

On May 18th, 1641, the House of Commons ordered that this publication be referred to the Committee for printing as concerning the printer; and that the Stationers' Company be strictly required to use all their endeavours to suppress those copies; and that John Turner, who names himself the author, be sent for as a delinquent for his boldness in causing a new belief to be printed without authority, during the sitting of parliament.[1]

The accompanying folding page contains an exact reprint, line for line, of this eccentric paper, of which a copy exists in the British Museum Library.

87.

The declaration of Colonel Goring to the House of Commons upon his examination concerning the late conspiracie against the state and kingdome. With the

1. Commons' Journals, vol. 2, p. 148.

THE
SAINTS
BELIEFE.

I Beleeve in one Almighty God, [a] *Creator and maker of all things,* [b] *distinguished in three, Father, Sonne, and Holy Ghost :* [c] *but not divided,* [d] *all working together in the Creation,* [e] *Redemption,* [f] *preservation,* [g] *and salvation of Man. The Son our* Lord Jesus Christ, [h] *God and Man ;* [k] *begotten and sent by the Father ;* [l] *conceived and born of the Virgin Mary,* [m] *suffered under the Roman power,* Pilate *being Judge ;* [n] *crucified* [o] *dead,* [p] *and his soule immediately received by* God *his Father ;* [q] *and his body buried ;* [r] *rose againe the third day according to the Scriptures ;* [s] *and ascended into heaven ;* [t] *sits at the right hand of* God ; [u] *whom the heavens must contain for a time ;* [w] *in whom all our sins are forgiven ;* [x] *and from thence he shall come to judge the living and the dead ;* [y] *before whom every one shall appeare,* [z] *to give an account* [a] *of every evill thought,* [b] *idleword,* [c] *vaine oath, and* [d] *wicked action. And I beleeve in the Holy Ghost,* [e] *sent by the Father and the Sonne to teach and leade* [f] *his Elect in all truth,* [g] *instituting by his Apostles particular Churches here on earth, and no other ;* [h] *every ordinance of* God *belonging to every one of them ;* [i] *all of equall authority, no one being greater or lesser then other, either in power or priviledges ;* [k] *who must serve him as he hath commanded in his holy Scriptures ;* [l] *both in ordinances,* [m] *and order,* [n] *in their own Faith ;* [o] *with a pure conscience ;* [p] *all Beleevers being bound in duty to have and hold communion in some one of them ;* [q] *and that every Church hath power from* GOD *to elect and ordaine their own Officers,* [r] *receive in Beleevers, and Excommunicate any one of them that lives in transgression, without the helpe or assistance of any ;* [s] *no one member being more free then another.* [t]*

And I beleeve I am bound in conscience to GOD *to honour and obey my Father, Mother, King, Master, and every Officer under him, whether they be Christians, irreligious, Idolaters, or Heathens. The Commandement requires obedience to every one of them of what Religion soever they be equall, and alike.* [u] *And I beleeve the bodies of the just shall rise to life everlasting,* [w] *and the wicked to everlasting perdition, &c.*

[a] Gen. 1, 1. Prov. 16, 4. [b] 1 Joh. 5, 7.
[c] Joh. 10, 30. 1 Joh. 5, 7. [d] Gen. 1, 2.
Joh. 1, 1, 2, 3. [e] Ro. 3, 24. Ephe. 1, 7.
[f] Psal. 97, 10. Phil. 4, 7. [g] Tit. 2, 11.
Jo. 11, 25. [h] Col. 2, 9.
Mat. 1, 23.
[i] 1 Tim. 2, 5.
Act. 2, 22. Heb. 7, 24.
[k] 1 Joh. 4, 9. Joh. 3, 17. [l] Isay. 7, 14.
Luk. 2, 7. [m] John 11, 48. John 19, 12, 15,
16. [n] Mat. 27, 35.
[o] Joh. 19, 33. [p] Luk. 23, 43, 46.
[q] Joh. 19, 41, 42, [r] 1 Cor. 15, 4. [s] Act. 1, 9, 10, 11.
Joh. 20, 17. [t] Heb. 1, 3. [u] Act. 3, 21.
[w] 1 Joh. 2, 12. Joh. 1, 29. [x] 1 Thes. 4, 16, 17. [y] Mat. 25, 32.
[z] Mat. 1, 2, 36. [a] Gen. 6, 5. 1 Cor. 3, 20.
[b] Mat. 12, 36. [c] Exo. 20, 7. Mat. 5, 34, 35, 36, 37. Jam. 1, 26.
[d] Rev. 22, 12. Mat. 25, 41, 45, 46.

[e] Joh. 14, 26. Joh. 15, 26. Joh. 16, 13. [f] Col. 3, 12. 1 Pet. 1, 2. Rom. 9, 11. [g] Mat. 18, 17, 18, 19, 20. Rev. 1, 11. Gal. 1, 2.
[h] 1 Cor. 3, 21, 22, 23. Psal. 149, 7, 8, 9. [i] 2 Cor. 12, 13. 1 Cor. 5, 12, 13. [k] Joh. 15, 10, 14. Joh. 5, 39. [l] Rev. 22, 18. Deut. 5, 32. Mat. 28, 20. [m] Col. 2, 5. 1 Cor. 14, 40. 1 Cor. 15, 2. Levi. 10, 1, 2. 1 Chro. 13, 9, 11. 1 Chro. 15, 13. Num. 15, 16.
[n] 2 Tim. 1, 13, 14. Mat. 9, 22. Mark 16, 16. Heb. 11, 6. [o] 1 Tim. 10, 1. Joh. 3, 20. [p] Heb. 10, 25. Mat. 18, 17, 18, 19, 20.
[q] Acts 6, 2, 3, 5. Act. 14, 23. Act. 1, 15, 23, 26. Ezek. 33, 2. Numb. 8, 10. [r] 2 Cor. 2, 7, 8. Joh. 3, 10. [s] Mat. 18, 17, 18, 19, 20.
1 Cor. 5, 12, 13, Acts 11, 2, 3, 4. [t] Ro. 2, 11. Deut. 1, 17. Jam. 2, 9. Acts 11, 2, 3, 4. [u] Ro. 13, 2, 3, 4, 5. Exo. 20, 12. Ephes. 6, 5, 10. 1 Cor. 15. Mat. 25, 34. [x] Isay. 30, 33. Mat. 25, 41, 46.

Pro. 22, 6.   Teach a Child in the trade of his way, and when he is old he shall not depart from it.

1 *Thes.* 5,   Try all things, keep that which is good.

Acts 17, 11. These were also more noble men then they which were of Thessalonica, which received the Word with all readinesse, and searched the Scriptures dayly, whether these things were so.

1 *Sam.* 15, 22. To obey is better then sacrifice, and to hearken then the fat of rammes.

By me JOHN TURNER, Prisoner of our *Lord Jesus Christ* (committed by the Bishops) neare 14 yeares ; for affirming CHRIST JESUS *hath left in his written word sufficient direction to order his Church and Children in his worship : So that nothing may be done, over nor above, nor besides, what is commanded therein, by a Precept, an Example, or a true gathered consequence ; which I dare not but affirme, though I die for the same. And now delivered (as abusively Imprisoned all this time) by the most Honourable Lords in Parliament, 1641.*

1 *Cor.* 15, 57. Thanks be unto God which hath given us victory through our Lord Jesus Christ.

report of that worthy gentleman, Mr. Fynes, to the House of Commons from the Committee upon the examination of severall gentlemen concerning the same, 19th June, 1641.

On June 28th, 1641, the House of Commons ordered that this book be referred to the Committee for printing, and they were to use their best diligence in enquiring as to the printer.[1]

88.

The Protestation protested, or a short remonstrance showing what is principally required of all those that have or doe take the last Parliamentary Protestation. 1641.

On July 10th, 1641, the House of Commons ordered that the Committee for printing should take this book into consideration, and examine the printer thereof, and discover the author; and on August 24th following, it was further ordered that Gregory Dexter, printer, who printed this pamphlet and was therefore committed prisoner to the Gatehouse, should be bailed.[2] A copy of this book is at the British Museum, and a manuscript note on the title page ascribes its authorship to H. Burton, of whom mention has been previously made.

89.

The Brownists' Conventicle: or an assemble of Brownists, Separatists, and Non-Conformists, as they met together at a private house to heare a Sermon of a brother of theirs neere Algate, being a learned Feltmaker. 1641.

On the title page of this curious tract (of which there is a copy in the British Museum Library) there is a woodcut which represents four men seated at a table after a meal, and listening to one who appears half an idiot, and is named "*simple Robin*"; on the right is a man kissing a woman, and saying, "*A little in*

1.　Commons' Journ., vol. 2, p. 190.
2.　Ibid, pp. 206, 269.

zeale good sister Ruth." The tract refers to the numerous "Hereticks, Schismaticks, Novellists, Separatists," and other sects of this time, including Thraskites or Sabbatarians, Banisterians, Brownists, Anabaptists, Familists, Adamists, "who have their private meetings when they will not heare the Word preached nor have the Sacrament administered unto them but naked, not so much as fig-leave breeches upon them, thinking thereby to imitate our first parents in their innocency." On July 12th, 1641, this tract was referred by the House of Commons to the Committee for printing.[1]

90.

The order and form for Church Government by Bishops and the Clergy of this kingdom. N. d.

On July 23rd, 1641, the House of Commons ordered that this pamphlet be referred to the Committee for printing; and that the author and printer be enquired after.[2]

91.

The Heads of severall Petitions and complaints made against, 1.—Sir John Connyers, Lieutenant Generall of the Horse in the Northerne expedition. 2.—Dr. Heywood, of St. Gyles in the Fields. 3.—The Parishioners of St. Mary Woolchurch. 4.—Dr. Fuller of St. Giles, Cripplegate. 5.—Mr. Booth, of St. Botolph's, Aldersgate, Touching the Rayles about the Communion Table, the Pictures in Glasse windowes, and weekely Lectures; and read before the Committee, October 16,1641. London, Printed for John Thomas, 1641.

On October 23rd, 1641, the House of Commons ordered that the Stationers' Company should enquire and inform the House who printed this "scandalous pamphlet."[3] A copy exists in the British Museum Library. It is in quarto, and contains four pages.

1. Commons' Journals, vol. 2, p. 206.
2. Ibid, p. 221.
3. Ibid, p. 293.

92.

A Petition directed to the House of Lords by the inhabitants of the County of Herts. 1642.

This is contained in a tract of which there is a copy in the British Museum Library, entitled: "Two Petitions of the Knights, "Gentlemen, Freeholders, and others of the Inhabitants of the "County of Hertford. The one to the Right Honourable House "of Peeres, the other to the Knights, Citizens, and Burgesses of "the Honourable House of Commons assembled in Parliament. "Delivered by at least 4000 Knights, Gentlemen, Freeholders, "and other Inhabitants of the County of Hertford, January 25, "1641. London. Printed by a perfect copy for John Wright, dwelling in the Old Bailey. 1642.

On the title page of this tract is a small woodcut representing an old man standing under a tree, from which he is lopping some branches, with a scroll over his head inscribed "noli altvm sapere."

On January 25th, 1642, the House of Commons ordered that a Committee should examine who printed this petition, and who was the author of it, and brought it to be printed. Martin Eldred, of Jesus College in Cambridge, on being brought to the bar, said that he did not compose the petition, but one Thomas Herbert, once of Trinity College, did compose it; and that he was in the company of Herbert when he composed it, and that it was composed at the Sign of the Antelope, and afterwards sold it to John Greensmith for two shillings and sixpence. John Greensmith the stationer was called in, and confessed that Eldred and Herbert brought the petition unto him, and that one Barnaby Alsop, of Bread Street, printed it; he also confessed that he had printed sundry pamphlets of these men's composing : viz.—*Good News from Ireland*, and *Bloody News*, and the *Cambridge Petition*, and that he had two shillings and sixpence a piece for them. It was thereupon resolved that Eldred and Greensmith should be committed prisoners to the Gatehouse, and that Herbert and Alsop should be sent for as delinquents; but shortly afterwards Eldred and Greensmith were liberated.[1]

The following is a copy of the petition complained of:—

1. Commons' Journals, vol. 2, pp. 393, 396, 408, 415.

"To the Right Honovrable the
"Hovse of Peeres now assembled
"in Parliament.

"The humble Petition of Knights, Gentlemen, Freeholders, and
"other inhabitants of the County of Hertford
"Sheweth,
"That the Petitioners having hitherto with much patience waited
"for, and with great confidence expected the happy progresse of
"this Parliament, and therein the removall of all those grievances
"under which they have a long time groaned, and the perfect
"Reformation of Church and Commonwealth, They are now con-
"strained to represent unto this Honourable House, the manifold
"feares, troubles, and distractions wherewith they are incompassed,
"ariseing from that hellish and bloody rebellion in *Ireland*, acted
"by the Papists against our Bretheren by Nation and Religion,
"apparently threatning the losse of that Kingdome, the extir-
"pation of the Protestants Religion there, and extreame prejudice,
"if not ruine of this Kingdome, From the want of timely and
"powerful supplies to suppresse those Rebells, the not granting
"ample Commissions to those who have bin ready to take up
"Armes against them, the not passing of the Acts for impressing
"Soldiers to that service, and the delayes in acceptance of the
"worthy offer of the South Nation to send 10,000 Soldiers thither,
"From the continuance of the Prelacy, and multitude of erronious
"and scandalous Ministers in this Kingdome; the Insolency of
"the Papists their being armed: the want of execution of Justice
"against Priests and Jesuits already condemned, and other
"notorious Delinquents; the many desperate plots and designes
"attempted against the Parliament and Kingdome by the Popish
"and Prelaticall party; the great and unparrelled breaches
"lately made upon the Priviledges of Parliament, endangering
"the overthrow of the very being thereof, and the destruction of
"divers of its Members, worthy Patriots of their Country; the not
"disclosing and punishing of those persons who counselled the
"same; The unpreparednesse of the sea Forts and other strenghts
"of this Kingdome by Sea and Land against any Invasions, and
"the continuance of divers of them in unsafe hands, wherein the
"Parliament (and in them the whole Kingdome) cannot confide,
"the delay of putting the Kingdome into a posture of Warre, for
"their better defence; the misunderstanding between his Majesty

" and the Parliament, and the want of Compliance by this Honour-
" able House with the House of Commons, in entertaining those
" many good Motions and passing those necessary Bils presented
" to you from that House for the Common good. All which
" springs and causes of your Petitioners' feares and distractions,
" having occasioned the totall decay of trade, and great scarcity
" of money, and thereby impoverishing and unsetlement of the
" whole Kingdome, and tending so exceedingly to the indangering
" of his Majestie's honour and dignity, and the peace and
" safety of this Kingdome :—the Petitioners doe verily beleeve,
" that as the same received their first being from the Popish and
" Prelaticall party, so have they hitherto beene continued, and
" will be (it is to be feared) daily increased by the Voting of the
" Popish Lords and Bishops in this Honourable House (whose
" interests in respect of Religion, their owne standings, or other-
" wise are at this time so contrary to the happinesse of this
" Kingdome) and by the continuance of wicked Councellors and
" evill Ministers of State about his Majestie.
" The Petitioners therefore humbly pray, that all the foresaid
" Causes and springs of their feares and troubles may be speedily
" removed: And (for the effecting thereof) that the evill
" Councellors and others hindring the publike good may be taken
" from his Maiestie, and the voting of the Popish Lords and
" Bishops removed out of this Honourable House; And that the
" Petitioners (who shall be ever ready to hazard their lives and
" Estates for the deffence of the King and Parliament, the
" Priviledges of the same, and in speciall those noble Lords and
" Gentlemen in both Houses, whose endeavours are for the
" publike good) may have liberty to protest against all those as
" enemies to this Kingdome, who refuse to joyne with those
" Honourable Lords and the House of Commons for the putting
" of the Kingdome into a way of safety under the Command of
" such persons as the Parliament shall appoint.
" And your Petitioners shall daily pray, &c.

93.

The Resolution of the Roundheads to pull downe
Cheapside Crosse. Being a zealous Declaration of the
Grievances wherewith their little Wits are consumed to

destruction.   And what things they in their wisedome
(yet left them) conceive fit to bee Reformed.   Also the
Answer to the Rattle-Heads, Concerning their fictionate
Resolutions of the Round-Heads.   Wherein is explained
every particular therein contained against them, with
many godly Counsells to Doctor *Little-wit*: the Com-
poser of their former scurrilous and illiterate Pamphlet.
London, printed 1641.

On February 1st, 164½, the House of Commons ordered that
this pamphlet should be referred to the Committee for printing;
and Stephen Buckle, in St. Martin's, London, who was said to
be the printer, was ordered to attend the Committee.[1]

A copy of this curious pamphlet is in the British Museum
Library.   It commences thus:—

"Whereas we are through our great ignorance and obstinacy
"growne to a most seditious and malignant head, and the hornes
"of that head (though of a maine length) not able to support our
"arrogant faction, as appeares by our last being soundly slasht
"and bastinadoed by a mad crew called the Cavallery; and
"whereas a great part of us have shut up our shops because wee
"could no longer keepe them open, which kind of shutting up
"proceedeth commonly from our vast expence in White broths,
"Custards, and other luxurious Dishes provided for the Edifica-
"tion one of another.   And whereas the multitude, called true
"Protestants, endeavour to hold up Bishops, to maintaine good
"Order, Discipline, and Orthodox preaching in the Church,
"Learning and Arts in the Universities, and peace in the
"Commonwealth; all which is nothing but Idolatry, superstition,
"prophanenesse, and plaine Popery: and further, whereas wee
"(who are nothing properly but *Roundheads* and *Prickeares*) who
"are in most scandalous manner termed Puritans, Holy Brethren,
"the Zealots of the Land, and which in sincerity wee never were,
"or ever will be:—

And then after stating various grievances, not without a considerable spice of indecency, the pamphlet proceeds thus:—

"All which grievances doe stand with much reason, and therefore
"are utterly against our tender Consciences, and never were

1. Commons' Journals, vol. 2, p. 408.

"allowed by any Synod of Moore-fields or Pimlico. That "therefore which we doe now resolve to maintaine, and desire to "have confirmed and never to be altered (till some new toy "tickle us in the *Pericranium*, which will be very shortly) is :—

"1.—That our religion, Tenents, and maners before mentioned "be established and maintained against all reason, Learning, "Divinity, Order, Discipline, Morality, Piety, or Humanity "whatsoever.

"2.—That the very names of Bishops shall be a sufficient Jury "and judge to condemne any of them, without any further "Evidence or circumstance.

"3.—That if any man whatsoever having knowledge in the "Latine Tongue (being a Popish Language) shall presume to "think he can save a soule by preaching, he be excommunicated "both in this world and in the World to come unlesse it be some "certaine Lecturers of whose approved rayling and ignorance we "are well assured, and have knowne to stand 6 houres on a "fasting day.

"4.—That the Felt-maker and the Cobler, two innocent cuckolds "may be instituted Primats and Metropolitans of the two Arch "Provinces, and the rest of the Sect preserved (preferred?) "according to their imbecilities of spirit, to such Bishopricks and "other Livings as will competently serve to procure fat poultry "for the filling of their insatiate stomacks; in which regard, "Church livings had more need to be encreased than diminished.

"5.—That no man whatsoever who beares the name of Caviler, "may be capable of making any of the Brethren a Cukold, unlesse "he cut his hair and altar his Profession, but be excluded from "the Conventicles as the King's friend and a Reprobate.

"6.—Lastly, That there bee two whole daies set apart to Fast "and pray, for the confusion of all that are not thus resolved.

"I come to charge yee
"That slight the Clergie,
"And pull the Miter from the Prelate's head;
"That you will bee wary,
"Lest you miscarry,
"In all these factious humours you have bred;
"But as for Brownists wee'l have none,
"But take them all; and hang them one by one.

" Your wicked Actions,
" Joyn'd in Factions,
" Are all but aymes to rob the King of his due,
" Then give this reason,
'· For your treason,
" That you'l be rul'd if he'l be rul'd by you ;
" Then leave these Factions, zealous brother,
" Least you be hang'd against each other.

" Your wit abounded,
" Gentle Roundhead,
" When you abus'd the Bishops in a Dity ;
" When as you sanged,
" They must be hanged,
" A Tinpence of malice made you witty,
" And though your hot zeale made you bold,
" When you are hang'd your a—e will be a cold.

" Then leave confounding,
'· And expounding,
" The doctrine that you preach in Tubs ;
" You raise this warring,
" And private jarring,
" I doubt, in time will prove the knave of Clubs ;
" It's for your lying, and not for your Oathes,
" You shall be hang'd, and Greg shall have your cloaths.

" We further agree amonst ourselves that whosoever shall not be
" of our owne Schismaticall opinion, they shall receive from us
" the Apellation of Papists, though never so innocent and harme-
" lesse ; and whatsoever shall be enacted by them as adornment
" to their Church, wee will terme it superstitious and Popish
" Innovation, if not approved by our sect.   But O ! the famous
" and illustrious Crosse in Cheapside, the Enigmaticall Embleme
" of impiety, in respect it has bin an eye-sore unto us so long,
" We order further, that we not onely proceed, but also perfect
" those our zealous beginnings in the confusion therof ; not only
" detracting armes and legges of the superstitious bodies, but
" also making it levell with the ground, to the utter abolishing
" of their Idoll, which they account the glory of this City ; after

"which, we will in recompence of these our ignorant brethren's "paines taken therein, infuse into them spiritual blessings, and "endow them with gifts far exceeding the abilities of the learned "stiffe-necked Protestants."

94.

A collection of speeches made by Sir Edward Dering, Knight and Baronet, in matters of religion. London, 1642.

This book was on February 2nd, 164½, voted by the House of Commons scandalous, and ordered to be burnt by the Common Hangman in Westminster, Cheapside, and Smithfield; the author disabled from sitting as a member, and ordered to be committed to the Tower; the printer was likewise prohibited from selling them. On February 5th it was also ordered that the Stationers' Company should have power to search the houses where they should be informed that Sir Edward Dering's books were printing, or to be sold, and seize them, and inform the House of the name of the printer.[1] Dr. Harris says that this book contains many curious particulars not elsewhere to be met with.

95.

Vox Hiberniæ.

This is a false copy of a sermon preached by the Archbishop of Armagh before the House of Lords on the Fast day, December 22nd, 1641. It was printed by one John Nicholson; but on the petition of the Archbishop it was ordered to be called in and suppressed by the House of Lords on February 11th, 1641.

96.

To your Tents, O Israel. By Henry Walker. 1642.

A seditious pamphlet, for which Walker was tried at the Old Bailey in July, 1642. On the trial the Queen's Attorney and two Serjeants at law after causing the indictment to be read "began "to show and did make it plain how odious the matter was, and "how it was a fact of a high nature; first against his Majesty, "to make him as it were odious to his people: *To your Tents, O*

1. Com. Journals, vol. 2, pp. 411, 414.

"*Israel;* as if the King were a Tyrant, bidding as it were every
"man to take his Sword and Armor; and oppose all Authority
"whatsoever, obeying no Law but that of their owne humour
"and will; what can there be more said, but that it was very
"plaine, but that this *Walker* did by those words labour to insti-
"gate and stir up the King's Subjects to a mutiny, and to cause
"tumults to arise in this Kingdome, nay, in the heart of this
"Kingdome, in the City of London too; not onely to teach these
"words, but to cause them at his owne charge to be printed,
"and to divulge the same through his Majestie's Kingdomes.
"Nor did this *Walker* rest himselfe therewith satisfied, but in an
"audacious way, and in a bold manner, as the King's Majesty
"passed through the City of London riding in his Coach, threw
"one of them into the very Coach itselfe, and in the very face
"of the King; what an affront was this? can any age paralell
"it, or any Chronicle make mention of the like, and in a Civill
"Commonwealth, and in a well governed City; I think not: nor
"is this all, for this *Walker* hath invented and writ divers
"Pamphlets and other scandalous Bookes, to the great distur-
"bance of his Majesty, and of his Liege people; a meere sower
"of division, an upholder of a new Government, an inventer of a
"new Doctrine; nay, he is become a Preacher and a deliverer of
"this his humour even in the Church, and openly in the Pulpit
"too, and on the Sunday: drawing after him, and seducing poore
"ignorant people to the very ruine of their soules, if it were
"possible. This act of his, it was done with much venome,
"malice, bitternes, and rankor considering the time; because
"the King and his Parliament were then at some difference, who
"did as much as in him lay to set his Majesty and his Subjects
"together at discord; it was drawne with cunning, and at such
"a time published that if envy itself had plotted it, it could not
"have come forth in a more dangerous season. He confessed it
"was his owne worke, and done by night, and the next day by
"him exposed to sale. It was a foule misdemeanour, and it was
"published with an ill intent. Nay, what is this *Walker* not,
"what wrong hee hath done let his owne conscience, his severall
"Bookes and Pamphlets, which hee hath both written, made, and
"printed them himselfe witnesse. Well, the Jury heares the
"information, the severall pleadings, the severall Witnesses that
"this *Walker* was the onely framer, inventer, publisher, and

"disperser of that Booke, *To your Tents, O Israel;* upon which
"severall Evidences the Jury withdrawes themselves (being 12
"honest men, and of a good rank and quality) to consider of the
"matter; which being truely weighed, and a long time debated
"and scanned, agreed all in one mind, calleth for *Henry Walker*
"to the Bar: who being come to deliver their Verdict, they all
"declared him by the voyce of their Foreman to be guilty both
"of the Trespasse and of the misdemenour. He was convicted,
"1.—For writing of it. 2.—For the composing of it. 3.—For
"the publishing of it himselfe at the Printer's house, and
"receiving money for them. Which done, he had nothing to say
"for himselfe, nor his Counsell neither, but onely he did it not
"with an ill intent to doe any harme. And now he is heartily
"sorrowfull for it, and begs the King's mercy, and the charitable
"censure of all men for his rashnesse and over hot zeale,
"especially of his sacred Majesty, whom he hath most offended;
"and for his Majestie's clemency to him, he will ever be bound
"to pray for him; because his Majesty did give Command that
"his Inditement should not be put against him for Treason, but
"onely for a misdemenor, which if it had bin preferred for
"Treason it might have bin as well found and have cost him his
"life, as for this fact of misdemenour; and so I, *H. Walker*, am
"heartily sorry, and desire God, his Majesty, and all his
"Majestie's Subjects to forgive me, and by my example to forsake
"these private and secret meetings, or rather conventicles; and
" so with teares I submit myselfe to the Law and the punishments
"whensoever it shall be denounced and inflicted upon me."
This account of Walker's trial is taken from his life and
recantation, collected and written by John Taylor, 1642.

97.

The Petition of Sir Philomy Oneale, Knight,
Generall of the Rebels in Ireland, and of the Lords,
Nobility, and Commanders of the Army of the Cath-
oliques in that Kingdome. Presented to the Right
Honourable the Lords and Commons now assembled in
the High Court of Parliament in England. London.
Printed by T. F. for John Thomas.

On March 8th, 164½, the House of Commons ordered that the consideration of this pamphlet be referred to the Committee for printing, and that they take some speedy course for repairing the honour of the Earl of Ormond, much wounded by this pamphlet, and for the corporal punishment of the printer and the contriver.[1]   A copy is in the British Museum Library.   It is in quarto, and contains six pages.

98.
Message of the House of Commons, sent in reply to his Majesty's last message.   1642.

On March 28th, 1642, the House of Commons resolved that John Franc the printer should be forthwith sent for as a delinquent by the Serjeant at Arms for causing this message to be printed without any licence.[2]

99.
The humble petition and declaration of both Houses of Parliament, of 23rd March, 164½.

On March 28th, 1642, the House of Commons resolved that John Wright the stationer and Gregory Dexter should be sent for as delinquents by the Serjeant at Arms for printing this petition without licence.[3]

100.
Two letters from the Hague.   1642.

On March 28th, 1642, the House of Commons resolved that William Humfreyvile should be sent for as a delinquent for feigning and making these two letters, and causing them to be printed.[4]

101.
Diurnal from March 14th to March 21st, 1642.

1. Com. Journals, vol. 2, p. 472.
2. Ibid, p. 500.
3. Ibid, p. 500.
4. Ibid, p. 501.

On March 28th, 1642, the House of Commons resolved that this Diurnal, printed by Robert Wood, was false and scandalous to the King and the parliament, and contained in it "divers seditious passages and of dangerous consequence," and that Wood should be sent for as a delinquent by the Serjeant at Arms for printing this Diurnal; and it was resolved that whoever should print or sell any act or passages of that house under the name of a Diurnal or otherwise without particular licence "should be "reputed a high contemner and breaker of the privilege of "parliament, and so punished accordingly."[1]

A copy of this Diurnal is among the King's pamphlets in the British Museum.

102.

A short treatise of Baptisme : wherein is declared that only Christ's disciples or beleevers are to be baptised ; and that the baptising of infants hath no footing in the word of God, but is a meere tradition received from our forefathers.   1642.

A little pamphlet of 13 pages, written by Thomas Kilcop, of which there is a copy in the British Museum Library.

On April 28th, 1642, the House of Commons ordered that the Lord Chief Justice should be required to proceed against Thomas Kilcop according to law "speedily and with effect" for the setting forth and publishing this " scandalous ignorant pamphlet."[2]

103.

A Letter sent by a Yorkshire Gentleman to a friend in London: Being a full and true Relation of the proceedings betweene his Majesty and the County of York, at *Heworth Moore*, upon *Friday*, June 3.   Also the most materiall passages of this weeke, from London, Westminster, &c.   N. d.

A pamphlet of eight pages, but without title; of which a copy exists in the British Museum Library.

1. Com. Journ., vol. 2, p. 501.
2. Ibid, p. 546.

On June 8th, 1642, the House of Commons ordered that this pamphlet should be referred to the Committee for printing, and that the printer should be immediately sent for to attend that Committee.[1]

104.

A true relation of the proceedings of the Scotts and English forces in the north of Ireland. 1642.

On June 8th, 1642, the House of Commons ordered that this pamphlet should be referred to the Committee for printing, and that the printers be sent for; and that Tobias Sedgewick, Francis Cowles, and Thomas Baites be forthwith sent for in safe custody. Cowles and Bates being called in before the Committee, confessed that one White, a printer, brought the copy thereof to them before it was printed, and offered to sell the impression thereof to them, and they accordingly bought it and published divers printed copies thereof. It was thereupon ordered that Cowles and Bates should be forthwith committed prisoners to the King's Bench, and that the Lord Chief Justice of the King's Bench be required to proceed against them as publishers of false news; and the book was ordered to be burnt by the Common Hangman in the new Palace Yard at Westminster.

On the next day, White, the printer of the pamphlet was called in, and confessed that he had received the letter, which was directed from one Pike in Ireland to one Tobias Sedgwick, from Sedgwick, a barber in the Strand; and that he carried this letter to Baites and Cowles the stationers and read it to them, and they thereupon hired him to print three reams of paper, and gave him therefore eighteen shillings; he presented to the house the original letter. It was then resolved that White should be forthwith committed to the King's Bench prison for printing and publishing a scandalous libel to the dishonour of the Scott's nation, and that he be referred to the King's Bench, to be proceeded with there according to law; but on the 15th June following all concerned were ordered to be forthwith discharged from any farther imprisonment.[2]

1. Commons' Journals, Vol. 2, p. 612.
2. Ibid, pp. 612, 613, 615, 626.

105.

A picture of Sir John Hotham on horseback upon the walls of Hull, his Majesty on foot before the walls. 1642.

Whether this is an independent picture unaccompanied by letter-press, or whether it is the illustration on the title page of a pamphlet I have not been able to discover. On June 10th, 1642, the House of Commons ordered that "this scandalous picture" should be burnt by the Common Hangman in the Palace Yard, and that all further sale or publication of them be strictly forbidden, and enquiry was to be made for the printer and publisher. On June 13th, the printer and designer of the picture was brought to the door of the House in custody: but no further proceedings against him appear among the Records of the House.[1]

106.

A Collection of Sundry Petitions presented to the King's most excellent Majestie. As also to the two most Honourable Houses, now assembled in Parliament. And others, already signed, by most of the *Gentry*, *Ministers*, and Freeholders of severall Counties, in behalfe of *Episcopacie*, Liturgie, and supportation of *Church-Revenues*, and suppression of *Schismaticks*. Collected by a faithfull Lover of the *Church*, for the comfort of the dejected *Clergy*, and all moderatly affected *Protestants*. Published by his Majesties speciall Command. Printed for William Sheares, 1642.

A pamphlet of 67 pages, of which there is a copy in the British Museum Library.

On June 14th, 1642, the House of Commons ordered that this book, which was printed for William Sheares, should be referred to the Committee for printing; and that Sheares the printer should be summoned to attend the Committee.[2]

1. Com. Journ., Vol. 2, pp. 617, 622.
2. Ibid, p. 623.

107.

New Orders new agreed upon by a Parliament of Roundheads. Confirmed by the Brethren of the New Separation. Assembled at Roundheads' Hall, without Cripplegate. With the great discretion of Master Longbreath, an upright new inspired Cobler, Speaker of the House. Avowed by Ananias Dulman, alias Prick-eares. Cler. Parl. Round. London, printed for T. U. 1642.

A pamphlet of which there is a copy in the British Museum Library. It commences thus :—

"In the spacious Theater of the Universe, the singular conditions
"of singular Persons are directly articulated in some expresse
"place. Wherefore the *Round-heads*, whose Pricke-eares are
"longer than their Haire, have erected an Image of their own
"Imaginations; a Synagogue, or a convenient place conduceab¹y
"to the obscured secrecy of their Conventicles : and they gave a
"plausible appellation to it, calling it *Round-heads'* Hall. Here
"did the Councell of *Fooles* meet usually, and called themselves
"*The Simple Senate of the Times.* There are severall places for
"severall Men appointed, yet I did alwaies wonder that one
"should be so long wanting. There is *Newgate* for Theeves,
"*Ludgate* for Debters, the *Counter* for Drunkards and misdemean-
"ors, *Bridewell* for Idle Persons, *Bedlam* for Mad-Men; but I
"wondered extreamely there should be no place appointed for
"*Fooles* : but the *Round-heads* have taken that into their serious
"consideration, and least a place should be wanting for *Fooles*,
"they have built *Round-heads'* Hall, wherein they seeme to have
"done a great Act of Charity : for Charity begins at home."
And it concludes thus :—

"Thus being conveened in this *Round-heads'* Hall, in this manner
"without any Order : for they say Order is prophanesse, and
"where no Order is, there can be no transgression upon any, and
"where no transgression is found, there can be no prophanesse,
"*Ergo*, It is holinesse to be without Order : They began to shew
"their simple Opinions, each Man at least foure houres, and after

"the minds of them all were knowne, and uttered by the instinct
"of the Spirit, they unanimously agreed to Order these things
"following."

> " *Orders made by the Parliament of Round-heads,*
> " *sitting at Round-heads' Hall, without Cripple-Gate.*

"Since the Lobs and Common Fooles assembled at *Round-heads'*
"*Hall*, have understood in sincerity the manifold distempers of
"Religion, the errors of People, and the malignity of some
"Popishly affected, and that they being sensible of the insolency
"of the Cavalleers, and what imminent danger that insolency
"may produce if not prevented in time, It is therefore by them
"ordered, 1.—Since a parity was first ordained by God himselfe,
" and that there needeth no Order or Degree of persons, because
"God is equall and no respecter of persons, Be it therefore
"ordered, that we have no King but *P.*

"2.—That we have no Bishops, because they are the Pope's Sons,
,, but that we send them either to the Tower or Tiburne.

"3.—That we have no Churches, for they are of a Popish con-
"struction, and were derived first from Rome.

"4.—That we have no Bels, Organs, or Babylonish Timpans, for
"they all tend to the prophanation of God's holy Word.

"5.—That we have no Crosses, for they are meere Popery, and
"tend to the Confusion and Opposition of Scripture; especially
"let the sight of Cheapeside Crosse be a detestation unto you
"all: and let those streets that are called Crosses, as Red-Crosse
"Street, and White Crosse, &c., be turned otherwise and called
"after the Names of some of our owne Family, as *Greene, Spencer,*
"&c., and call it rather *Green Street* then Red Crosse Street, &c.,
"that thus all prophanesse being rooted and extirpated from
"our conventions, nothing but holinesse may remaine amongst
"us.

"6.—That there be no tolleration of Surplices, because it was the
"defiled Smocke of Pope *Jone*; who being great with Childe,
"had her Smocke made the wider, which is now commonly called
"a Surplesse.

"7.—That we assume no other Names to ourselves but *Round-*
"*heads*, and that this *Round-heads' Hall* shall be our meeting
"place.

"8.—That we have no pictures of Saints, Cherubims, &c.,
"because they leade the way to Idolatry and Abomination.

"9.—That any *Round-head* (being God's anointed) may and shall
"have authority by Us, the Parliament of *Round-heads*, to Preach,
"teach, Pray, and Instruct in any place soever; whether it be in
"a Barne, Chamber, Stable, Loft, Garret, Field, Ditch, Saw-pit,
"in Woods, or under Hedges, either by Land or Sea, without the
"prohibition of any Place; provided onely, That it be not taught
"in a Pulpit, for that tends to the advancement of Popery, there-
"fore it is more convenient in a Tub.

"10.—That in our Prayers a singular caution be made, not to
"pray for the King, Queene, Prince, or State: but especially not
"for Bishops or Universities; and that it be no set forme of
"Prayer, but such as the Spirit doth suggest into the heart, yea,
"the Lord's Prayer is not to be used amongst us Holy ones as
"lawfull.

"11.—That Salvation be Preacht to none but *Round-heads*, because
"we are the only Children of Grace, and to us belongeth the
"Kingdome: for at the latter day of judgment it shall be said,
"*Come ye Round-heads, &c.*, but *Depart yee Rattle-heads and
"Cavaleers, &c.*

"12.—That instead of Matrimony, if any Brother taketh affection
"to any Sister, or if any Sister mutually reflects her love to any
"Brother, they may (if they agree in the affectionate community
"of the Spirit) take one another's word, without any other foolish
"circumstance as the Church of *England* ignorantly useth.

"13.—That in the Buriall of the Dead, Prayer is as needlesse as
"superfluous, and therefore no words are to be expressed,
"because it is Popery to pray for the Dead.

"14.—That none ought to be Baptised before they be foureteen
"years of age, and have their names written in the Book of the
"Faithfull.

"15.—That the *Common Prayer* is *Porrage*, and made by the *Pope's*
"Cook, being the Rubbish of Babilonish opinions, and therefore
"ought not to be used but as *Apocrypha*.

"16.—That everything be common amongst the Brethren, one
"Man's Wife for another, when the candle of iniquity is exting-
"uished, and the Spirit moves, as to the Exposition of that place
"in Scripture, *Increase and Multiply*.

"17.—That no kneeling at the Sacrament be allowed of, but
"that it shall be received at Night in an upper Roome, only by
"twelve together sitting all round.

"That none shall weare long haire, for as Souldiers are known
"only by their Colours they weare, so we will be known to be
"*Round-heads* onely by our long Eares.

"19.—That our Diet be very provocative, and whatsoever is
"effectuall to the accomplishment of this purpose, that it be
"esteemed as a Soveraign Antidote to expell the contagious
"infection of despaire, and very co-operative to revive our dead
"and fainting Spirits, because they will be much weakened with
"such holy zeale, and will want some lively nourishment; there-
"fore let our bodies be alwaies well tempered, that our pulses
"may beat hard when the flesh riseth.

"20.—That all Learning, Order, Discipline, and the Universities
"be abrogated from all our Brethren as being Popery.

"21.—That every Yeare there shall be the *Round-heads'* Feast
"Celebrated, a well lung'd long-breathed Cobler shall preach
"a Sermon six houres, and his Prayers two houres long, and at
"every Messe in this Feast shall be presented a goodly Dish of
"*Turnips*, because it is very agreeable to our Natures; for a
"*Turnip* hath a round head, and the anagram of *Puritan* is
"A TURNIP.

"22.—That whosoever shall not agree and condescend to the due
"observation of each particular Order by us here establisht, they
"shall be held as the malignant party, enemies to the State of
"the *Round-heads*, and worthy to be renounced, suspended, or
"excommunicated, and never to be re-admitted into the Society
"of the Brethren."

On June 15th, 1642, the House of Commons ordered that
Stephen Buckley, dwelling in St. Martin's near Aldersgate, who
printed "this scandalous pamphlet," should be sent for as a
delinquent.[1]

108.

Three Speeches, being such Speeches as the like were
never spoken in the City. The first by Master Warden
to the Fellowes of his Company, touching the Affaires
of the Kingdome. The second by Mistriss Warden,
being her observations on her Husband's Reverent

1. Com. Journals, vol. 2, p. 624.

Speech, to certain Gentlewomen of Ratliffe and Wapping. The third by Mistriss Warden's Chambermaid, as she was dressing her Mistriss; the Wisdome and Learning whereof will amaze your judgements. Published by Antibrownistus Puritanomastix. London 1642.

A tract with a woodcut on the title page which is divided horizontally, the lower part being unequally divided by a pillar, as of an arcade. In the upper portion ten men, in official civic robes, sit at a long table, and are addressed by another who is at the head of the table. "*Militia*" is printed near the head of the last man. What appear to be the balusters of a staircase are under an arch, on our left; under another arch, on our right, a window and a table appear.

In the lower division on our left, six women sit at a round table; one of them addresses her companions in an animated manner; "*I am Mistris Warden*" is written at her side. The compartment on our right shows a woman adjusting her head-dress before a mirror, which hangs against a latticed window; near her stands a second woman, with reference to whom "*the Maid*" is printed over her head.

Mr. Warden's speech commences thus :—

"Brethren and fellow Counsellors, I begin with an acknowledg-
"ment of thanks for your election of me to wagge my beard
"amongst you this day for the good of the Common-wealth. I
"confesse myselfe as very a Woodcock as the best of you, yet
"(with your patience) I will express my simple affection to the
"Weale publick, to shew the spleene of my shallow capacity.
"Be pleased first to consider the Liturgy of the Church, now
"generally spoken against by grave and Orthodox Coachmen,
"Weavers, and Brewers' Clarkes, and growne odious to our she
"divines, who looke asquint with the very thought of it, what
"this Liturgy is I know not, nor care not; yet as simple as I am,
"I beleeve it is a hard word, either Greeke or Latine or both:
"whence I conclude if no hard word, no Greeke or Latine nor
"any that know them ought to come within the Discipline of
"the Church, but plaine Hebrew and English. Let us then avoyd
"this Liturgy, and if it concerne the Common Prayer, (as my

" singular good wife saith) then questionlesse if the new Convo-
" cation be but as wise as himselfe they will doome it to be burnt,
" nay and consum'd as the loggs in Lincolne in Feilds were; for
" it hath caused the Gospell to prosper so slowly under Preaching
" Tradesmen and Lay Clergymen, who have coupled in laborious
" conjunction to procreate young Saints in this new faith, making
" Barnes, Stables, Woods, Saw-pits, old Ditches, Cellers, open
" houses of Office their private Synagogues, where unseene of the
" wicked they may doe what I will not speake, but speake I will
" againe of and against this Liturgy, the Heathen word Liturgy,
" which if blotted out of the Church, they would encrease and
" multiply spirituall Children, and make them swarme in
" Parishes. For having liberty and being strong of spirit,
" through high fare, they are so zealously impudent that they
" would go toot in the streetes; but I will conclude with good
" man Greene's Hebrew Exhortation, *Quicquid liber cuquodlibet*,—
" away with the Liturgy, and so say I."

On June 15th, 1642, the House of Commons ordered that
Nicholas Vavasor, who dispersed this pamphlet, should be forthwith summoned and brought in safe custody to answer to the
House; and the Stationers' Company were called in and were
enjoined by the Speaker to be very careful and diligent in
searching after anything that was printed which might reflect
upon his Majesty; and it was resolved that an ordinance be
drawn for preventing the printing or publishing any scandallous
or libellous pamphlet that might reflect upon the King, the kingdom, or the parliament, or Scotland, and for suppressing such as
already had been printed.[1]

109.

The Petition of the Nobilitie, Gentrie, Burrows,
Ministers, and Commons of the Kingdom of Scotland
to The Lords of His Majestie's most Honourable Privie
Councell. London. Printed by Robert Barker. 1642.

A pamphlet of five pages, of which a copy exists in the
British Museum Library. On June 15th, 1642, the House of
Commons ordered that Robert Barker, the King's Printer, be

1. Com. Journ., vol. 2, p. 624.

required to satisfy the House by what authority he printed this
paper, and that he be farther enjoined to stay the sale thereof
till the House should take further order.[1]

110.
A Declaration or Resolution of the County of Hereford. 1642.

A printed paper, on a single sheet, commencing thus:—

"Wheras the Kingdom for many yeers past hath groned under
"Taxes of Loans, Shipmoney, and the like dismall effects of an
"Arbitrary Government and a high stretcht *Prerogative*, for the
"cure of which distempers a *Parliament* was held to be the onely
"good old way of *Physick* to cleanse the Body Politique from
"oppressing Crudities (which was heartily desir'd). but not by
"overstrong Purgations to weaken it in the principall Part,
"charging it to receive a disposition to the like distemper, or a
"Relapse into the same, or a worse Disease, which instead of
"restoring it to its primitive vigour and health, must needs drive
"it to a fatall Period.   Such is our misery, such the just judg-
"ment of God upon our Sins.

"This wholsome *Physick* hath not wrought in us that blessed
"effect, as was either believed by some or hoped for by all men:
"but as if God had answered our importunity for a Parliament,
"as hee did the old Israelites for a King in his anger; we drive
"on with much more haste then good speed to the other extream,
"which portends no lesse Symptomes of ruine and destruction
"than the former.   So that having maturely considered what
"hath proved destructive to this or other Parliaments, we may
"the more easily avoid those Rocks upon which others have split
"themselves, *viz.* 1.   The venting of particular ends of Avarice
"and Ambition in the publike Cause.   2.   Private Combinations
"or Chamber conventicles to resolve before-hand what shall be
"done in the House.   3.   Hindring the freedom of speech by
"imprisonment of their persons.   4.   Denying information by
"the humble way of Petitions from the County, as that most
"excellent Orthodox Petition of our Brethren of *Kent*, and of
"rejecting information of Letters to our Knights and Burgesses.
"5.   The ready swallowing of informations and jealous rumours

1. Commons' Journals, Vol. 2, p. 625.

"against his Majesty, the styling them the malignant party and
"enemies to the State, which were onely, truely and conscionably
"his friends. 6. The private if not publike mutinous rabble,
"which ill Spirit was ready at all times to be raised by a whisper
"from any of those worthy Members, Emphatically so called, if
"not exclusively, as if all Justice, Reformation, and Government
"were onely to be expected from them. 7. The now unheard of
"State-law and Logick to style and believe that a Parliament
"that is divided in itselfe, is sévered from the King the Head
"thereof: if they may be remedied (as we hope they are not
"past cure) we shall rather desire to change some of our
"Physicians then Physick, there being no better way, nor more
"necessary to preserve the health of a Common-wealth, than a
"well temper'd Parliament. Wherefore we as faithfull Subjects
"to his Majesty, as free-born Englishmen, doe joyne in an
"unanimous resolution to maintain.

1. *The Protestant Religion.*
2. *The King's just power.*
3. *The Laws of the Land.*
4. *The Liberty of the Subject.*

After expatiating upon these four resolutions, the paper
concludes thus :—

"As wee conceive ourselves obliged by the Law of God, the
"Law of the Land, by the Dictates of Nature and reason to
"maintaine all these; so by God's grace assisting us, we hope
"we shall not be terrified or compelled to yeeld any active
"obedience to any dis-joyned part of *Parliament* without the
"consent of the whole (which we heartily desire may be united)
"or to any uncertaine Debates, Votes or Ordinances, that are
"not digested or setled into Lawes; nay which seemes to
"contradict former Lawes, and yet are tender'd to us with so
"much earnestnes, as some dare hardly deny them with safety
"or obey with Conscience.

"Nor shall we ever yeeld ourselves such Slaves, or so betray
"the liberty purchased by our Forefathers blood, and bequeathed
"unto us as to suffer our selves to be swayed by any Arbytrary
"Government whatsoever, or stand with too much contention of
"Spirit to cast off the yoake of our Tyrany to endure many worse.

"*And seeing his Majestie is graciously pleased to maintaine the true*
"*Protestant Religion; his owne just Power, The Lawes of the Land,*

" *The* Liberty *of the* Subjects *and that these waters of* Reformation
" *having beene longe stirred*; *we want onely the favour of his Princely*
" Majestie *to let us in and heale us*; *So we doe reciprocally declare*
" *that we conceive our selves bound to maintaine him in all the*
" *Premisses with our lives and Fortunes.*"

On July 8th, 1642, the House of Commons resolved that this
printed paper should be referred to the Committee for printing,
and that Hammon the printer should be forthwith summoned to
attend the House. Mr. Maddison was then called in, and averred
that he being at a stationer's shop and reading this pamphlet,
and saying that this was a foul scandal upon the Parliament, and
that the author of it deserved to be whipt; one Sir William
Boleter told him that he deserved to be whipt for saying so; and
that he would justify every word of it; and that, by God he
would slash him; and while he was talking with him one
Mr. Dutton a minister came to him, and likewise said that he
deserved to be whipt; and he asked him wherefore? And he
replied, for speaking Nonsense, and for saying it was a Libel.
It was then resolved that Mr. Dutton the Minister should be
forthwith committed a prisoner to the Gatehouse, during the
pleasure of the House for carrying himself in a scornful manner
in the House, and for, as much as in him lay, justifying the
foulest and most scandalous pamphlet that ever was raised or
published against the Parliament.

Sir Robert Harley reported from a conference had with the
Lords, that the Lords had brought unto them a printed paper
which is a scandalous and infamous libel in the name of the
County of Hereford, and they desired that the Commons would
join with them in desiring the Knights that serve for that County
to send down to know who in that County would avow the same ;
and if any did, that they should be prosecuted to the utmost for
setting forth such an infamous libel.[1]

111.

Animadversions upon those notes which the late
Observator hath published upon the seven doctrines
and positions which the King by way of Recapitulation
(he saith) layes open so offensive. London. 1642.

1.   Commons' Journals, Vol. 2, pp. 661, 662, 679, 683, 690, 691.

On July 22nd, 1642, the House of Commons ordered that this pamphlet should be referred to the Committee for printing.[1] A copy exists in the British Museum Library.

112.

King James, his judgment of a king and of a Tyrant. Extracted out of his own speech at Whitehall, to the Lords and Commons in Parliament, 1609. With certaine notations anent the same. Also 28 questions, worthy due consideration and solution in these dangerous times of England. 1642.

On September 12th, 1642, the House of Commons ordered that this pamphlet should be referred to the Committee for printing, to enquire out the author, and the printer and publisher; and also that it should be burnt.[2] A copy is preserved in the British Museum Library.

113.

A pamphlet by Sir William Denny of Norwich. (1642.)

I have not been able to meet with a copy of this pamphlet, neither can I give any idea of its title. The only book by Sir William Denny mentioned in Watts's Bibliotheca Britannica, is the "Pelecanicidium, or the Christian adviser against self-murder, together with a guide, and the Pilgrim's Passe to the Land of the Living. London, 1653,"—of which there are two copies in the British Museum Library.

On September 16th, 1642, the House of Commons resolved that Sir William Denny should be forthwith sent for as a delinquent by the Sergeant at Arms, for spreading and divulging this scandalous pamphlet and libel to the dishonour of both Houses of Parliament, and Thomas Hill, Sir William Denny's clerk, and Michael Philips, Mr. Corye's servant, were summoned to attend the House. On October 7th, Denny's examination was referred to the Committee for informations, but on the 19th December it was ordered that he should be released from the Sergeant's custody.[3]

1. Commons' Journals, Vol. 2, p. 685.
2. Ibid, p. 762.
3. Ibid, pp. 769, 798, 894.

114.

A most exact and true relation of the proceedings of His Majestie's Armie at Shelborne. Written by a lover of truth. London. 1642.

On September 16th, 1642, the House of Commons ordered that the two Stationers, Badger and Marriott, who caused this "false and scandalous book" to be printed, should be forthwith summoned to attend that House to answer for the doing thereof.[1] A copy is preserved in the British Museum Library. It contains five pages.

115.

The King's Majestie's Desires and Propositions to all his subjects in Scotland, declaring his royall intentions and determination to all the Lords of his Privie Councell, concerning this Kingdome, signed with his Royall Signett, and now published by authority. 1642.

A pamphlet of six pages, of which there is a copy in the British Museum Library. On September 16th, 1642, it was referred by the House of Commons to the Committee for printing to enquire who were the printers and authors of this book.[2]

116.

A speedy post from Heaven to the King of England. Never put out by any before. Written by A. H. London. 1642.

On October 5th, 1642, the House of Commons resolved that this pamphlet should be forthwith publicly burnt, and the books all called in, and the booksellers charged not to publish or sell them; and it was referred to the Committee of printing to enquire who was the author or printer of it.[3] A copy of this pamphlet, which consists of six pages, exists in the British Museum Library.

1. Commons' Journals, Vol. 2, p. 769.
2. Ibid, p 769.
3. Ibid, p. 795.

117.

A Letter sent from the Lord Falkland, Principal Secretarie to His Majestie, unto the Right Honourable Henry, Earle of Cumberland, at York, September 30. 1642, concerning the late conflict before Worcester, with the State of His Majestie's Armie now at Shrewsbury. Printed at York, October 1st, and now reprinted at London for J. T., October 7. 1642.

On October 8th, 1642, this pamphlet was brought before the notice of the House of Commons. John Thomas, who printed it, was called in, and confessed that he printed some 1300 copies of it; and that Browne, a bookseller by Christ Church, brought him the original thereof, and that the said Browne said he had it from the servant of a Parliament man as he said. It was thereupon resolved that Thomas should be committed a prisoner to Newgate, and that Browne should be sent for in safe custody; and that these pamphlets now in the custody of one Mr. Browne in Cheapside should be burnt, one half in Cheapside, and half in the Palace Yard.[1] A copy exists in the British Museum Library.

118.

The examination of Sir Ralph Hopton, Sir John Winter, Sir John Stowell, and two other Knights upon their knees at the Barre in the House of Commons the 14 day of this instant October. With articles of High Treason exhibited against them by the House of Commons. London. 1642.

On October 18th, 1642, the House of Commons ordered that this pamphlet should be referred to the Committee for printing to enquire out the author and the printer.[2] A copy exists in the British Museum Library.

119.

Some few and short considerations on the present distempers. By J. P. 1642.

1. Commons' Journals, Vol. 2, p. 801.
2. Ibid, p. 12.

A pamphlet of eight pages written by Dr. John Price against the Parliament. On November 2nd, 1642, the House of Commons ordered that Sir Peter Wentworth, Mr. Rous, Mr. Rigby, and Mr. White should search the studies, libraries, and papers of Dr. John Price, and that they prepare an impeachment against him; also that he should be forthwith committed prisoner to Newgate during the pleasure of the House for composing and publishing this book "very much derogatory to the proceedings of Parliament."[1]

120.

The Resolving of Conscience, *upon this question*, whether upon such a supposition or case, as is now usually made (the King will not discharge his trust, but is bent or seduced to subvert Religion, Laws and Liberties) Subjects may take Arms and resist? and whether that case be now? Resolved, I.—*That no Conscience upon such a Supposition or Case can finde a safe and cleare ground for such resistance. II.— That no man in conscience can be truly perswaded, that the resistance now made is such, as they themselves pretend to, that plead for it in such a case. III.—That no man in Conscience can be truly perswaded that such a case is now*, that is, *that the King will not discharge his trust, but is bent to subvert*, &c. *Whence it followeth*, That the resistance now made against the Higher Power is unwarrantable, and according to the Apostle, Damnable, *Rom.* 13. Also that the shedding of bloud in the pursuit of this resistance is Murder. By H. Fern, D.D., &c. Cambridge. 1642.

On December 24th, 1642, the House of Commons resolved that Dr. Fearne should be forthwith sent for as a Delinquent for composing and publishing this "seditious book," and on the 2nd February, 164$\frac{2}{3}$, there was produced to the House the

1.   Commons' Journals, Vol. 2, p. 831.

warrant under Dr. Holdsworth's hand for printing this book, whereupon it was resolved that Dr. Holdsworth should be forthwith sent for in safe custody. It appears that this book was printed by Roger Daniel, printer to the University of Cambridge.[1]

121.

A complaint to the House of Commons. 1642.

On January 2nd, 164$\frac{2}{3}$, the House of Commons ordered that John Wright should be committed to the Compter in Wood Street, for publishing this "scandalous book against the Parliament;" and the book itself was ordered to be burnt by the Common Hangman in the new Palace at Westminster and in Smithfield. The Serjeant's man was also to search the shops in and about Westminster for the books, and to take into custody any persons having the same in their possession. On February the 3rd following it was also ordered that Luke Norton, printer, and Mr. Sheres, stationer, should be forthwith committed prisoners to Newgate for printing this book; and it was also referred to the Committee for informations to consider of some effectual course for the speedy suppressing the printing of scandalous pamphlets, and the inordinate licentiousness of printing.[2]

122.

Two Speeches made in the House of Peeres on Munday the 19 of December, for and against accommodation. The one by the Earl of Pembroke, the other by the Lord Brooke. The latter printed by order of the House of Commons. Lond. 1642.

A pamphlet of eight pages, of which a copy exists in the British Museum Library. On January 13th, 164$\frac{2}{3}$, the House of Commons ordered that the Committee for printing should enquire after the printer and publisher of this pamphlet.[3]

1. Commons' Journals, Vol. 2, pp. 900, 951.
2. Ibid, pp. 910, 911, 953.
3. Ibid, p. 925.

123.

The reasons of the Lords and Commons in Parliament, why they cannot agree to the alteration and addition in the articles of cessation offered by His Majesty: with His Majestie's gracious answer thereunto, April 4, 1643. Printed by His Majestie's command at Oxford by Leonard Lichfield, Printer to the University. 1643.

On April 12th, 1643, the House of Commons ordered that Sir Frederick Cornewallis be forthwith sent for in safe custody for dispersing this book (which he brought with him from Oxford) printed without the order of the House; and the printers were enjoined not to proceed in the printing, publishing, or dispersing the said book. On the 19th April however, Sir Frederick Cornwallis was ordered to be discharged from custody.[1]

This is a pamphlet of 25 pages, a copy of which is preserved in the British Museum Library, bound with others in a volume, on one of the fly leaves of which there is this interesting note :—
"Memorandum y^t Col. Will. Legg and Mr. Arther Treavor wer "imployed by his Matie K. Charles to gett for his present use, a "Pamphlet, wch his Matie had then occasion to make use of, and "not meetinge wth it, they both came to me, havinge heard y^t I "did imploy my selfe to take up all such thinges from ye begin-"inge of that Parlement. And findinge it wth me, tould me it "was for ye kinges owne use, I tould them all I had were at his "Maties command and service, and wthall tould them if I should "part wth it, and loose it presuminge y^t when his Matie had done "wth it, y^t litle accompt would be made of it, and soe I should "loose it by y^t losse a Limbe of my Collection, wch I should be "very loth to doe, well knowinge it would be impossible to "supplie it if it should ha$\mathit{p}$ pen to be lost, wth wch answer they "returned to his M$\mathit{a}$jestie at Hampton Court, (as I take it) and "tould him they had found y^t peece he soe much desired, and "wth all how loath he y^t had it was to part wth it, he much fear-"inge its losse; whereuppon they were both sent to me againe "by his Matie to tell me y^t upon y^e word of A Kinge, (to use "their owne expressions) he would safely returne it, thereuppon "immediatly by them, I sent it to his Ma$^{tie.}$

1. Commons' Journals, Vol. 3, pp. 40, 52.

"Who havinge dun wth it, and havinge it wth him when he was
"goinge towardes y^e Isle of Wight let it fall in y^e durt; And
"then callinge for y^e two persons before mentioned (who attended
"him) delivered it to them, wth a charge, as they would answer
"it another day, y^t they should both speedyly and safly returne
"it to him, from whom they had received it. And wthall to desier
"y^t partie to goe on and continewe what had begun, wch Booke
"togeather wth his Maties signification to me, by those worthy and
"faithfull gent, I received both speedyly and safely.

"W^{ch} volume hath y^t marke of Honor upon it, wch noe other
"volume in my Collection hath. And very dilligently and care-
"fully I continewed ye same, until ye most happie restoration and
"Coronation of his most gratious Matie Kinge Charles ye Second,
"whom God Longe Preserve."

Geo. Thomason."

124.

A discourse, or Parley, continued between *Partricius*
and *Peregrine* (upon their landing in France) touching
the Civill Wars of England and Ireland. 1643.

On August 11th, 1643, this pamphlet was referred by the
House of Commons to the Committee for examinations.[1] It
seems never to have been finished, for in the British Museum
Library there is a portion of it extending to 24 pages, but with
no title page ; and a manuscript note on one of the fly leaves says
that it was written by James Howell, and that it was taken while
printing, when Howell was in prison in the Fleet, and that no
more of it was printed.

125.

A discourse of a true hearted Englishman. 1644.

On July 3rd, 1644, the House of Commons ordered that the
author and printer of this pamphlet should be enquired for.[2]

126.

A book by one Williams, concerning the tolerating
of all sorts of Religion. 1643.

1. Commons' Journal, Vol. 3, p. 202.
2. Ibid, p. 549.

Owing to the vagueness with which this book is mentioned in the Commons' Journals, I have not been able to identify it at all. On August 9th, 1644, the House of Commons ordered that all the copies should be publicly burnt.[1]

127.

Lex, Rex, the Law and the Prince. A dispute for the just Prerogative of King and People. Containing the reasons and causes of the most necessary defensive wars of the Kingdom of Scotland, and of their Expedition for the ayd and help of their dear Brethren of England. In which their Innocency is asserted, and a full answer is given to a seditious pamphlet intituled *Sacro-sancta Regum Majestas*, or the Sacred and Royall Prerogative of Christian Kings; Under the name of J. A., but penned by Jo. Maxwell the Excommunicate P. Prelat. With a scripturall confutation of the ruinous grounds of W. Barclay, H. Grotius, H. Armisæus, Aut. de Domi. P. Bishop of Spalato, and of other late Anti-Magistratical Royalists; as, The Author of Ossorianum, D. Fern, E. Symmons, the Doctors of Aberdeen, &c. In XLIV questions. Published by authority. London: Printed for John Field, and are to be sold at his house upon Addle-Hill, near Baynards-Castle. Octob. 7, 1644.

This book was written by Mr. Samuel Rutherford. A copy is preserved in the British Museum Library. It is in quarto, and contains 467 pages. It was ordered to be burnt by the hands of the Common Hangman.

128.

A True Relation of the most Chiefe Occurrences, at, and since the late Battell at Newbery, untill the disjunction of the three Armies, of the Lord Generall, the

1. Commons' Journals, Vol. 3, p. 585.

Earle of Manchester, and Sir William Waller, together with the London Brigade, under the command of Sir James Harrington. Published upon necessity, both to undeceive the mistaken multitude, and to vindicate the Earle of Manchester from many undeserved aspersions commonly cast upon him, either through ignorance or prejudice. Penned by Simeon Ash, who as his Chaplaine did waite upon his Lordship, in the Westerne Expedition. London, Printed by G. M. for Edward Brewster, at the Signe of the Bible at Fleete-Bridge. 1644.

A pamphlet of 12 pages, of which there is a copy in the British Museum Library. On January 20th, 1644, the House of Commons ordered that enquiry should be made who was the author, printer, and divulger of this book.[1]

129.

The Speech of their Excellencies the Lords Ambassadours Extraordinary from the High and Mighty States General of the United Provinces of the Netherlands, taking their leave of both the Honourable Houses of Parliament assembled at Westminster, 10 April, 1645. Translated out of French into English, and printed by their Excellencies order. Steph. Taylor, Secr. Together with a moderate answer by a private Gentleman. Printed according to order. London. Printed by M. B. for Robert Bostock at the King's Head in Paul's Church-yard, 16 April, 1645.

A pamphlet of 6 pages, of which there is a copy in the British Museum Library. On April 15th, 1645, the House of Commons, on being informed of this printed paper, ordered that the consideration of its printing and publishing should be referred to the Committee of both Kingdoms, who were to give an account thereof the next morning.[2]

1. Commons' Journals, Vol. 4, p. 25.
2. Ibid, p. 111.

130.

The Scottish Dove.   1645.

On May 23rd, 1645, the House of Commons ordered that the Committee of Examinations should send for the writer of this pamphlet to examine him touching some passages in one of his pamphlets "laying some aspersions upon the Prince of Orange, complained of by the States Ambassadors."[1]

131.

Various books and treatises by one Paul Best, alleged to be of a blasphemous and irreligious nature.

I have not been able to discover the titles or even the existence of these books. On June 10th, 1645, the Assembly of Divines attended the House of Commons, and being called in represented the blasphemies of one Paul Best against the Deity of our Saviour Jesus Christ, and of the Holy Ghost, contained in books, treatises, and notes of his, and in his answer to twelve Interrogatories drawn out of the writings of the said Paul Best; and they desired that the Parliament would use that authority they were intrusted with, for executing of condign punishment upon an offender of so high a nature; that, in reference to the crime, he might be made exemplary: "that all the world may know, how much you detest such prodigious blasphemies, and heresies of so fearful a nature." It was thereupon referred to the Committee of plundered ministers, to examine, with all diligence, the truth of the fact of the informations against Paul Best, of divers prodigious blasphemies against the Deity of our Saviour and the Holy Ghost, contained in notes and writings of the said Paul Best, and that they bring their opinions to the House with all speed, what they think fit to be done in the business, and it was resolved that Best should be forthwith committed close prisoner to the Gatehouse Prison. On January 28th, 164$\frac{5}{6}$, it was further resolved that an ordinance be prepared and forthwith brought in for punishing with death Paul Best for his "abominable, prodigious, horrid blasphemies.[2]

1. Commons' Journals, Vol. 4, p. 152.
2. Ibid, pp. 170, 420.

132.

Comfort for Beleevers about their Sinnes and Troubles, in a treatise showing that true Beleevers, how weake soever in faith, should not be opprest, or perplexed in heart by anything whatever befalls them either in sin or afflictions.   By John Archer, Master of Arts, sometime Preacher of All Hallowes, Lumbard Street, London.   London, 1645.

On July 14th, 1645, this book was brought before the notice of the House of Commons by the Assembly of Divines, and its scope was stated to be, "that true believers, how weak soever in "faith, should not be oppressed or perplexed in heart by anything "whatever befals them either in sin or afflictions." The author's words were, "God is and hath an hand in, and is the author of "the sinfulness of his people; and that God is more in their "sins and their sorrows than they themselves," &c. The author, the Rev. John Archer, a minister, was said to be dead. The book was thereupon ordered to be publicly burnt by the Common Hangman; some of them in the Palace Yard, and other some in Cheapside, Smithfield, Paul's Church-yard, and the Exchange; and the Stationers' Company was to search for and seize upon the same, and deliver them to the Sheriffs of London and Middlesex, who were to see this order put in due execution. The Assembly of Divines were also to appoint some of their members to be present at the burning of these books; and to declare to the people the abominableness of it; and if there be cause, to vindicate the author. And it was referred to the Committee of Examinations to find out the author and printer of this book, and who brought the same to the press.[1]   A copy exists in the British Museum Library.

133.

England's Birthright justified against all arbitrary usurpation, whether regall or parliamentary, or under what vizor whatever.   With divers Queries, Observations, and Grievances of the People, declaring this

1. Commons' Journals, Vol. 4, p. 206.

Parliaments present Proceedings to be directly contrary to those fundamentall principles, whereby their actions at first were justifyable against the King, in their present illegall dealings with those that have been their best friends, advancers and preservers; and in other things of high concernment to the Freedom of all the Freeborn People of England ; by a Well Wisher to the just cause for which Lieutenant Col. John Lilburne is unjustly imprisoned in Newgate.

A pamphlet of 49 pages, of which there is a copy in the British Museum Library. On November 8th, 1645, this pamphlet was referred by the House of Commons to a Committee to report their opinions thereupon to the House.[1]

134.

Divers papers presented to the Honourable Houses of Parliament by the Commissioners of the Kingdome of Scotland. London, printed by M. B. for Robert Bostock, at the Kings Head in Pauls Church Yard. 1645.

On November 14th, 1645, the House of Commons ordered that the Committee of Examinations should send for the printer of this book, and examine him by what direction or authority the same was printed. On the 18th November the Committee reported that Robert Bostock, stationer, being examined, said that he caused the first impression of these papers to be made; that they were licensed by Mr. Crauford, minister; and were brought to him by Mr. Buchanan without any knowledge or consent of the Scotts Commissioners that he knew of.[2] A copy exists in the British Museum Library.

135.

A word to the wise. Displaying great augmented grievances, and heavie pressures of dangerous conse- quence. Appearing by certain materiall weighty

1. Commons' Journals, Vol. 4, p. 336.
2. Ibid, pp. 342, 348.

passages of speciall concernment. Remonstrating the
great dangers which the Counties of Cumberland and
Westmoreland are in (though now in the hands of the
Parliament) but like to be possessed by the enemy,
who aimeth at it, above all other landing places, from
foraign parts; the said Countries being most hazard-
able, sith that Mr. Richard Barwis (a member of the
House of Commons) hath (as is set forth by the
Commissioners for the well affected, in their charge)
betrayed his trust, and placed traytors, and disaffected
officers in the said Counties, tending to the ruine of
the well affected, and to the incouragement and
upholding of the malignant party. All which being
certified by Mr. John Musgrave, Commissioner, for and
in the behalfe of those Countries aforesaid, who gave
in the charge against Mr. Richard Barwis. And the
House having referred the same to a Committee, instead
of prosecuting the charge brought against the said Mr.
Barwis, Mr. Musgrave aforesaid was illegally committed
to Fleet Prison (although he still offereth, and is still
able to prove his charge by a cloud of sufficient competent witnesses) and although the same day (in which
he was committed by the House) certain and true
intelligence came to the Parliament that the enemy
had entered the said County, yet notwithstanding is
this worthy gentleman, still most unjustly and ungrate-
fully retained in prison against all Law, and Justice;
and though he (the said Mr. John Musgrave) hath
petitioned the House in behalf of his Country, for
redresse of the said grievances, yet are not the grievances redressed, but the Traytors and disaffected are
still there retained in their offices. All which is
apparent by these following producements.

A pamphlet of 20 pages, of which there is a copy in the British Museum Library. On January 27th, 164⅚, the House of Commons referred to the Committee of Examinations to make a strict enquiry after the author, printer, and divulger of this pamphlet, and to give a speedy account thereof to the House.[1]

136.

A Confession of Faith of seven Congregations or Churches of Christ in London which are commonly but unjustly called Anabaptists. Published for the vindication of the truth, and information of the ignorant; likewise for the taking off of those aspersions which are frequently both in Pulpit and Print unjustly cast upon them. The second impression corrected and enlarged. Published according to order. London, printed by Matthew Simmons, and are to be sold by John Hancock in Pope's Head Alley. 1646.

On January 29th, 164⅚, the House of Commons resolved that the Serjeant should apprehend Benjamin Cox and Samuel Richardson, the parties who delivered this pamphlet at the door to the members of the House, and to take bail of them to appear from time to time at the Committee for plundered ministers; and that it be referred to that Committee to examine the book, and the parties whose names are subscribed; to send for the licenser and printer, and state the business to the House with all speed, and that the Committee of plundered ministers should have power to advise with such of the Assembly of Divines as they should think fit to send for upon this business. It was also ordered that the Stationers' Company should take diligent care to suppress the pamphlet, and the Serjeant at Arms was to send some of his servants immediately to seize and suppress the said books. The parties who delivered the pamphlet at the door were also ordered to be called in, and asked by what order and authority the pamphlet was published, and who licensed it. Whereupon Samuel Richardson and Benjamin Cox were called in, and being demanded who printed the said pamphlet, said,

1. Commons' Journals, Vol. 4, p. 419.

One Simonds; and that he got it licensed: and Richardson said, that the printer told him that Mr. Downeham licensed it: that this was a second edition: that they had meetings every first day of the week: that there were seven congregations of them English and one French: and that the subscribers were two of every congregation.[1] A copy of this book exists in the British Museum Library.

137.
Another word to the wise. 1646.

On February 23rd, 164$\frac{5}{6}$, the House of Commons referred to the Committee of Examinations to find out the author, printer, and dispersers of this pamphlet, which was also ordered to be suppressed; and the author, printers, publishers, sellers, or dispersers of the same were to be committed to prison.[2]

138.
The last warning to all the Inhabitants of London.

On March 21st, 164$\frac{5}{6}$, the House of Commons referred this pamphlet to the Committee for Examinations, to find out the author, printer, and publisher.[3] A copy exists in the British Museum Library. It is in quarto, and contains eight pages, but is without title page, date, or author's name.

139.
Justiciarius justificatus. The Justice justified. Being an Apologeticall Remonstrance, delivered to the Honourable Commissioners of the Great Seale, by George Wither Esquire and occasioned by Sir Richard Onslow Knight with some others, who moved to have him put out of the Commission of the Peace in Surrey. In which private defence many things are expressed verie pertinent to publike consideration, and to the vindication of the liberties of the subject, in generall, and of Magistrates in particular.

1. Commons' Journals, Vol. 4, p. 420.
2. Ibid, p. 451.
   Ibid, pp. 483, 505, 516.

A tart and libellous remonstrance on being thrust out of the Commission for the peace and gaol delivery in Surrey, which act Wither ascribed to Sir Richard Onslow's malice. On April 10th, 1646, the House of Commons being informed of this pamphlet, resolved that Wither should be forthwith sent for as a delinquent, and the book was referred to the consideration of the Committee of Examinations. On the 7th August following it was further resolved that the matters contained in this book which reflected upon Sir Richard Onslow were "false, scandalous, and injurious," and that Wither should pay him £500 for damages. The book was ordered to be burnt at Kingston upon Thames and at Guildford, upon the market days there.[1]   A copy is preserved in the British Museum Library. It is in quarto, and contains fifteen pages, but has no title page or date.

140.

Truth its manifest, or a short and true relation of divers main passages of things (in some whereof the Scots are particularly concerned) from the very first beginning of these unhappy troubles to this day. London.   1645.

This book was written by Mr. David Buchanan. On April 13th, 1646, the House of Commons resolved that Buchanan should be sent for as a delinquent by the Serjeant at Arms and brought to the bar of the House the next morning, for writing this book; also that the book itself contained in it many matters false and scandalous; and order was given that it should be forthwith burnt by the Common Hangman. On the 20th April the Lords were desired to concur in this order.[2]   A copy of this book exists in the British Museum Library. It is in duodecimo and contains 142 pages.

141.

Some papers of the Commissioners of Scotland given in lately to the Houses of Parliament concerning the Propositions of Peace.   London, printed for Robert Bostock, dwelling at the Sign of the King's Head in Paul's Church-yard, April 11, 1646.

1.   Commons' Journals, Vol. 4, pp. 505, 531, 639.
2.   Ibid, pp. 505, 507, 517.

PART III.]   [TO BE CONTINUED.

INDEX

EXPURGATORIUS

ANGLICANUS:

OR

A DESCRIPTIVE CATALOGUE OF THE PRINCIPAL BOOKS

PRINTED OR PUBLISHED IN ENGLAND,

WHICH HAVE BEEN SUPPRESSED,

OR BURNT BY THE COMMON HANGMAN,

OR CENSURED,

OR FOR WHICH THE AUTHORS, PRINTERS, OR PUBLISHERS

HAVE BEEN PROSECUTED.

BY W. H. HART, F.S.A.

PRICE TWO SHILLINGS.

LONDON:

JOHN RUSSELL SMITH, 36, SOHO SQUARE.

1874.

HART, PRINTER,]   [SAFFRON WALDEN.

On April 13th, 1646, the House of Commons resolved that this book contained matters "scandalous and false," and it was ordered to be burnt forthwith by the Common Hangman. It was also declared that "the author and publisher thereof was an Incendiary between the two kingdoms of England and Scotland," and search was to be made for him.

It was also ordained by both Houses of Parliament that the Epistle and Tract intituled "The State of the Question concerning Propositions of Peace" comprised in the before mentioned book, contained in it matters scandalous and false, and that only the said Epistle and Tract should be forthwith burnt by the Common Hangman, and it was declared and ordained that the author was a person highly disaffected to the Parliament of England, and had endeavoured to raise sedition against the Parliament and kingdom.[1]

A copy of this book exists in the British Museum Library. It is in quarto, and contains 26 pages. The "Epistle" before referred to was written by Mr. David Buchanan.

142.

An open sheet containing a print entitled "Dictated thoughts upon the Presbyterians late Petition for compleat and universal power (in divine ordinances) as represented by a heart borne on the wings of "Tender· Conscience Religiously affected."

A copy of this curious print is preserved in the British Museum Library, with this M.S. note thereon. "London, 14 April, 1646." From the heart issue two labels inscribed

"*The more* { *ye wound my tender dear & pretious Heart* { *yo[r] seered on's shall feel most bitter smart.*

All three to Injure me as mortall foe } Reve., c. 8, v. 13.
Encreaseth yo[r] eternall woe, woe, woe. }

The "*Papa*" holding a book inscribed "*Latin Mass*," a "*Prelat*" holding another book, "*Liturgi*," and an "*Antichristian Presbiter*" holding a third book, "*Directorie*," have their legs fastened to one chain, and are piercing the heart with swords. The arm of "*Presbiter*" is kept down by a heavy weight; he is trampling upon the crown.

1. Commons' Journals, Vol. 4, pp. 507, 508, 510, 511, 516, 517.

On April 20th, 1646, the House of Commons referred to the Committee of Examinations to find out the author and printer of this "scandalous paper," and to report the same to the House on Wednesday morning next, but no further proceedings seem to have been taken.[1]   A copy is preserved in the British Museum Library.

143.

An Alarum to the House of Lords : against their insolent Usurpation of the Common Liberties, and Rights of this Nation.   Manifested by them in their present Tyrannioall Attempts against that worthy Commoner, Lieutenant Col. John Lilburne, Defendour of the Faith, And of his Countries Freedoms, both by his Words, Deeds and Sufferings, against all Tyrants in the Kingdome ; whether Black-Coats, Papists, Kings, Lords, &c.   1646.

A pamphlet of 12 pages, of which there is a copy in the British Museum Library.   On August 11th, 1646, Overton was summoned to the Bar of the House of Lords for being concerned in printing this book, and was committed to Newgate.   On January 5th, 164⅚, his house was searched, when was found another treasonable work, entitled *Regal Tyranny Discovered*, &c. On his wife refusing to give any account of its author, she was committed to Bridewell for contempt.[2]

144.

The Scottish Dove.   Number 146 from Wednesday 5° Augusti till 12° Augusti, 1646.

On September 10th, 1646, the House of Commons referred to the Committee for Foreign Affairs to examine who was the printer and publisher and likewise the author of this pamphlet, and to report their opinion to the House.[3]

1.   Commons' Journals, Vol. 4, p. 517.
2.   Lords' Journals, Vol. 8, pp. 645-50, 657, 658.
3.   Commons' Journals, Vol. 4,p. 664.

145.

Yet another word to the wise : showing that the lamentable grievances of the Parliament's friends in Cumberland and Westmerland presented by their Commissioner Mr. John Musgrave to the House of Commons above two yeares agoe, are so far yet from being redressed, that the House of Commons not only protecteth Mr. Richard Barwis one of their owne Members from the Law, being accused of High treason, as appeareth by the great charge against him in this treatise contained. As also against Sir Wilford Lawson, Commander in Chiefe of Cumberland, who betrayed that County into the enemies hands. And after he was Commissioner of array, carried Men and Arms out of the Countrey for the King against the Parliament. But instead of doing justice either against them or other accused Traytors to the Common-wealth, they have most unjustly committed that worthy gentleman, Mr. John Musgrave, (their Accuser and prosecuter) to the Fleet Prison above these 12 moneths, without any kind of allowance to himselfe or family, or so much as any appearance yet of any faire hearing, triall, or deliverance. *Matters worthy all the freemen* of Englands serious observation. 1646.

On October 3rd, 1646, the House of Commons ordered that this "scandalous pamphlet tending much to the breach of the "privilege and the great scandal and contempt of this House" should be referred to the Committee formerly appointed for complaints concerning any breach of the Articles for surrender of Oxford, to examine and find out the author, printers, and publishers thereof, and to take care for the suppressing thereof.[1] A copy exists in the British Museum Library.

1. Commons' Journals, Vol. 4, p. 682.

146.

Mercurius Rusticus.   The Country's Complaint, recounting the sad events of this unparalleled war. (1646.)

The author was Bruno Ryves, of whom an account will be found in Wood's Athenæ Oxonienses, (ed. Bliss), Vol. 3, p. 1110. On October 3rd, 1646, the House of Commons referred to the Committee formerly appointed for complaints concerning any breach of the Articles for surrender of Oxford to examine and find out the author, printer, and publisher of this "scandalous book," and to take care for the suppressing thereof.[1]   A copy is preserved in the British Museum Library.

147.

An unhappy game at Scotch and English.   Or a Full answer from England to the Papers of Scotland. Wherein their Scotch Mists and their Fogs; their sayings and gaine-sayings; their Juglings, their windings and turnings; hither and thither, backwards and forwards, and forwards and backwards again; Their breach of Covenant, Articles and Treaty, their Kingcraft present design against the two Houses of Parliament and People of England, their plots and intents for Usurpation and Government over us and our children detected, discovered, and presented to the view of the World, as a dreadfull Omen, All-arme, and Warning to the Kingdome of England.   Edinburgh, Printed (as truly as the Scotch papers were at London) by Evan Tyler, Printer to the Kings most excellent Majestie, and are to be sold at the most Solemn Signe of the *Blew Bonnet*, right opposite to the two Houses of Parliament.   1646.

1. Commons' Journals, Vol. 4, p. 682.

A pamphlet of 26 pages, of which there is a copy in the British Museum Library. On November 30th, 1646, the House of Commons ordered that all the copies of this "scandalous pamphlet" should be forthwith burned by the Common Hangman; some in the New Palace Yard at Westminster, and the remainder at the Royal Exchange; and' the Committee of Complaints was to enquire and find out the author, printers, and publisher thereof.[1]

148.

A Protestation attested before Anthony Luther, Esquire, one of the Justices of the Peace for the County of Essex, upon June 10, 1644, as the causes why the Protestators could not hear in the publick assemblies of the Church of England and so join in worship. N.d.

On December 2nd, 1646, the House of Commons resolved that the party who distributed these papers be forthwith sent for as a delinquent by the Serjeant at Arms; and that the examination of the business be referred to the Committee of Complaints, to consider of the making of this Protestation and of the printing and dispersing the same.[2]

149.

The humble petition of many well affected freemen and covenant engaged citizens of the City of London. 1646.

On December 2nd, 1646, the House of Commons ordered that the examination of this business be referred to the Committee for complaints, to examine and enquire out the authors, dispersers, printers, and publishers, and to report their opinions what is fit to be done in this business; and in the meantime to suppress the dispersing of them.[3] A copy of this paper did exist in the British Museum Library; it is entered in the old seven-volume catalogue, but is now marked as missing.

1. Commons' Journals, vol. 4, pp. 731, 732.
2. Ibid, p. 735.
3. Ibid.

150.

London's Account: or a Calculation of the Arbitrary and Tyranicall Exactions, Taxations, Impositions, Excises, Contributions, Subsidies, Twentieth Parts, and other Assessements, within the Lines of Communication, during the foure yeers of this Unnaturall Warre. What the totall summe amounts unto, what hath beene disbursed out of it, and what remaines in the Accomptants hands. 1647.

A pamphlet of 12 pages, of which a copy exists in the British Museum Library. On February 3rd, 164⅚, a Committee of the House of Commons was directed to examine and enquire who were the authors, publishers, and printers of this, as also of the three following pamphlets; and they were to have further power to " consider of an ordinance for the suppressing of these and all " such like scandalous pamphlets, and to prevent the publishing " and vending of the like for the future; and to suppress the " publishing in the streets, by ballad singers, pamphlets and " ballads scandalous to the Parliament; and to give order that " the venders and singers of such might be punished according " to law."[1]

151.

The Oppressed Man's Oppressions declared : or An Epistle written by Lieut. Col. John Lilburn, Prerogative prisoner (by the illegall and arbitrary Authority of the House of Lords) in the Tower of *London*, to Col. *Francis West*, Lieutenant thereof : in which the oppressing cruelty of all the Gaolers of *England* is declared, and particularly the Lieutenants of the Tower. As also, there is thrown unto *Tho. Edwards*, the Author of the 3 *Ulcerous Gangrænes*, a bone or two to pick : In which also, divers other things are handled, of speciall Concernment to the present times.

1. Commons' Journals, vol. 5, pp. 72, 73.

A pamphlet of 39 pages, but without title. A copy exists in the British Museum Library.

152.

Bellum Hybernicale: or IRELAND'S WARRE *Astrologically* demonstrated from the late Celestiall-congresse of the two Malevolent Planets, *Saturne* and *Mars*, in *Taurus*, the Ascendent of that Kingdome. Wherein likewise, their future *opposition* in the signs *Sagittary* and *Gemini*, (most ominous to London, and many other of the *South* and *West* parts of *England*) is *Mathematically* handled. The *Ignorance, Malice, Mistakes, Errors, Insolencies*, and *Impertinencies*, of John Booker, (in his *Astrologicall Observations* upon the said *Conjunction*, in a late Pamphlet of his, styled, *A Bloody Irish Almanack*, &c.) discovered, corrected, refuted, and retorted. And the Author further vindicated, from his, and Master *Lilly's* former frivolous, false, and malicious Aspersions, throughout the whole Discourse. *By Capt.* GEO. WHARTON, *Student in Astronomy*. Printed in the yeere 1647.

A tract of 36 pages, of which a copy is preserved in the British Museum Library.

153.

No *Merline*, nor *Mercurie*; but A new *Almanack* after the old fashion, for the year of our Redemption 1647. Delivering exactly the Eclipses, Lunations, Quarterly ingresses, and other congresses and configurations of the celestiall bodies, with their effects probably to happen on this Planet (the Earth). Wherein likewise a few of the many grosse errours and impertinences of Mr. William Lilly are plainly discovered, modestly refuted, and the Author vindicated from his former Aspersions. Calculated exactly for the Honourable Citie of York.

Whose {Latitude is 54 degrees, 20 minutes.
{Longitude is 23 degrees, 30 minutes.

By George Wharton, student in Astronomy. Printed Anno Dom. 1647.

A copy of this pamphlet is preserved in the British Museum Library.

154.

The out-cryes of oppressed Commons. Directed to all the Rationall and understanding men in the Kingdome of *England* and Dominion of *Wales* (that have not resolved with themselves to be Vassells and Slaves unto the lusts and wills of Tyrants). From Lieut. Col. *John Lilburne,* prerogative prisoner in the Tower of *London,* and *Richard Overton,* prerogative prisoner in the infamous Gaole of *Newgate. Febr.,* 1647.

On March 9th, 164⁶₇, the House of Commons ordered that this pamphlet should be referred to the examination and consideration of Sir Robert Pye and others, to enquire out the authors, printers, and publishers thereof.[1] A copy exists in the British Museum Library. It consists of 20 pages.

155.

The Scots Apostacy.

A folio broadside containing the following set of verses.

" Is't come to this ? what ? shall the Cheekes of Fame
" Stretch't with the breath of learned *Lowden's* name
" Be flagg'd againe, and that great peice of Sence
" As rich in Loyaltie, as Eloquence,
" Brought to the Test, be found a tricke of State ?
" Like Chimists tinctures prov'd Adulterate ?
" The Divell sure such language did atcheive,
" To cheate our un-fore-warned Grandame *Eve* ;

1. Commons' Journals, vol. 5, p. 109.

"As this Impostor found out to besot
"Th' experienc't *English* to beleeve A *Scot*.
"Who reconcil'd the Covenants doubtfull Sence?
"The Commons Argument, or the Cities Pence?
"Or did you doubt persistance in one good
"Would spoyle the fabrick of your Brotherhood,
"Projected first in such a forge of sinne,
"Was fit for the grand Divel's hammering.
"Or was't Ambition that this damned fact,
"Should tell the world you know the sines you act.
"The infamie this super-Treason brings,
"Blasts more then Murders of your sixtie Kings.
"A crime so blacke as being advis'dly done,
"Those hold with this no Competition.
"Kings only suffer'd then, in this doth lie,
"Th' Assacination of Monarchye.
"Beyond this sinne no one step can be Trod
"If not t'attempt deposing of your God.
"Oh were you so engag'd that we might see,
"Heavens angry lightning 'bout your eares to flee;
"Till you were shriveld into dust, and your cold land,
"Parcht to a drought beyond the *Libian* sand;
"But 'tis reserv'd, and till heaven plague you worse
"Be Objects of an Epidemick curse.
"First may your Brethren to whose viler ends,
"Your power hath banded cease to count you friends;
"And prompted by the Dictate of their reason
"Reproach the Traytors; though they hug the Treason.
"And may their Iealousies encrease and breed,
"Till they confine your Ships beyond the *Tweed*.
"In forreigne Nations may your loath'd name be,
"A stigmatizing brand of Infamie.
"Till forc't by generall hate you cease to rome
"The world, and for a plague goe live at home;
"Till you resume your povertie, and bee
"Reduc'd to begge where none can be so free,
"To grant; and may your scabbie Land be all,
"Translated to a generall Hospitall.
"Let not the Sun afford one gentle ray,
"To give you comfort of a Summers day.

" But as a Guerdon for your Trayterous warre,
" Live cherisht only by the Northerne Starre.
" No stranger deigne to visite your rude Coast,
" And be to all but banisht Men, as lost.
" And such in Hightening of the infliction due,
" Let provok't Princes send them all to you.
" Your State a Chaos be, where not the Law ;
" But Power, your lives and liberties may awe.
" No Subject 'mongst you keepe a quiet brest,
" But each man strive through blood to be the best ;
" Till for those Miseries on us yo've brought,
" By your own sword, our just revenge be wrought.
" To summe up all— let your Religion be,
" As your Allegiance, mask't hypocrisie.
" Untill when *Charles* shall be compos'd in dust,
" Perfum'd with Epithites of good and just ;
" *He sav'd ; Incensed Heaven may have forgot,*
" *To afford one act of mercy to a* Scot.

Finis."

On March 9th, 164⁶⁄₇, the House of Commons referred this
paper to the examination and consideration of Sir Robert Pye
and others, to enquire out the authors, printers, and publishers
thereof.[1]   A copy is preserved in the British Museum Library.

156.

A warning for all the Counties of England to awake
spedily out of their dreames and apply themselves to all
just meanes for the recoverie and preservation of their
Liberties ; because of a present designe, to expell the
most Faithfull out of their House of Commons, and to
frustrate all the Countries good Elections, that so the
Malignant party may bring the free Commons of
England now (after all their bloody sufferings) into
cruel Thraldome, and make themselves Lords over
them.

On March 25th, 1647, the House of Commons ordered that
enquiry should be made who were the " authors, contrivers,

1.   Commons' Journals, Vol. 5, p. 109.

designers, printers, publishers, and venders" of this "scandalous seditious pamphlet," and the Stationers' Company were forthwith to seize the same, and all other scandalous pamphlets of the like nature, and suppress them; and the Sergeant at Arms was to do the same.[1]

A copy exists in the British Museum Library. It is in quarto, and contains 20 pages. It commences thus:—

"JER. 5. 1. 2.

" *Run to and fro thorough the streetes in* Jerusalem, *(as it may be* " *truly said of* Westminster *and* London*) and see now, and know,* " *and seeke in the broad places thereof, if ye can finde a man, if there* " *be any that executeth judgement, that seeketh the Truth, and I will* " *pardon it.*

"And though they say the Lord liveth, surely they sweare "falsly.

HOSEA. 10. 4.

" *They have spoken words swearing falsly, in making a Covenant.*

"Wee the free Commons of *England,* have been (for the "general part) like Marchant Adventurers, who according to the "Poet, *per varios casus, per tot discrimina rerum,* &c., through "many great difficulties and dangers do saile into farr Countries, "with great costs and charges to fetch home rich Treasures, the "which when they have gotten, they do returne therewith joy-"fully: & yet upon their own Coasts, or in the very harbour at "home, through the negligence, or ambition, pride, covetous-"nesse, falshood, or contention of the Ships-Master, or his "Mariners, do suffer wrack, and loose the fruit of all their Costs, "Adventures, and travells."

157.

A new found Stratagem framed in the old forge of Machivilisme, and put upon the Inhabitants of the County of Essex. To destroy the Army under his Exeellency Sir Thomas Fairfax, and to inslave all the Free-born of England on a Sudden, manifested and laid down, in certain animadversions, upon a clandes-tine, illegall petition, contrived, made, and privatly

---

1. Commons' Journals, Vol. 5, pp. 123, 124.

printed, by a destructive party in London: and then by them sent down to the Ministers of the County of Essex, to publish as on the last Lord's day, 4. April, to the people, with directions to take their subscriptions in two sheets of paper; which being done: So many of the Subscribers as can, are to be desired to meet at Stratford Langton, the 18. instant Aprill, and so to come and present the same to both Houses, as the Petition and sense of the whole County: whereas it was never propounded to the County, not even heard of among them, before it came down ready in print, from London, to be published by their Ministers, in there severall Parishes. With certain Observations and Cautions on the same, conducing to the information, and publick good of the whole Kingdome. Published principally for the Meridian of the County of Essex, but may serve for all the Counties of England. 1647.

A pamphlet of 15 pages, a copy of which exists in the British Museum Library. On April 23rd, 1647, the House of Commons referred the consideration of this paper, as also of the paper described in the next article, to a Committee, to examine and find out the "authors, inventors, contrivers, publishers, and dispersers" thereof, and how, and by what hands, and to what ends they were dispersed and sent down to the army.[1]

158.

An Apollogie of the Souldiers to all their Commission Officers in Sir Thomas Fairfax his Armie. 1647.

A sheet of two pages, quarto size, of which a copy exists in the British Museum Library. For its condemnation by the House of Commons see preceding article.

1. Commons' Journals, vol. 5, p. 153.

159.

The unlawfulnesse of subjects taking up armes against their Soveraigne in what case so ever. Together with an answer to all objections scattered in their severall Bookes. And a proofe that notwithstanding such resistance as they plead for, were not damnable, yet the present warre made upon the King is so, because those cases, in which onely some men have dared to excuse it, are evidently not now; His Majesty fighting onely to preserve himselfe, and the rights of the subjects. Written by Dudley Diggs, Gentleman: late Fellow of All-Soules Colledge in Oxford. Printed in the yeare of our Lord, 1647, Since the 25. day of March.

On May 11th, 1647, this book was referred by the House of Commons to the Committee of Complaints, and the printer and publisher were ordered to be tried at the King's Bench.[1]

A copy exists in the British Museum Library.

160.

Lex Terræ: or a briefe Discourse collected out of the Fundamentall Lawes of the Land, wherein it is proved that the Supream power in this Kingdome is in the KING onely, and not in the two Houses of Parliament. The ignorance of which hath been the visible cause of the late unnaturall warre, and all the sad calamities that now lye heavy upon this realme. Whereunto are added divers other small tracts of the same nature, (viz.) a Vindication, Declaration, Cordiall, The Armies Indemnity, The inconvenience of long-continued Parliaments, and an Apology for the Army. Written and published for the Common Good, and

---

1. Howell's State Trials, vol. 4, p. 926.

recommended to the practise of the present times and posterity. By David Jenkins, Prisoner in the Tower of London. London. Printed for John Gyles, 1647.

On May 11th, 1647, the "Vindication," which is contained in the Lex Terræ, was referred by the House of Commons to the Committee of Complaints, and the printers and publishers thereof were to be tried at the King's Bench; but proceedings appear never to have been carried on, and Judge Jenkins was pardoned in 1651.[1] A copy of the Lex Terræ is preserved in the British Museum Library.

161.

A true impartiall Narration, concerning the Armies preservation of the King; by which it doth appear, that the Army doth intend the Good, Life, Propertie, and Libertie of all the Commons of England.

A pamphlet of 12 pages, but without title. On June 26th, 1647, the House of Commons referred this pamphlet to the Committee of Complaints, to send for the printer and to enquire into and examine the business.[2]

162.

Twelve arguments drawn out of the Scripture, Wherein the commonly received Opinion touching the Deity of the Holy Spirit is clearly and fully refuted. To which is prefixed a Letter tending to the same purpose, written to a Member of the Honourable House of Commons. And to which is subjoyned an exposition of five principall Passages of the Scripture, alleadged by the Adversaries to prove the Deity of the Holy Spirit; together with an Answer to their grand Objection touching the supposed Omnipresence of the Holy Spirit. By John Bidle, Master of Arts. Printed in the yeare 1647.

1. Howell's State Trials, Vol. 4, p. 926.
2. Commons' Journals, vol. 5, p. 224.

For writing this book John Biddle was summoned to appear at the bar of the House of Commons, and being asked whether he owned that book and the opinions therein, he answered yea, and that they were his; whereupon being remitted to his prison, they ordered on September 6th, 1647, that the said book, blasphemous against the Deity of Christ, be called in and burnt by the Common Hangman in Cheapside and the New Palace Yard at Westminster. It was also referred to the Committee of Plundered Ministers to examine Biddle concerning this pamphlet, and to commit him if they saw cause, and they were to appoint divines to confer with him and to endeavour to remove him from his blasphemous and dangerous opinions. The Assembly of Divines sitting at Westminster made their endeavours to Parliament that he might suffer death in May, 1648; this however did not take place, and he was kept in close confinement. In February, 1651, a general act of oblivion was passed, by means of which Biddle was restored to liberty.[1] A copy is preserved in the British Museum Library.

163.

The Parliament's agreement for a personall treaty with the King, the Conditions thereof, and his Majesties Reasons, that the said Treaty may be at London to settle a firme peace in the three kingdomes. Also a message to be sent, and 4. new Propositions to be first signed by his Majestie. London. Printed by B. Alsop, and are to be sold at the Royall Exchange. 1647.

On November 27th, 1647, the House of Commons ordered that the debate concerning the printing of this pamphlet should be taken up.[2] A copy is preserved in the British Museum Library.

164.

Mercurius Elenchicus
and
Mercurius Pragmaticus.

These were periodical pamphlets. No. 1 of the Elenchicus appeared on November 5th, 1647, and No. 1 of the Pragmaticus

1, Commons' Journals, vol. 5, p. 293. Wood's Athen. Oxon, (Bliss), vol. 3, p. 594.

2. Commons' Journals, vol. 5, p. 370.

on September 21st, 1647. On November 27th, 1647, the House
of Commons ordered that a Committee should enquire after the
licensers, authors, printers, and publishers of these pamphlets, or
any other pamphlet of the like scandalous or seditious nature,
and all unlicensed pamphlets, and to cause the licensers, authors,
printers, and publishers thereof to be apprehended and imprisoned; and to seize all such seditious and scandalous
pamphlets and cause them to be burnt; and to destroy and take
away the presses and letters and all materials and instruments of
printing.[1] The publication, however, of these periodicals was
continued for some considerable time, notwithstanding the vote of
censure passed on them by the House of Commons.

165.

The answer of the Commissioners of the Kingdome
of Scotland, to both Houses of Parliament, upon the
New Propositions of Peace, and the Foure Bills to
be sent to his Majestie.   London, Printed for Robert
Bostock, dwelling at the sign of the Kings Head in
Panls Church-yard.   1647.

On December 21st, 1647, the House of Commons referred to
the Committee for printing to send for Bostock and Walkeley and
all others who had been concerned in prihting this paper, and to
know by what authority they printed the same, and to proceed
with them in such manner as they should think fit according to
the power granted to that Committee.[2] A copy is preserved in
the British Museum Library.

166.

The People and Souldiers Observations on the Scotch
Message to the Parliament concerning the King; 5. of
November, 1647.   By the scope whereof, all who will
be satisfied with Reason, or with men's practises more
than their words, may have full resolution to this more
usuall then doubtfull question : Whether the King,

1.   Commons' Journals, Vol. 5, p. 371.
2.   Ibid, p. 395.

Lords, Commons, Scotts, City, Clergy, City, and Officers of the Army, have sought more their own private ends then the publick weale of this Nation?

On December 25th, 1647, the House of Commons referred to the Committee of Complaints to enquire who was the author and printer of this "scandalous libellous pamphlet."[1] A copy exists in the British Museum Library. It is in quarto, and contains sixteen pages.

167.

The humble petition of Agnes Corbett, a most distressed widow from Ireland. (1647.)

On December 25th, 1647, the House of Commons referred to the Committee of Complaints to enquire who was the author and printer of this pamphlet.[2]

168.

A Just and Solemn Protestation of the Free born People of England, and Free Citizens of London, against a Clause in the late Ordinance to deprive them of their Free Elections, and enslave them.

On January 12th, 164⁷⁄₈, the House of Commons referred this broadside to the Committee for Complaints, to enquire after the printers, publishers, divulgers, and abettors of it, and of the affront done to an officer that pulled it down from a post or some other public place where it was fixed in Cheapside.[3] A copy is preserved in the British Museum Library.

169.

The Parliament's Ten Commandments; the Parliament's Pater-noster, and the Articles of their Faith. (164⁷⁄₈.)

A single sheet containing a parody on the Commandments, commencing thus:—"1. Thou shalt have no other Gods but US "the LORDS and COMMONS assembled at Westminster;" a

1. Commons' Journals, vol. 5, p. 405.
2. Ibid.
3. Ibid, p. 428.

parody on the Lord's Prayer commencing thus, "Our Fathers, which think your Houses of Parliament to be Heaven;" and a parody on the Apostles' Creed commencing thus, "I beleeve in "CROMWELL, the Father of all Schisme, Sedition, Heresy, and "Rebellion." A copy is preserved in the British Museum Library.

On February 19th, 164⅞, the House of Commons resolved that a reward of £100 should be bestowed on the discoverer of the author or printer of this "vile blasphemous pamphlet;" and a few days afterwards it was further ordered that all the copies should be collected together and be burnt by the Common Hangman in three of the most public places of London and Westminster, upon a market day.[1]

170.

Ecce the New Testament of our Lords and Saviours, The House of Commons at Westminster and the Supreame Councell at Windsor. Newly translated out of their owne Heathenish Greek Ordinances, with their former proceeding; diligently compared and revised and appointed to be read in all Conventicles. Cum Privilegio. Printed in the yeare, 1648.

A Parody upon the commencement of the Gospel of St. Matthew, commencing thus:—

"The Booke of the Generation of JOHN PIM, the sonne of "Judas, the sonne of Belzebub," &c.; and it concludes with this:—

A Psalme, to be sung as the 15. of David.

" Good Lord confound King Oliver,
    and all his holy Crew,
" With Rainsborow that Leveller,
    and Pride that precious Jew.

"Let Say once more, we doe thee pray,
    into a Saw-pit fall,
" Let Martin purge his Pocks away
    within some Hospitall.

1.   Commons' Journals, vol. 5, pp. 469, 471.

" Let Hammon *have his brains knockt out*
 with his owne bunch of Keyes,
" Let Watson *and his zealous rout*
 visit the Hebrides.

" Let the two Houses fight and scratch,
 like wives at Billingsgate,
" And let them ne're a Peace up patch,
 untill it bee too late.

" That so upon each House of clay
 King Charles *may mount his Throne,*
" Heare us (O Father) wee thee pray,
 our hope's in thee alone."

This pamphlet was condemned to be burnt under the vote of
the House of Commons which consigned the Parliament's Ten
Commandments to the flames. (See last article.) A copy exists
in the British Museum Library.

171.

A motive to all loyal subjects to endeavour the
preservation of his Majesty's Royal person. 1648.

On June 27th, 1648, the House of Commons resolved that this
"scandalous and seditious paper" should be referred to the
Committee for suppressing of libels, with power to examine who
printed and published the same, and who set up the same, or
advised the knocking down of Lieut. Col. Bellamy; and it was
further ordered that the said Committee should draw up something and present to the house for vindication of the honour of
Major General Skippon. On the 10th July, upon Mr. Challoner's
report from the Committee, it was resolved that this paper,
wherein Major General Skippon was slanderously charged with
notorious, falsities "was a malicious and scandalous Libel: and
" also this House doth declare, That it doth appear to them, that
" Captain Rolfe, charged by Mr. Osborne to conspire the Taking
" away of his Majesty's Life is not Son-in-law to Major General
" Skippon; neither hath any Relation unto him, as is falsly
" charged in the said Paper. Also, that it doth appear to this
" House, That Mr. Rolfe who is Son-in-Law to Major General
" Skippon, hath no Command in this Army, or hath, or ever had,

"any Command in the Isle of Wight. Also, that the foul
"aspersions in the said Libel, cast upon Major General Skippon,
"tended to blast him in his Reputation, to raise Mutiny and
"Sedition, and to stir up the Hatred of 'the People against
"him, thereby to render him useless in these distracted Times,
"he being a Person of such eminent Worth." And it was finally
resolved that these Votes should be forthwith printed, and set
up in the most publick Places of the City, " to discover to the
"People the wicked Designs of these Libels; and to vindicate
"Major General Skippon in his Honour, from the false Calumnies
"thereby cast upon him.[1]

172.

A treatise of Magistracy.   N. d.

On January 6th, 164⅞, the House of Commons ordered that this
pamphlet should be referred to the Committee for printing unlicensed pamphlets.[2]

173.

A Salva Libertate, sent to Collonell Francis West,
Lieutenant of the Tower of London, on Fryday the
fourteenth of September 1649. by Lieutenant Collonell
John Lilburne, unjustly, and illegally imprisoned in
the said Tower, ever since the 28. of March, 1649.
Occasioned by the receipt of a Verball Command (which
in law is nothing, nor signefies nothing) whereby the
said Lieut. was seemingly authorized, to carry the said
John Lilburne before Mr. Prideaux the nicknamed,
and falsly so called Atturney Generall, on Fryday, 14.
Sept. 1649.

A folio sheet, signed "As much a Christian and an Englishman
as ever, JOHN LILBURNE. From my Chamber in the Tower of
London, this 14. of Sept., 1649." A copy is preserved in the
British Museum Library.

1. Commons' Journals, vol. 5, pp. 614, 630.
2. Ibid, p. 420.

For writing and printing this and the four following pamphlets, Lilburne was prosecuted and tried in October, 1649, but was acquitted. The proceedings are given at great length in Howell's State Trials.

174.

An Impeachment of High Treason against *Oliver Cromwel*, and his son-in-law *Henry Ireton*, Esquires, late Members of the late forcibly dissolved House of Commons, presented to publique view; by *Lieutenant Colonel John Lilburn*, close prisoner in the Tower of London, for his real, true, and zealous affections to the Liberties of his Native Country. In which following Discourse or Impeachment, he engageth upon his life, either upon the principles of Law (*by way of indictment, the only and alone legall way of all tryals in England*) or upon the principles of Parliaments ancient proceedings, or upon the principles of reason (*by pretence of which alone they lately took away the King's life*) before a legal Magistracy, when there shall be one again in *England* (*which now in the least there is not*) to prove the said *Oliver Cromwel* guilty of the highest Treason that ever was acted in England, and more deserving punishment and death then the 44 Judges hanged for injustice by *King Alfred* before the Conquest; or then the Lord *Chief Justice Wayland* and his associates tormented by Edw. I. Or, then Judge *Thorpe*, condemned to dye for Bribery in Edw. 3. time; Or, then the *two disthroned Kings* Edw. 2. *and* Rich. 2. Or, then the Lord Chief Justice *Tresillian*, (*who had his throat cut at Tyburn as a Traitor in Rich. 2. time, for subverting the Law*) and all his associates; Or, then those two grand Traytorly subverters of the Laws and Liberties of England, *Empson* and *Dudley*, who therefore as

Traytors lost their heads upon Tower-hill, in the beginning of Henr. 8 raign; Or, then trayterous Cardinal *Wolsey*, who after he was arrested of Treason, poysoned himself; Or, then the late trayterous *Ship-Money Judges*, who with one Verdict or Judgment destroyed all our propertie; Or, then the late trayterous Bishop of *Canterbury*, Earl of *Strafford*, Lord-Keeper *Finch*, Secretary *Windebanck*, or then Sir *George Ratcliff*, or all his Associates; Or, then the two *Hothams*, who lost their heads for corresponding with the Queen, &c.; Or, then the late King *Charls* whom themselves have beheaded for a *Tyrant* and *Traytor*. In which are also some Hints of Cautions to the Lord Fairfax, for absolutely *breaking his solemn Engagement with his souldiers, &c.*, to take head and to regain his lost Credit in acting honestly in time to come; in helping to settle the Peace and Liberties of the Nation, which truly, really, and lastingly can never be done, but *by establishing the principles of the Agreement of the Free People;* that being really the peoples interest, and all the rest that went before, but particular and selvish. In which is also the Authors late Proposition sent to Mr. Holland, June 26. 1649, to justifie and make good at his utmost hazard (upon the principles of *Scripture, Law, Reason, and the Parliaments and Armies ancient Declarations*) his late actions or writings in any or all his Books. London. 1649.

A copy of this pamphlet is preserved in the British Museum Library. It is in quarto, and contains 66 pages.

175.

An outcry of the young men and Apprentices of London : or an Inquisition after the lost Fundamentall

Lawes and Liberties of England. Directed (August 29. 1649) in an Epistle to the private Souldiery of the Army, especially all those that signed the solemne Ingagement at Newmarket-Heath, the fifth of June, 1647., But more especially to the private souldiers of the Generalls Regiment of Horse, that helped to plunder and destroy the honest, and true-hearted Englishmen, trayterously defeated at Burford the 15. of May, 1649. Signed by Charles Collins, Anthony Bristlebolt, William Trabret, Stephen Smith, Edward Waldegrave, Thomas Frisby, Edward Stanley, William White, Nicholas Blowd, John Floyd, in the name and behalf of themselves, and the young-men and apprentices of the City of London. Who are cordiall approvers of the Paper, called, The Agreement of the Free People, People, dated May 1. 1649 and the defeated Burfordmens late Vindication, dated the 20. of August 1649.

A quarto pamphlet of 12 pages, of which there is a copy in the British Museum Library.

176.

The Legall Fundamentall Liberties of the People of England, Revived, Asserted, and Vindicated. Or an Epistle written the eighth day of June 1649, by Lieut. Colonel John Lilburn (Arbitrary and Aristocratical prisoner in the Tower of London) to Mr. William Lenthall, Speaker to the remainder of those few Knights, Citizens, and Burgesses that Col. Thomas Pride at his late purge thought convenient to leave sitting at Westminster (as most fit for his and his Masters designes, to serve their ambitious and tyrannical ends, to destroy the good old Laws, Liberties, and Customs of England, the badges of our freedom (as the Declaration against the King, of the 17. of March 1648, pag. 23. calls them) and by force of arms to rob the people of their lives, estates, and properties, and subject them to perfect vassalage and slavery, as he cleerly evinceth in his present case &c. they have done) who (and in truth no otherwise) pretendedly stile themselves (the Conservators of the peace of England, or) the Parliament of England, intrusted and authorised by the consent of all the people thereof, whose Representatives by election (in their Declaration last mentioned, *pag.* 27. they say) they are; although they are never able to produce one bit of a Law, or any piece of a Commission to prove, that all the people of *England*, or one quarter, tenth, hundred, or thousand part of them authorised *Thomas Pride*, with his Regiment of Souldiers, to chuse them a Parliament, as indeed he hath *de facto* done by this pretended mock-Parliament : And therefore it cannot properly be called the Nations or Peoples Parliament, but Col. Pride's and his associates, whose really it is; who although they have beheaded the King for a Tyrant, yet walk in his oppressingest steps, if not worse and higher. London, Printed in the grand yeer of hypocriticall and abominable dissimulation. 1649.

A tract of 75 pages, of which there is a copy in the British Museum Library. It was written by Lilburn, while he was imprisoned in the Tower of London, and is thus dated by him:—
"From my close, unjust, and causelesse captivity without allow-
"ance (the legall right of all men in my case) in the Tower of
"London this 8. of June 1649). The first yeer of England's
"declared Freedom, by the lying and false pretended Conserva-
"tors thereof, that never intended it." At the end is this note.

"The Printer to the Reader.
"Reader, As thou the faults herein dost spy,
"   I pray thee to correct them with thy Pen:
"The Author in Close Prisonn, knows not why;
"   And shall have Liberty, he knows not when.
"   But if he falls; as he hath Liv'd, he Dies
"   A Faithfull Martyr for our Liberties."

177.

A preparative to a Hue and Cry after Sir Arthur Haslerig, (*a late Member of the* forcibly *dissolved House of Commons, and now the present wicked, bloody, and tyrannical Governor of Newcastle upon Tine*) for his severall ways attempting to *murder*, and by *base plots, conspiracies, and false Witnesse* to take away the life of Lieutenant Colonel *John Lilburn* now *Prisoner* in the *Tower* of London: As also for his *felonious Robbing* the said Lieut. Col. *John Lilburn* of betwixt 24 and 2500.*l.* by the *meer* power of his *own will*, without ever fixing any *reall* or pretended *crime* upon the said *Lieutenant Col.* or so much as affording him any *formall* proceedings, though upon a paper Petition. *In which action alone*, he the said *Haslerig* hath outstript the Earl of *Strafford, in traiterously subverting* the fundamentall *Liberties of England*, and (in time of Peace) exercising *an arbitrary and tyrannicall Government, over and above Law*, and better and more justly deserves to die therefore, then ever the Earl of *Strafford* did (especially, considering he *was one* of his Judges, that for such actions condemned him to *lose his head as a Traytor*) by which *tyranicall* actions the said Haslerig is become a *Polecat*, a *Fox*, and a *Wolf*, (as a subverter and destroyer of humane society) *and may and ought to be knockt on the head therefore*, by the very words of Solicitor *S*⁺· *John's* own doctrine against the said Earl of *Strafford*. All which the said Lieutenant Col. *John Lilburn* hath cleerly and evidently evinced *in his following Epistle of the* 18 *of August* 1649, to his Uncle *George Lilburn Esquire* of *Sunderland*, in the County of *Durham*.

A copy of this pamphlet is preserved in the British Museum Library. It is in quarto, and contains 40 pages.

178.

A Breife Memento to the present Unparliamentary Junto Touching their present Intentions and Proceedings to *Depose* and *Execute*, CHARLES STEWARD, their lawfull KING. By *William Prynne* Esquire: *A Member of the House of Commons*, and Prisoner under the Armies Tyranny ; who, it seemes, have *leavyed Warre* against the Houses of *Parliament*, their *quondam Masters*; whose *Members* they now forcibly take and detaine *Captives*, during their *lawlesse Pleasures*. London, 1648.

On January 5th, 16$\frac{48}{49}$, the House of Commons ordered that Mr. Humphrey Edwards and Mr. Fry should repair to Mr. Prynne and show him this "scandalous book or pamphlet," and to know of him if he would own and avow the same book. The next day Mr. Edwards reported Mr. Prynne's answer touching his owning this pamphlet, which was a characteristic one, viz. : "I "will give no answer until I am commanded by a lawful "authority." On January 10th, it was resolved that Mr. Prynne by this answer had disowned the authority of that House, and that he should therefore be forthwith sent for in safe custody by the Serjeant at Arms. But Prynne refused his attendance, for the next day the servant to the Serjeant at Arms who was sent to take Mr. Prynne gave the following information to the House; that he repaired to Mr. Prynne, and served the warrant upon him, that Mr. Prynne thereupon gave him this answer, viz. that upon the sixth of December last as he was coming to do his duty in the House of Commons, he was taken by Colonel Pryde and Sir Hardres Waller, and by them imprisoned he knew not for what cause; that he yet remained under that restraint and was not yet discharged from that imprisonment; and that therefore he would not come upon that warrant.[1]

A copy is preserved in the British Museum Library. It is in quarto, and contains 16 pages.

179.

A vindication of the Ministers of the Gospel in, and about London, from the unjust aspersions cast upon their former actings for the Parliament, as if they had promoted the bringing of the King to capitall punishment. With a short exhortation to their people to keep close to their Covenant-Ingagement. London. 1648.

On February 3rd, 164$\frac{8}{9}$, the House of Commons ordered that this book should be taken into consideration, and that the authors, publishers, printers, and subscribers to the same should be examined; and that a Committee should take information of such as had already preached, published, or printed seditiously the proceedings in bringing the King to justice; and also that they should prepare and bring in an ordinance to restrain public preaching and printing anything against the proceedings of the House of Commons and the High Court of Justice in relation to bringing the King to justice.[2] A copy is preserved in the British Museum Library. It is in quarto, and contains 11 pages.

180.

To the Right Honourable, the Supreme Authority of this Nation, the Commons assembled in Parliament: An Appeal, in the humble claim of justice, against Tho. Lord Fairfax General of the English Army, raised and declared to be raised, for the propagation and

1. Commons' Journals, Vol. 6, pp. 111, 112, 115, 116,
2, Ibid, p, 131,

defence of impartial Justice, and just Liberty in the
Nation; by Captain William Bray. For, and on the
behalf of himself, and all the Officers and Souldiers,
and other the free People of this Nation, that are for
Righteousnesse, Settlement, and Peace. London.
1649.

On March 19th, 164⅘, Captain Bray appeared before the House
of Commons, and being demanded whether this was his book or
not, and whether it was an appeal of all those in whose name it
was made, he answered that it was his book, but it was done
without the consent or knowledge of any of the soldiery or people
on their behalf, and he doubted not that they would justify and
engage for it. Being again asked why he did it, and by whose
licence it was printed, he answered that "although it be a
"declared principle by the army, that it is contrary to the
"privilege of the nation, to answer to any interrogatories at all;
"but he having formerly prepared an appeal, which he laid
"aside, expecting the proceedings of the army would have been
"according to justice and equity, he engaged himself freely for
"the public, and for execution of justice; but finding himself to
"be dealt with as he hath remonstrated, and the case being thus,
"he appealed to this supreme authority: wherein he expects
"relief according to justice and righteousness; and shall sit
"down in such sentence: and saith, it was printed by the
"authority of reason and justice; which is declared to be
"supreme to all men." And being demanded by whose com-
"mission he was made a captain; he answered, by the General's
Commission in Colonel Lilburne's regiment, in one case remonstrated in the Petition, and in another case by the Committee of
Kent; but that he had not the punctilio of a commission in the
last business; but his engagement with Colonel Reynolds, for
maintenance of truth and righteousness, far above any punctilio
of commission "according to right, reason, justice, and righteousness."

It was thereupon resolved that this book was "scandalous as
"to the General and Council of War; and tending to stir up
"sedition in the people and mutiny in the army," and that Captain
Bray should be committed to Windsor Castle during the pleasure

of the House.[1] A copy of this pamphlet is preserved in the British Museum Library. It is in quarto, and contains 19 pages.

181.

The Alcoran of Mahomet translated out of Arabique into French by the Sieur Du Ryer, Lord of Malezair and Resident for the King of France at Alexandria. London. 1649.

On March 19th, 164$\frac{8}{9}$, the House of Commons ordered that this book, which was then in the press, should be seized, and the printer taken into custody, and subsequently the Council of State was directed to suppress all the books, and the further imprinting of the same.[2]

182.

The Paper called the Agreement of the People taken into consideration, and the lawfulness of subscription to it examined, and resolved in the negative by the Ministers of Christ in the Province of Lancaster. Published by them especially for the satisfaction of the Conscience, and guiding of the practise of our entirely honored and beloved, the People of our several Churches committed to our charge; and for the general good of this Church and Nation. London, Printed for Luke Fawne, and are to be sold at his shop at the signe of the Parrot in Pauls Church-yard. 1649.

A pamphlet of 36 pages, of which there is a copy in the British Museum Library. On March 21st, 164$\frac{8}{9}$, the House of Commons referred to the Committee of plundered Ministers to consider of this book; to examine the business and to send for the printer, and to report it to the House.[3]

1. Commons' Journals, Vol. 6, p. 169.
2. Ibid, pp. 168, 170.
3. Ibid, p. 170.

183.

The second Part of Englands New Chaines discóvered : Or a sad Representation of the uncertain and dangerous condition of the Commonwealth : directed to the Supreme Authority of England, the Representors of the People in Parliament assembled. By severall wel-affected persons inhabiting the City of *London*, *Westminster*, the Borough of *Southwark*, *Hamblets*, and places adjacent, presenters and approvers of the late large Petition of the Eleventh of *September*, 1648. London, 1649.

On March 27th, 1649, the House of Commons resolved that this printed paper contained "much false, scandalous, and "reproachful matter; and was highly seditious and destructive "to the present Government; as it is now declared and settled "by Parliament; tends to Division and mutiny in the army, and "the raising of a new war in the Commonwealth, and to hinder "the present relief of Ireland; and to the continuing of Free "Quarter." And it was further declared that the authors, contrivers, and Framers of the said paper were guilty of High Treason; and should be proceeded against as Traitors : and that all persons assisting them should be esteemed as traitors to the Commonwealth ; and be proceeded against accordingly. And it was referred to the Council of State to examine and find out the authors, contrivers, and framers, printers and publishers of the said paper; and to proceed therein as they should find just and necessary, for preventing tumults, and for preservation of the peace of the Commonwealth, and thereof to give an account speedily to the House. On April 11th, 1649, the House of Commons ordered that the Attorney General should prosecute Lieut. Col. Lilburne, Mr. William Walwyn, Mr. Richard Overton, and Mr. Thomas Prince, in the Upper Bench, touching the publication of this book.[1] A copy is preserved in the British Museum Library. It is in quarto, and contains 18 pages.

1. Commons' Journals, Vol. 6, pp. 174, 183.

184.

A Remonstrance and Declaration of the Generall Assembly of the Church of Scotland, concerning present and imminent dangers and concerning duties relating thereto. Edinburgh. Reprinted at London for Robert Bostock, dwelling at the sign of the King's Head in Paul's Church Yard. 1649.

On August 14th, 1649, the House of Commons ordered that the printer of this pamphlet should be sent for, and, if necessary, committed.[1] A copy is preserved in the British Museum Library. It is in quarto, and contains 16 pages.

185.

The Moderate: Impartially communicating Martial Affaires to the Kingdom of England. From Tuesday August 7. to Tuesday August 14. 1649. Number 57.

On August 14th, 1649, the House of Commons ordered that the author of this pamphlet, and the licenser of it should be sent for, and, if necessary, committed.[2] A copy is preserved in the British Museum Library. It is in quarto, and contains 12 pages.

186.

Anarchia Anglicana: or the History of Independency. The second part. By Theodorus Verax. 1649.

On October 24th, 1649, the House of Commons ordered the Council of State to use all diligent endeavour to find out the authors, printers, and publishers of this book, and to examine the whole business, and report the same to the House.[3] The author was Clement Walker, who was born at Cliffe in Dorsetshire; he became M.P. for Wells in 1640, and was a zealous Covenanter. He was imprisoned in the Tower for writing the Anarchia, and died there in 1651. "This work," says Bishop Warburton, "gives an admirable idea of the character of the times, parties, "and persons."

1. Commons' Journals, Vol. 6, p. 278,
2. Ibid.
3. Ibid, p. 312.

187.

A Fiery Flying Roll: or Word from the Lord to all the Great Ones of the Earth, whom this may concerne. Being the last Warning Piece at the dreadfull day of *Judgement.* Imprinted at *London,* in the beginning of that notable day, wherein the secrets of all hearts are laid open; and wherein the worst and foulest of villanies, are discovered, under the best and fairest outsides. 1649.

On February 1st, 16$\frac{49}{50}$, the House of Commons resolved that this book contained "many horrid blasphemies and damnable "and detestable opinions, to be abhorred by all good and godly "people;" and that all the printed copies thereof should be burnt by the Hangman at the New Palace Yard, Westminster, the Exchange in Cheapside, and the Market Place in Southwark. On the 27th September following, it was also ordered that Abiezer Copp, the reputed author of this book, should be examined, and that the author and publisher thereof should be discovered.[1] A copy is preserved in the British Museum Library. It is in quarto, and contains 15 pages.

188.

The doctrine of the Fourth Commandment deformed by Popery, reformed and restored to its primitive purity. By James Okeford. 1649.

On March 1st, 16$\frac{49}{59}$, a letter from the Mayor of Sarum, dated February 27th, enclosing one of these books, was read before the House of Commons, and it was referred to the Committee of plundered ministers to peruse the same, and report to the House thereon. On March 8th, the House resolved that this book "ascertaining the observation of the Jewish Sabbath, and con-"demning the observation of the Lord's Day as the Christian "Sabbath," was "erroneous, scandalous, and profane, contrary "to the practice of the apostles and of all the Christian "Churches;" and all the printed copies of the same were to be burnt, and the author was to be apprehended and imprisoned.[2]

1. Commons' Journals, Vol. 6, pp. 354, 475.
2. Ibid, pp. 374, 378.

189.

An Act of the Commons assembled in Parliament for erecting an High Court of Justice for trying and judging of Charles Stuart King of England. 1649.

This "traiterous cursed writing in parchment" was read by the House of Commons on May 27th, 1661, and ordered to be burnt on the following day in Westminster Hall by the Common Hangman.[1]

190.

An Act for subscribing the engagement. 1649.

This "treasonable parchment in writing" was read by the House of Commons on May 27th, 1661, and was ordered to be burnt on the following day at the Old Exchange, London, by the Common Hangman, at full Exchange time, between the hours of twelve and one o'clock.[2] A printed copy is preserved in the British Museum Library. It is in folio.

191.

The Obstructours of Justice. Or a Defence of the Honourable Sentence passed upon the late King, by the High Court of Justice. Opposed chiefly to the serious and faithfull Representation and Vindication of some of the Ministers of London. As also to the Humble Addresse of Dr. Hamond to His Excellencie and Councel of Warre. Wherein the Justice and Equitie of the said Sentence is demonstratively asserted, as well upon clear texts of Scripture, as principles of Reason, grounds of Law, Authorities, Presidents, as well Forreign as Domestique. Together with a brief Reply to Mr. John Geree's Book, intituled *Might overcoming Right :* wherein the Act of the Armie in garbling the Parliament, is further cleared. As

1. Commons' Journals, Vol. 8, p. 259.
2. Ibid.

also, some further Reckonings between the said Dr.
Hamond, and the Authour, made straight. By John
Goodwin. London. 1649.

After the Restoration of King Charles the Second, this book
was called in by proclamation, and burnt by the Common
Hangman. John Goodwin, the author, was chaplain to Oliver
Cromwell, and a Nonconformist, but of a different stamp to the
generality of them. He had a clear head, a fluent tongue, a
penetrating spirit, and a marvellous faculty in descanting on
scripture, and must be owned to have been a very considerable
man.[1] A copy is preserved in the British Museum Library. It
is in quarto, and contains 146 pages, and a postcript of one page.

192.

The Royal Charter granted unto Kings by God
himself: and collected out of his Holy Word in both
Testaments. By T. B., Dr. in Divinitie. London.
1649.

Thomas Bayly was the author of this work, and for writing
the same he was committed to Newgate. A copy is preserved in
the British Museum Library. It is in octavo, and contains 144
pages.

193.

An Act declaring and constituting the people of
England to be a Commonwealth and Free State. 1649.

This "traiterous writing in parchment" was read by the
House of Commons on May 27th, 1661, and ordered to be burnt
on the following day by the Common Hangman at the Old
Exchange in London, at full Exchange time, between the hours
of twelve and one o'clock.[2] The burning of this and other Acts
was witnessed by Samuel Pepys, as appears from the following
passage in his Diary: "1661. 28th May. With Mr. Shipley
"to the Exchange, and there saw the hangman burn, by vote of

---

1. Timperley's Encyclopœdia of Literary and Typographical Anecdote,
(second edition) p. 547.
2. Commons' Journals, Vol. 8, p. 259.

"Parliament, two old Acts; the one for constituting us a
"Commonwealth, and the other I have forgot; which still do
"make me think of the greatness of this late turne, and what
"people will do to-morrow, against what they all, through profit
"or fear, did promise and practise this day.[1] A printed copy is
preserved in the British Museum Library. It is in folio.

194.

'ΕΙΚΟΝΟΚΛΑΣΤΗΣ, in answer to a Book entitled
'ΕΙΚΩΝ ΒΑΣΙΛΙΚΗ, the Portraiture of his Sacred
Majesty in his solitudes and sufferings. By John
Milton. 1649.

Defensio pro populo Anglicano contra Claudii Salma-
sii Defensionem Regiam. 1650. By the same.

On June 16th, 1660, the House of Commons ordered that these
books should be burnt by the Common Hangman; and a proclamation was issued for calling in and suppressing them.

195.

The Clergy in their colours or a brief character of
them. Written from a hearty desire of their Reformation, and great zeal to my Countrymen, that they may
no longer be deceived by such as call themselves the
Ministers of the Gospel, but are not. By John Fry, a
Member of the Parliament of England. London.
1650.

An octavo pamphlet of 68 pages, of which there is a copy in
the British Museum Library.

The Accuser sham'd; or a Pair of Bellows to blow
off that dust cast upon John Fry a Member of Parliament by Col. John Downs, likewise a Member of
Parliament, who by the confederacy and instigation of
some, charged the said John Fry of Blasphemy and

1. Pepys' Diary, Vol. 1, p. 236, (third edition).

Error to the Honorable House of Commons. Whereunto is annexed a word to the Priests, Lawyers,
Royalists, Self-Seekers, and Rigid Presbyterians. Also
a brief Ventilation of that chaffie and absurd opinion,
of *Three Persons or Subsistences in the Godhead.* By
the accused John Fry. London. Febr. 1648.

A quarto pamphlet of 23 pages, of which there is a copy in the
British Museum Library.

On January 31st, 16$\frac{50}{51}$, the House of Commons referred these
books to the Committee of plundered ministers, to state the
exceptions against them and to report the same to the House;
and also ordered that their author, Mr. John Fry, a member of
Parliament, should attend the House. On February 20th following, the Committee made their report to the House, in which are
contained particulars of the various blasphemous and irreligious
opinions contained in these books, and two days afterwards the
House of Commons ordered that both the books should be burnt
by the Common Hangman.[1]

196.

A single eye all *Light* no Darkness; or *Light* and
Darkness One: In which you have it purely discussed,
1. The Original of Darkness. 2. What Darkness is.
3. Why it is called Darkness. As also what *God* is
Within, and what *Without;* how he is said to be *One,*
yet *Two;* when *Two* and not *One,* yet then *One,* and
not Two. Likewise a word from the Lord touching
the onely Resurrection of the Body, in, from, and to
the Lord. With a certain parcel of Quæries to be
answered from Heaven or Hell. This Revealed in
L. C., one of the Universality. Imprinted at London,
in the yeer that the Powers of Heaven and Earth was,
is, and shall be shaken, yea damned, till they be no
more for ever.

1.   Commons' Journals, Vol. 6, pp. 529, 536, 539.

On June 21st, 1650, the House of Commons ordered that search should be made for the author, printer, and publisher of this pamphlet, and on the 27th September following; the confession of Laurence Clarkson "touching the making and "publishing of this impious and blasphemous book" was reported to the House; and it was resolved that Clarkson should be forthwith sent to the House of Correction for one month, and 'from that time "to be banished out of the Commonwealth and "the territories thereof, and not to return upon pain of death." The book itself was to be burnt by the Common Hangman in the New Palace at Westminster, and upon the Exchange.[1] A copy is preserved in the British Museum Library. It is in quarto, and contains 16 pages.

197.

A petition of Josiah Prymat.   1651.

A folio broadside, of which the following is a copy:—

"   To the Supream Authority of this Nation, the Parliament of "the Commonwealth of England.

"   The humble petition and appeal of Josiah Prymat of London, "Leatherseller, sheweth,

"That your Petitioner, by his under-tenants, George Lilburn "Esquire, and George Gray the younger, Gentleman, both of the "County of Durham, being in the years 1647, 1648, and 1649, "in a just and quiet possession of the Collieries, or Seams of Cole, "in Harraton, in the County aforesaid, called the Five-quarter "and Nine-quarter Cole, (and having spent near £2000 to win "the same), which lay drowned and lost, from 1642 to 1647; Sir "Arthur Haslerig, in September, 1649, procuring Colonel Francis "Wren, one of the Committee of that County, and Colonel George "Fenwick, to joyn with him, made an Order, (against which the "rest of the said Committee present protested) to sequester the "said Collieries, under colour of an untrue suggestion that Sir "Wm. Armyn had sequestred the same in 1644, as belonging to "one Thomas Wray, a Papist Delinquent: and thereupon the "said Sir Arthur violently dispossessed your Petitioner's tenants, "and seized their goods; and lett the said Collieries to Colonel "Francis Hacker, and several of the Officers of his own "Regiment."

1.   Commons' Journals, Vol. 6, pp. 427, 444, 474, 475.

"That your Petitioner hath petitioned to the Commissioners
"for compounding for relief; but, by the power and influence of
"the said Sir Arthur, upon most of the said Commissioners, your
"Petitioner hath been delayed, and denied the ordinary course
"of proceedings in all Courts of Justice: and at last, coming to
"hearing, the said Sir Arthur appeared every Day of the hearing;
"and took upon him, not only to plead against your Petitioner
"(which is humbly conceived to be contrary to Law, he being a
"Member of the Supream Authority) but also Authoritatively to
"prejudge your Petitioner's case, and to direct the said Commis-
"sioners what to judge therein; and by his power and influence
"upon the said Commissioners, he over-awed most of them, and
"after full hearing, judgment being respited from day to day,
"the said Sir Arthur kept private correspondence with some of
"the said Commissioners, about finding some new colour or
"pretences to detain your petitioner's possession from him,
"whereupon he produced new pretended evidence after full
"hearing; and thereupon the major part of the said Commiss-
"ioners, not daring (as is humbly conceived) to oppose the will
"and pleasure of the said Sir Arthur, have contrary to clear
"evidence before them for your petitioner, refused to relieve him;
"and have punctually pursued in their Judgment, the directions
"publickly given by the said Sir Arthur."

"   That the said Commissioners being the onely persons author-
"ized by the Parliament to hear and determine all cases about
"sequestred estates, your Petitioner cannot be relieved from the
"oppression and tyranny of the said Sir Arthur, save by the
"Parliament or their special Order and Directions: And your
"Petitioner hath been kept from his Possession above two years,
"and the said Sir Arthur hath declared the said Collieries to be
"worth, at least, £5000 per annum.

"   May it therefore please the Parliament, in respect
"to the Public Justice of the Commonwealth, to cause
"the truth of the Premises to be speedily examined,
"and to provide for your Petitioner's relief from the
"oppression and Tyranny of the said Sir Arthur Hasle-
"rigg, and for the dispensation of Justice, without fear
"or favour; as to your Wisdoms shall seem most just.
"And your Petitioner shall pray, &c.

"Joseph Primatt."

On January 15th, 16$\frac{51}{52}$, the Parliament approved and affirmed the judgment and resolutions of the Commissioners for compounding in the case of Josiah Prymate, and after having proceeded with the matter of crime charged in the petition, it was resolved that this petition was false, malicious, and scandalous, and that the printing, publishing, and dispersing of the same was a high breach of privilege of Parliament; and also that all the printed copies should be burned by the Common Hangman at the Old Exchange, London, and in the New Palace, Westminster, on Tuesday and Wednesday next, also that Prymate should be fined £3000, to be paid to the use of the Commonwealth; also £2000 more, to be paid to Sir Arthur Haslerig; also £2000 more to be paid to James Russells, Edward Winslow, William Molins, and Arthur Squibb, Esquires, four of the Commissioners for compounding. It was then ordered that Prymat should be committed to the Fleet till the aforesaid sums were paid. The House then proceeded against Lieutenant Colonel John Lilburne, who confessed that he had dispersed several of the printed copies of this petition, and similar fines were imposed upon him, as well as perpetual banishment from the Kingdoms of England, Scotland, and Ireland.[1]

A copy is preserved in the British Museum Library.

198.

A just reproof to Haberdasher's-Hall: or, An Epistle writ by Lieut. Colonel John Lilburn, July 30. 1651. to four of the Commissioners at Haberdasher's Hall, viz. Mr. James Russel, M. Edward Winsloe, M. William Mollins, and M. Arthur Squib, wherein is set forth their unjust and unrighteous dealing in severall cases; with the relations of the said John Lilburn, and their captiving their understandings to the Tyrannical will of Sir Arthur Haslerigge, who hath most unjustly endeavoured a long time together, the extirpation of the Family of the said John Lilburn.

1. Commons' Journals, Vol. 7, pp. 71, 72, 73.

On January 16th, 16$\frac{51}{52}$, the House of Commons resolved that this book contained matters "false, scandalous, and malicious," and all the printed copies of the same were ordered to be burnt by the Common Hangman.[1] A copy is preserved in the British Museum Library. It is in quarto, and contains 40 pages.

199.

The Racovian Catechisme; wherein you have the substance of the Confession of those Churches, which in the Kingdom of Poland, and Great Dukedome of Lithuania, and other Provinces appertaining to that Kingdom, do affirm, That no other save the Father of our Lord Jesus Christ, is that one God of Israel, and that the man Jesus of Nazareth, who was born of the Virgin, and no other besides, or before him, is the onely begotten Sonne of God.   Printed at Amsterledam for Brooer Janz, 1652.

On February 10th, 16$\frac{51}{52}$, this book was referred by the House of Commons to a Committee, who on the 2nd April reported to the House a collection of the principal blasphemous errors in the book, which are set out in the Journals.   These errors consist of a denial of our Saviour's divinity, together with "many other "gross errors concerning predestination, the fall of man, Christ "adding to the Commandments, Free-will, the Priesthood and "Sacrifice of Christ, Faith, Justification, Baptism, and the Lord's "Supper."   It was thereupon resolved that the book contained matters "blasphemous, erroneous, and scandalous," and that all the copies should be burnt at the Old Exchange, London, and in the New Palace at Westminster.

On June 22nd, 1652, the House of Commons also referred to the Committee of plundered ministers to examine and find out the authors, printers, and publishers of this Catechism.[2] A copy is preserved in the British Museum Library.   It is in octavo, and contains 176 pages.

1.   Commons' Journals, Vol. 7, p. 73.
2.   Ibid, pp. 86, 113, 144.

200.

The three grand impostors. N.d.

On June 22nd, 1652, the House of Commons referred to the Committee of plundered ministers to find out the authors, printers, and publishers of this book.[1] As far as the editor's opportunities have extended, no clue can be found to the full title or author of this book.

201.

An answer to the Declaration of the Imaginary Parliament of the unknowne Commonwealth of England, concerning the Affaires past betwixt them of England, and the High and Mighty Lords the States Generall of the United Provinces: wherein their Frivolous Reasons are cleerly refuted; and their unjust proceedings in the Treaty of the aforesaid Affaires, as in all their Actions, manifestly discovered. At Rotterdam, by John Pieterson. 1652.

On October 26th, 1652, the House of Commons referred to the Council of State to examine and find out the authors, printers, and publishers of this pamphlet, and to peruse and consider thereof, and report the same to the Parliament.[2] A copy is preserved in the British Museum Library. It is in quarto, and contains 16 pages.

202.

Merlini Anglici Ephemeris; or Astrologicall Predictions for the year 1653. By William Lilly, Student in Astrology. London. 1653.

On October 26th, 1652, the House of Commons referred this book to the consideration of the Committee for plundered ministers; with power to send for the author and secure him.[3] A copy is preserved in the British Museum Library. It is in octavo.

1. Commons' Journals, Vol. 7, p. 144.
2. Ibid, p. 195.
3. Ibid.

203.

Mercurius Britannicus. 1652.

The Faithful Scout. 1652.

On December 28th, 1652, the House of Commons referred to the Council of State to take care to suppress these pamphlets, or any other books that go out to the dishonour of the Parliament and prejudice of the Commonwealth; and to examine the authors, printers, and publishers of the Mercurius Britannicus and the Scout or any other books of that nature, with power to imprison the offenders.[1] These were weekly periodicals, of which there are several preserved among the King's pamphlets in the British Museum Library.

204.

Colonel Shapcott (Knight of Devonshire). His Speech in Parliament the 30 of October, 1654. With the case of the secluded members. 1654.

On November 7th, 1654, it was resolved by Parliament that this printed pamphlet was "treasonable, false, scandalous, and seditious," and it was referred to the Committee for printing to enquire after the author, printers, and publishers of the same, and to suppress the same; and the Serjeant at Arms was to seize all the printed copies of this pamphlet, and all persons selling or publishing the same.[2] A copy of this pamphlet is preserved in the British Museum Library. It is in quarto, and contains six pages.

205.

The apostolical and true opinion concerning the Holy Trinity revived and asserted; partly by twelve arguments levyed against the traditional and false opinion about the Godhead of the Holy Spirit: partly by a Confession of faith touching the three persons. Both which having been formerly set forth in those

1. Commons' Journals, Vol. 7, p. 236.
2. Ibid, p. 383.

yeers which the respective titles bear, are now so altered, so augmented, what with explications of the Scripture, what with reasons, what finally with testimonies of the Fathers, and of others, together with observations thereupon, that they may justly seem new. 1653.

The original work was published in 1647, and was condemned to be burnt; it is described in a previous part of this work, (see ante p. 144). This 1653 edition is a reissue. On December 12th, 1654, the House of Commons resolved that this book contained "impious and blasphemous opinions against the Deity of the "Holy Ghost," and all the printed copies were to be burnt by the Common Hangman. On January 15th, 16$\frac{54}{55}$, the House of Commons further resolved that this book "is full of horrid, "blasphemous, and execrable opinions; denying the Deity of "Christ, and of the Holy Ghost; and particularly asserting

" 1. That God the Father only, separate from the Son and "Holy Ghost, is the First Cause of all things that pertain to "salvation, *Art.* 1, *p.* 1.

" 2. That God the Holy Ghost is a created Spirit, *p.* 3. and "*p.* 2, not God: That Christ is a made Lord; and neither the "Son, nor the Holy Spirit, the most High God, *p.* 4.

" 3. That Christ is the Second Cause of all Things pertaining "to our Salvation, *Art.* 2. And that the Son is not equal with "the Father, 16.

" 4. That Christ hath no other than a human nature, *Art.* 3, "*p.* 19.

" 5. That Christ is not the most High God, the same with the "Father, but subordinate to him," *Art.* 4, *p.* 29.

" 6. That the Holy Ghost is the only principal Minister of "God and of Christ, singled out of the number of other "Heavenly Ministers, or Angels, *Art.* 6, 44.

" That Christ is not the supreme and independent Monarch "*Jehovah, p.* 44.[1]

A copy of this book exists in the British Museum Library.

---

1. Commons' Journals, Vol. 7, pp. 400, 416.

206.

A Twofold Catechism: the one simply called A Scripture Catechism; The other, A brief Scripture Catechism for Children. Wherein the chiefest points of the Christian Religion being Question wise proposed, resolve themselves by pertinent Answers taken word for word out of the Scripture, without either consequences or Comments. Composed for their sakes that would fain be Meer Christians, and not of this or that Sect, inasmuch as all the Sects of Christians, by what names soever distinguished, have either more or less departed from the simplicity and truth of the Scripture. By John Biddle, Master of Arts of the University of Oxford. London. 1654.

A brief Scripture Catechisme for children. Wherein, notwithstanding the brevity thereof all things necessary unto life and Godliness are contained. By the same. London. 1654.

These were originally printed as one book; but the brief Scripture Catechism was printed again by itself in a small octavo the same year. The British Museum Library contains copies in the twofold form, from which the preceding titles are taken.

On December 12th, 1654, the House of Commons resolved that a Committee be appointed to consider of this book, with power to send for the author, and to restrain him, and to suppress his school. The next day Biddle was brought to the bar of the House, and on examination acknowledged the authorship, but denied that he kept a school, and also that he had a congregation. Being asked who printed the book, he said "Hitherto he hath "answered as a Christian, to give an account of the hope that is "in him: What the law of Christ doth warrant him to answer, "he will do: but beyond that he will not: the Law of Christ "enjoins him not to betray his brethren. Being asked, Whether "the Law of Christ did enjoin him to believe the Holy Ghost "is not God; saith, the Law of Christ doth no-where tell him, "the Holy Ghost is God." And being demanded by Mr. Speaker

"Whether the Holy Ghost be God? Saith, He hath examined "the Scriptures; and doth nowhere find, in the Old or New "Testament, that the Holy Spirit is God: He doth own the "Books, and his opinion is sufficiently declared in them.

" Being demanded whether Jesus Christ be God from Ever-"lasting to Everlasting; answered, He doth own the Books, and "therein hath declared his judgment; But saith, He doth not "find, in Scripture, where Jesus Christ is called the Most High "God, or God from Everlasting to Everlasting.

" Being asked, Whether God be confined to a certain Place; "saith, this is not to the Hope that is in a Christian: Therefore "there is no necessity lying on him to answer.

" Being asked, Whether God have a bodily Shape; saith, He "hath answered sufficiently to that already."

It was thereupon ordered that Biddle should be committed prisoner to the Gatehouse in Westminster. On January 15th, 165$\frac{4}{5}$, the House of Commons resolved that the whole drift and scope of this book was "to teach and to hold forth many "blasphemous and heretical opinions," and that in the preface the author thereof did "maintain and assert many blasphemous "and heretical opinions, and doth therein cast a reproach upon "all the catechisms now extant;" also "that report be made to "the House of the manner of the author's venting his said errors, "together with several particular errors and blasphemies in the "said book contained; that the manner is by proposing a "blasphemous and dangerous opinion, by way of question, and "by mis-applying of Scripture, by way of answer to the same."

"The several particulars are as followeth:"

" 1. That the Infinite God is confined to a certain Place. " Cat. p. 5. 6.

" 2. That God hath a bodily shape; that God hath a Right "Hand, and Left, in a proper Sense, 2. Cat. p. 6.

" 3. That there are Passions in God. 1. Cat. 11.

" 4. He denies the Omniscience and Immutability of God, "1. Cat. from the 14 to the *.

" 5. He denies that all the Three Persons are to be loved "with our whole Heart, 1. Cat. 21.

" 6. He denies that Jesus Christ hath the nature of God "dwelling in him, p. 27, 28, 29, ad 35, and p. 40 to the 60.

"That Christ hath only a divine Lordship, without a Divine "Nature.

" 7. He denies the Godhead of the Holy Ghost, 1. *Cat. p.* 21. "2. *Cat. p.* 16.

" 8. He denies that Christ was a Priest, whilst he was on "Earth, *p.* 64; or died to reconcile God to us, *p.* 68; or that "God doth justify any because of the full Price that Christ paid "to him in their stead, *p.* 83.

" 9. He affirms Justification by Works, *p.* 96.

" 10. He denies the Righteousness of Christ is imputed to "Believers, *p.* 82.

" 11. He affirms that Works give Vigour to Faith, and so "makes it able to justify, 2. *Cat.* 26; and affirms that Works "give Right to Eternal Life, 1. *Cat. p.* 86, 87; 94, 95; 98.

" He affirms that true Saints may turn Apostates finally, "1. *Cat. p.* 99.

" He denies that the Wicked do continue to live in Hell, under "the sense of everlasting Torment; but saith, That they are "destroyed, and cease to be, 1. *Cat. p.* 134, 135, 136, &c."

It was then resolved that this book should be burnt by the Common Hangman.

207.

Dissertatio de Pace, &c. or a Discourse touching the peace and concord of the church. Wherein is elegantly and acutely argued, that not so much a bad opinion, as a bad life, excludes a Christian out of the Kingdom of Heaven; and that the things necessary to be known for the attainment of salvation, are very few and easie; and finally, that those, who pass amongst us under the name of Hereticks, are notwithstanding, to be tolerated. London. 1653.

On Decmber 21st, 1654, the House of Commons referred this book to a Committee, to examine the substance thereof, and who were the authors, printers, and publishers, and also that all the copies should be seized.[1] A copy is preserved in the British Museum Library.

1. Commons' Journals, Vol. 7, p. 405.

208.

Thunder from the Throne of God against the Temples of Idols. 1652.

A quarto pamphlet of 36 pages, of which there is a copy in the British Museum Library. This and the book described in the next article were written by one Samuel Chidley, who for so doing was summoned to the bar of the House of Commons on October 20th, 1656, and committed to the custody of the Serjeant at Arms; and the book was referred to a Committee.[1]

209.

An Epistle directed to the Parliament of the Commonwealth of England.

A quarto pamphlet of 4 pages, but without title. A copy is preserved in the British Museum Library. For its condemnation see preceding article.

210.

A healing question propounded and resolved upon occasion of the late publique and seasonable call to humiliation, in order to love and union amongst the honest party, and with a desire to apply Balsome to the wound before it become incurable. London. 1656.

For writing this book, Sir Henry Vane was summoned before the Council at Whitehall, and having attended there on Thursday, August 21st, 1656, it was ordered that if he should not give good security in £5000 bond by Thursday next, to do nothing to the prejudice of the present government and the peace of the Commonwealth, he should stand committed. This security he refused to give, and on the 4th September, he was ordered to be apprehended and taken in safe custody to the Isle of Wight, there to be delivered to the Governor of the Island, to be disposed of according to the order of the Council.[2] A copy of this book is preserved in the British Museum Library. It is in quarto, and contains 24 pages, and a postcript, but no title.

1. Commons' Journals, Vol. 7, p. 442.
2. Howell's State Trials, Vol. 5, p. 791.

211.

An Act for renouncing and disannulling the pretended title of Charles Stuart, etc.   1656.

On May 27th, 1661, this "treasonable parchment writing" was ordered by the House of Commons to be burnt in Westminster Hall on the following Wednesday by the Common Hangman.[1]   It is printed in Scobell, p. 371.

212.

Choice Drollery, with songs and sonnets.   Printed by J. G. for Robert Pollard.   1666.

This book "giving great offence to the saints of that time, "who esteem'd it a lewd and scandalous thing, it was order'd by "the Protector's Council to be burnt on the 8th May the same "year."   *Ant.* à *Wood.*

213.

An Act for the security of his Highness the Lord Protector his person and continuance of the nation in peace and safety.   1656.

On May 27th, 1661, this "treasonable parchment writing" was ordered by the House of Commons to be burnt in Westminster Hall on the following Wednesday by the Common Hangman.[2]   It is printed in Scobell, p. 372.

214.

A Holy Commonwealth, or political aphorisms opening the true principles of government: for the healing of the mistakes and resolving the doubts that most endanger and trouble England at this time: if yet there may be hope.   And directing the desires of sober Christians that long to see the kingdoms of this world become the kingdoms of the Lord, and of his Christ. Written by Richard Baxter at the invitation of James Harrington esquire.   London.   1659.

1.   Commons' Journals, Vol. 8, p. 259.
2.   Ibid.

This book was burnt by the University of Oxford in the year 1688.[1]

215.

The Lord's Loud Call to England: being a true Relation of some late, various, and wonderful judgments, or Handy-works of God, by Earthquake, Lightening, Whirlwind, great multitudes of Toads and Flyes; and also the striking of divers persons with sudden death, in several places; for what causes let the man of wisdome judge, upon his serious perusal of the Book itself. Also of the strange changes, and late alterations made in these three Nations. As also of the odious Sin of Drinking Healths. With a Brief of Mr. Pryn's solid arguments against it, and his Epistle to the late King Charles to redress it. Published by H. J. a Servant of Jesus the Christ, and Lover of Peace and Holiness. London, Printed for L. Chapman in Popeshead Alley, and for Fr. Smith, at the Elephant and Castle neer Temple-Bar. 1660.

This book was the subject of proceedings against Francis Smith. He was imprisoned three times, according to his own account, for its publication.[2] It was written by Mr. H. Jessey, as appears from a pamphlet written in answer by one John Gadbury.

A copy is preserved in the British Museum Library. It is in quarto, and contains 44 pages.

216.

The Speeches and Prayers of some of the late King's Judges, viz. Major General Harison, Octob. 13. Mr. John Carew, Octob. 15. Mr. Justice Cooke,

1. D'Israeli's Amenities of Literature, Vol. 3, p. 325.
2. Howell's State Trials, vol. 7, p. 946. See also a Tract published by Smith, entitled "An account of the injurious proceedings of Sir George Jeffreys, Knight, late Recorder of London, against Francis Smith, Bookseller."

Mr. Hugh Peters, Octob. 16. Mr. Tho. Scott, Mr. Gregory Clement, Col. Adrian Scroop, Col. John Jones, Octob. 17. Col. Daniel Axtell, and Col. Fran. Hacker, Octob. 19, 1660, The times of their Death. Together with severall occasionall speeches and passages in their imprisonment till they came to the place of execution. Faithfully and impartially collected for further satisfaction. Printed Anno Dom. 1660.

Simon Dover and Thomas Brewster were tried at the Old Bailey on Feb. 22, 16$\frac{63}{64}$, for printing and publishing this book, and were found guilty. They were fined, ordered to stand upon the pillory, and then imprisoned. The proceedings will be found in Howell's State Trials, vol. 6, p. 518. A copy is in the Editor's possession. It is in quarto, and contains 96 pages.

217.

Mercurius Veridicus.   1660.

On June 25, 1660, on the House of Commons being informed of this printed paper, wherein this clause is printed, viz. "It "was moved by Major Beake, that Sir Richard Temple might be "one of the twenty excepted persons; and he gave several reasons "for it; among others that Sir Richard had been a menial "servant to Cromwell, and a great promoter of his Interest; but "the House at length waived the further debate of it;" it was ordered that a Committee be appointed to examine this particular case; and in order thereunto they were to send for Maxwell the printer; and they were to consider of the great liberty taken by divers persons, in printing, without warrant, several votes and proceedings of this House; and to prepare an order for restraining all persons whatsoever from printing any of the votes or proceedings of the House without special order. And they were to send for Mr. William Saunderson, and to examine him, by what warrant he printed, in his History, a speech in the name of Sir Harbottle Grimston, Baronet, Speaker of the House, and several other speeches, as the speeches of Members of Parliament, and other passages reflecting on Members of Parliament; and they were to take into consideration any other books or pamphlets, reflecting on any Member of the House, or other persons; and to report to the House what was fit to be done in the several cases.[1]

A copy of Mercurius Veridicus, No. 1, from Tuesday the 5th of June, to Tuesday the 12th, 1660, is in the British Museum Library, but it is not the number of which the House of Commons complained. There are no others, as far as the Editor can ascertain.

218.

The long Parliament revived; or an Act for continuation and the 'not dissolving the long Parliament called by King Charles the First in the year 1640 but by an Act of Parliament, with undeniable reasons deduced from the said Act to prove that that Parliament is not yet dissolved. Also Mr. William Prynne's five arguments fully answered, whereby he endeavours to prove it to be dissolved by the King's death, &c. By Thomas Phillips, Gentleman, a sincere Lover of the King and Country. 1660.

This pamphlet was written by William Drake under the assumed name of Thomas Phillips, and for the writing, printing, and publishing the same he was impeached by the House of Commons, and on the impeachment being carried up to the Lords on the 4th December, 1660, they ordered that Drake should be apprehended as a delinquent, and brought before them the next morning to answer to his charge; which being done, and he confessing his fault, the Lords, in consideration of the shortness of time for proceeding further in this business, left him to be prosecuted in the King's Bench by the Attorney General. No further proceedings however can be met with.

The following is a copy of the impeachment:—[2]

1. Commons' Journals, Vol. 8, p. 74.
2. Commons' Journals, Vol. 8, pp. 183, 186, 192, 194, 198. Howell's State Trials, Vol. 5, p. 1363.

"The Knights, Citizens, and Burgesses, the House of Commons,
" in the Name of themselves, and all the Commons of England,
" do hereby declare, complain, and shew, against William Drake
" Citizen and Merchant of London,

" That whereas, this present Parliament, through the Blessing
" of God upon their Endeavours, and the incomparable Grace
" and Goodness of his Majesty's Royal Condescensions, have
" proved the happy Instruments of repairing the Breaches of this
" Kingdom; restoring the ancient Foundations; and passing
" many good and wholsome Laws, for the Safety and Quiet of
" the People; and are daily preparing such others, as may yet
" seem to be wanting:

" Nevertheless the said William Drake, in contempt of his
" Majesty's Crown and Dignity, and of the Laws and Govern-
" ment of this kingdom; and out of a wicked and malicious
" intention, to scandalise and subvert the authority and being of
" this present Parliament, and to raise and stir up sedition and
" division in this Kingdom; and against the Peace of our
" Sovereign Lord the King; hath lately, that is to say, upon or
" before the eighteenth day of the month of November last, at
" Westminster in the County of Middlesex, written, printed, and
" published, in the name of one Thomas Phillips Gent. a certain,
" false, wicked, malicious and seditious Pamphlet intituled, *The*
" *Long Parliament revived &c.;* in which said scandalous and
" seditious pamphlet, the said William Drake, amongst many
" other wicked expressions, clauses, and assertions therein con-
" tained, doth falsely, maliciously, and seditiously, affirm and
" declare,

" Page 6. First, That all other Parliaments have no legal
" Capacity, till this (meaning the Long Parliament, called in the
" year 1640) be legally dissolved.

" Page 14. Secondly, The Act (meaning the Act of Parlia-
" ment to which the Title of the Pamphlet refers) is herein
" express, That by no other Way or means, but by an Act of
" Parliament, it shall be dissolved: Which, being it cannot be
" done by the dead King, but may be done by the Successor, it
" ought to be so dissolved; or else it must and doth, by virtue
" of this Act, still remain legally in full Being and Authority.

" Page 17. Thirdly, How much it were to be wished, that the
" Legislative Authority might revert into that Channel, meaning

." the Long Parliament aforesaid ; by which the Peace and Settle-
"ment of the Nation, through his Majesty's most gracious
" Influence, might durably, and without Question, be provided
" for and preserved.

"Page 21. Fourthly, If That be a lawful Parliament,
" (speaking of the long Parliament aforesaid, which he else-
" where affirmed to be in being) then this can be none, nor no
" other, till this be legally dissolved.

" All which practices for stirring up of sedition, the Commons
" are ready to prove, not only by the general Scope of the said
" Book, but likewise by several Clauses therein contained, besides
" these before mentioned, and such other Proofs as the Cause,
" according to the course of Parliament, shall require ;

" And do pray, that the said William Drake may be put to
" answer all and every of the Premises ; and that such Proceed-
"ing, Examination, Trial, Judgment, and exemplary Punish-
" ment, may be thereupon had and executed, as is agreeable to
" Law and Justice.

A copy of this book is in the British Museum Library.

219.

Mirabilis Annus, or the year of Prodigies and Won-
ders, being a faithful and impartial collection of several
signs that have been seen in the Heavens, in the Earth,
and in the Waters; together with many remarkable
accidents and judgments befalling divers persons,
according as they have been testified by very credible
hands; all which have happened within the space of
one year last past, and are now made publick for a
seasonable warning to the people of these three kingdoms speedily to repent and turn to the Lord, whose
hand is lifted up amongst us. 1661.

Francis Smith, in his account of the injurious proceedings of
Sir George Jeffreys before referred to, gives the following piteous
account of the way he was treated for the publication of this
book :—

"In August, 1661, a certain book was printed and published, "entitled, "Mirabilis Annus," or the year of Prodigies. Then "did a person of quality yet living, give me great encouragement "for its publication as a book grateful to the authority, and of "general caution to the nation, both to behold and consider the "works of God, and also to tremble for fear of his judgments; but "it so happened contrary to my expectation, that the very day it "was published, one of his Majesty's messengers came to my "shop, with a warrant both to seize the book and my person, "and carried me before the then Secretary of State, where after "examination, I was committed to the Gatehouse Prison by this "warrant inserted."

"It is his Majesty's pleasure that you take into your custody the "person of Francis Smith, Stationer, for having a hand in print-"ing and compiling dangerous books, and that you keep him "close prisoner till further order from his majesty, and for so "doing this shall be your warrant. Dated at the court at "Whitehall this 15th day of August, 1661.

Edw. Nicholas.

"To the Keeper of the Gatehouse,
"Westminster, or his deputy.

"This word in my warrant 'close prisoner' proved a fatal "word to me, as many still living can witness, for the keeper "improved it to a tittle; there I was truly buried alive, it being "a prison famous for oppression of poor prisoners, as many "besides myself can notoriously witness.

"For as soon as I was brought thither, a stern gaoler locked "me up, and said, I must not see, nor have the liberty of any "relations to visit me, without special order from the Secretary "first obtained. This looked like cold entertainment to one "unacquainted with such a condition. But this, and much more "I found as truly performed as promised, being locked up in a "room, where I had neither chair nor stool to rest on, and yet "ten shillings per week must be the price, and before I had been "there three nights £7. 15. 0 was demanded for present fees. "That is to say, five pounds to excuse me from wearing irons, "ten shillings for my entrance week lodging, five shillings sheets, "five shillings garnish money, the rest for turnkey fees; upon "which I gave this answer, that I did not understand any just

"cause for imprisonment, much less to pay such fees, and for
"wearing of irons I would not pay five groats to be excused, if
"he could by law impose irons on me, I would wear them.
"Upon this many cruel endeavours were used, whereby to exact
"consent of these fees from me; and my afflicted wife not suffered
"to speak with me but in the presence of the keeper, after
"chargeable orders, for so much privilege first obtained, nay
"many times orders denied for my friends admittance; in the
"presence of the keeper, and my window casements must be
"nailed up that I should not have the benefit of that common air
"which is every slave's birthright. And when provision was
"sent for my necessary support, yet was that many times kept
"back and frequent fasts imposed upon me, and what was sent
"for my dinner at 12 o'clock, must be given me four or five hours
"after, which I usually breakfasted with, and should be sure to
"want beer or bread, so I was forced to devise a way by a bag
"and a string to be let down in the night at a window, to convey
"some necessary food to me. Things continued thus several
"weeks, in which time for receiving a note at the keyhole by an
"open prisoner, sent from my poor wife then sick and weary with
"grief, and successless travels at my release, I was taken out of
"this room, and locked up in a trap-door room about 20 days,
"where I could hardly be heard with hallooing, it being a place
"for such as were condemned to die; to be usually secured in.
"At this time above thirty pound was spent to attempt my release
"but all ineffectual.

"Then was application made to the judges of the King's
"Bench, Westminster, and I had three chargeable Habeas
"Corpus's before the cruel gaoler would obey to bring me to the
"bar, where upon my appearance, care was taken, that I carried
"in my hand the copy of my commitment, and presented it to
"the Lord Chief Justice Forster, who gave patient hearing to all
"my complaints, disdaining the usage I had met with, and told
"the keeper, if it should happen before my legal release I should
"die by such usage, the keeper should be indicted for his life.
"At this time, to my great amazement, a new copy of commit-
"ment was produced in court, the contents whereof here
"followeth :—

"The prison of the Gatehouse, Westminster.
"I, Edward Broughton, knight, keeper of the prison of our lord

"the King of the Gatehouse, Westminster in the County of
" Middlesex, to the lord the king humbly certifieth, that before
" the coming of the writ to me directed to this schedule annexed,
" to wit, the fifteenth day of August in the year of the reign of
" our said lord the king that now is, the 13th, Francis Smith
" in the said writ named was taken at Westminster in the County
" of Middlesex and there in the prison of our said lord the king
" of the Gatehouse aforesaid, under my custody detained by
" virtue of a certain warrant to me directed. The tenor whereof
" followeth in these words :

"These are to will and require you in his Majesty's name, to
" take into your custody, and safely keep the body of Francis
" Smith of London, Stationer, for that traitorously and seditiously
" he compiled, printed, and published a treasonable and seditious
" book, intitled Several prodigies and apparitions seen in the
" heavens from August 1st 1660, to the latter end of May 1661,
" containing a collection of several former prodigies, mischievous
" events thereupon to princes, and a forgery of divers late false
" and feigned prodigies and impostures of the same kind, prog-
" nosticating thereby the like events to his majesty, and thereby
" did traitorously and seditiously instil into the hearts of his
" majesty's good subjects, a superstitious belief thereof, and a
" dislike and hatred of his majesty's person and government,
" and prepared them to effect a damnable design for the destruc-
" tion of his sacred majesty, and to introduce a change of the
" government established ; and for so doing, this shall be your
" warrant.   Given at our Court at Whitehall the 15th day of
" August 1661.   Edward Nicholas, To the Keeper of the prison
" of the Gatehouse, Westminster, or his Deputy. And this is
" the cause of the taking and detaining of the said Francis Smith
" in the prison of our lord the king, under my custody, whose
" body at the day and place in the said writ contained, I have
" ready as by the said writ is commanded me.

Edward Broughton, knight.

" My counsel pleaded they knew nothing of that copy till now,
" and gave evidence that the copy I produced was taken from the
" clerk of the prison for which he had five shillings, upon which I
" was remanded back again to prison till the next term following;
" and here it may be remembered as an addition to the habit
" of cruelty attending that prison; (the gaoler notwithstanding

" what the Lord Chief Justice Forster had said to him) forced
" me to go down into the dungeon for above 20 days because
" I could not raise him £7 towards chamber rent at that
" instant. Then upon renewed complaints and counsel charge,
" obtained order to be taken out of the dungeon, and put upstairs
" into a chamber where I was again turned out within a week,
" at eight o'clock at night, while my poor wife and two of my
" children were eating, and they at that time of the night in the
" depth of winter, forced to seek their lodging amongst strangers
" in Tothill Street, Westminster, and myself constrained to lie
" upon the bare boards in an open entry, where I continued the
" rest of my time till bailed out, being several weeks, sometimes
" lying on the ground; the rest in a hammock.

" In this time I was sent for to Whitehall, and in the presence
" of a gentleman of quality yet living and several others, was
" offered £100 and present discharge, but to declare my know-
" ledge (upon an imprecation) of the authors or printers of the
" aforesaid book. Yet rather than occasion hurt to any, gave
" myself up to their utmost displeasure; and had recourse to
" many chargeable Habeas Corpus's before I could obtain bail.
" By this imprisonment, I lost my shop and trade for two years,
" to above £300 charge and damage, towards which I can truly
" say to this day, I never had directly or indirectly to the value
" of £20 reparation from any person or persons whatsoever;
" though it hath been often suggested both by persons in author-
" ity and others, that competitors bore me out, which occasioned
" my bonds to be aggravated."[1]

On June 29th, 1661, Thomas Creake, of Little Britain, was
examined before the Secretary of State, when he stated that he
had in printing 2000 copies of this book; he had struck off the
first sheet, and delivered 1000 copies to one George Thresher for
binding.[2]

Among the State Papers of July, 1661, there is preserved the
draft of a warrant from the Secretary of State for the apprehension of one Cole, dwelling at the Sign of the Printing Press, near
the Old Exchange, and for search in his house, shop, &c., for
copies of the "Mirabilis Annus," or any other prohibited books.[3]

1. Howell's State Trials, Vol. 7. p. 946.
2. Domestic State Papers, Charles II, Vol. 38, Nos. 56, 57, 58.
3. Ibid, Vol. 39, No. 132.

On October 4th, 1661, a warrant was issued by the Secretary of State to the Keeper of the Gatehouse, to receive into custody Elizabeth, wife of Giles Calvert, bookseller, for printing and publishing a treasonable and seditious book called "*Several Prodigies and Apparitions seen in the Heavens, from August* 1. 1660 *to the latter end of May*, 1661, "being a forgery of false and " feigned prodigies, prognosticating mischievous events to the " King, and instilling into the hearts of subjects a superstitious " belief thereof, and a dislike and hatred of His Majesty's person " and government, and preparing them to effect a damnable " design for his destruction, and a change of government."[1]

In a communication from Mr. Ashmole to the Secretary of State, dated October 30th, 1661, the authorship of this book is attributed to Mr. George Cockain, a preacher, who had weekly meetings at an alehouse in Ivy Lane.[2]

On December 8th, 1661, Mr. Jessey, a minister, was examined before the Secretary of State in relation to this book, when he stated that he had long been in the habit of collecting notes of remarkable events; one of which described the strange death of Major Orde in the Bishopric of Durham, whch was in the Annus Mirabilis; he visited Mr. Cockain, and had written out prodigies for him, and heard them from him.[3]

On December 19th, 1661, Francis Smith, the printer before referred to, was examined by the Secretary of State, when he denied any knowledge of the book, "never heard of it, contributed " to it, read it, nor delivered it out."[4]

A copy of this book is in the Editor's possession. It is in quarto, and contains 88 pages.

220.

The fastening of St. Peter's Fetters by seven links or propositions, or the efficacy and extent of the solemn league and covenant asserted and vindicated against the doubts and scruples of Dr. John Gauden's anonymous Questionist. St. Peter's bonds not only loosed

1. Domestic State Papers, Charles II, Entry Book 5, p. 39,
2. Ibid, Vol. 43, No. 130.
3. Ibid, Vol. 45, No. 28.
4. Ibid, Nos. 74, 75.

but annihilated by Mr. John Russel, attested by John Gauden, D.D. The league illegal falsely fathered on Dr. Daniel Featley; and the reasons of the University of Oxford for not taking (now pleaded to discharge the obligation of) the Solemn League and Covenant. By Zechariah Crofton, Minister of the Gospel at S. Botolph's Algate, London. Printed for Ralph Smith at the sign of the Bible in Cornhill, near the Royal Exchange. 1660.

A quarto pamphlet of 159 pages, of which a copy is preserved in the British Museum Library. For the condemnation of this book see next article.

221.

Berith Anti-Baal, or Zach. Crofton's appearance before the Prelate-Justice of Peace, vainly pretending to bind the Covenant and Covenanters to their good behaviour. By way of rejoynder to, and animadversion on Dr. John Gauden's reply a vindication of his analysis from the (by him reputed) pitiful cavils and objections; but really proved powerful and convincing exceptions of Mr. Zach. Crofton's Analepsis. By the author of the Analepsis, and (not by the Dr. observed) Analepsis Anelephthe, to the continuing of S. Peter's bonds, and fastening his fetters against Papal and Prelatical Power. London. Printed by M. S. for Ralph Smith at the three Bibles in Cornhil; and for Thomas Parkhurst at the three Crowns over against the great Conduit in Cheapside. 1661.

A quarto pamphlet of 68 pages, with long introductory matter. A copy is preserved in the British Museum Library.

This, as well as the book mentioned in the preceding article, fell under the condemnation of the government; and on March 23rd, 1661, Crofton, having been imprisoned, was examined before the Secretary of State, when he admitted the authorship. Soon afterwards he addressed the following petition to the king.

"To the Kings most Excellent Majestie.

"The humble peticion of Zachariah Crofton, your Majesties "prisoner in the Tower of London.

"Most humbly sheweth

"That your Petitioner hath (according to the duty of his "allegiance) in the worst of times with constant and conscientious "Loyalty to the frequent hazard of his life and all that is deare "to him and with the actual losse and prejudice of his estate, by "sequestracion and imprisonment asserted, adhœred unto, and "in his place and capacity advanced your Majesties interest and "undoubted right to the Crowne, Dignity, Rule, and Govern- "ment of these your Kingdomes, and given publique testimonies "as well since as before your Majesties happy retourne to the "same.

"That your Petitioner haveing by rashly publishing some "inconsiderate expressions about matters out of his spheare, in "his late writings fallen under your Majestie's displeasure "Throweth himselfe down at your Royall feete, and most "humbly craveth your Majesties leave to professe, hee hath not "spoken or written anything of a malicious mind or intent, to "obviate or disturbe the peace and settlement of these your "kingdomes under your Royall Government. And that hee "retaineth towards your Majestie a most Loyall heart and "resolucion to acquiesse and submitt unto your Royall pleasure "whenever it shalbee signified, published and made knowne.

"The premisses considered, your Petitioner most humbly "prayeth That the rayes of your Royall grace, favour and "pardon may bee extended to him, and his numerous "family to the enlargement of his liberty that they may "not sitt alone in sadnes, butt pertake of that generall. "joy, by which your approaching happy Coronacion shall "revive your Majestie's kingdome, whose subjection to, "and happy settlement, under your Majestie's most "righteous, gracious, long and prosperous Reigne shalbee "the study and prayers of

"Your most Loyall subiect,

"ZECHARIAH CROFTON."[1]

1. Domestic State Papers, Charles 11, Vol. 33, No. 23.

Ralph Smith, the printer of this book, was also imprisoned for being concerned in its publication, and he also petitioned the King in the following manner:

" To the Kings most Excellent Majesty.

" The humble petition of Ralph Smyth, stationer,
" Humbly sheweth

" That your Petitioner had the ill fortune to publishe a booke
" written by one Zachary Crofton for which hee hath suffered
" imprisonment but by your Majesty's gracious clemency is at
" present inlarged under bail.

" That your Petitioner is and ever hath been a loyal subject to
" your Majesty and hath severall tymes adventured his life and
" fortune towards your Majesty's restoration particularly in Sir
" George Booth's buisnes.

" That your Peticioner was not privy to the wryting of the
" said booke, and by reason of a long sicknes was not able to
" read the same many weekes after it was printed but in order
" to a small support for his wife and six small children in the
" way of his trade did ignorantly suffer the same to be printed in
" his name.

" Your Peticioner being senceable that hee hath deserved
" your Majestie's displeasure for this his great crime
" most humbly submitteth to your mercy and implores
" your Majestie's most gracious pardon.

" And hee as bound in duty shall pray
" RALPH SMITH."[1]

Whether Crofton received any specific punishment for writing these books, and when he was liberated from prison, does not at present appear. He was a Nonconformist divine, born and chiefly educated at Dublin. Being a zealous Royalist during the Commonwealth, and refusing the engagement, he was deprived. He afterwards obtained the living of St. Botolph, Aldgate, London. He was ejected for nonconformity, and died in 1672.

222.

A Phenix, or, The Solemn League and Covenant. Whereunto is annexed I. The Form and manner of his Majestie's Coronation in Scotland. With a sermon

[1]. Domestic State Papers, Charles II, Vol. 34, No. 64.

then preached on that occasion by Robert Douglas of Edenburgh.   II.   A Declaration of the King's Majesty to all his loving subjects of the Kingdomes of Scotland &c. in the yeare 1650.   III.   The great danger of Covenant-breaking &c., being the substance of a sermon preached by Edm. Calamy the 14 of Jan. 1645 before the then Lord Mayor of the City of London, Sir Thomas Adams together with the Sheriffs, Aldermen and Common-Councell of the said City: being the day of their taking the Solemn League and Covenant at Michael Basenshaw, London.   Edinburgh. Printed in the year of Covenant-breaking.

On July 23rd, 1662, the Solemn League and Covenant of Scotland was torn and burnt by the heralds at the Cross of Edinburgh, by order of the Parliament then sitting there.

Thomas Brewster was tried at the Old Bailey, London, on February 22nd, 166$\frac{3}{4}$, for printing the Phenix, and found guilty. He was fined, ordered to stand on the pillory, and then imprisoned.   The proceedings will be found in Howell's State Trials, Vol. 6, p. 514.

223.

A treatise of the execution of justice, wherein is clearly proved that the execution of judgment and justice is as well the people's as the magistrate's duty, and if the magistrates pervert judgment the people are bound by the law of God to execute judgment without them and upon them.   1663.

For printing this book, John Twyn of London, stationer, was tried at the Old Bailey on February 20th, 1663, and being convicted received sentence as in cases of high treason, and was executed accordingly.[1]   A portion of this pamphlet is preserved among the State Papers of the period.   It is a sheet containing pp. 25 to 32, with a note attached that it was taken when printing by Twyn.[2]

1. Howell's State Trials, Vol. 6, p. 513.
2. Domestic State Papers, Charles II, Vol. 88, No. 76.

224.

The Mayor of Northampton's case. 1663.

On April 7th, 1663, the House of Commons ordered that this printed paper, containing "matter of scandal against several "persons of quality," should be referred to the Committee of privileges and elections.[1]

225.

The Child's Instructor; or a new and easy Primmer.

For writing and publishing this book, Benjamin Keach, of Winslow, in the County of Bucks., was tried at the Aylesbury Assizes on the 8th of October, 1664, and found guilty; and the following sentence was passed on him by the Judge.

"Benjamin Keach, you are here convicted of writing and pub-"lishing a seditious and scandalous Book, for which the Court's "judgment is this, and the court doth award, That you shall go "to gaol for a fortnight, without bail or mainprise; and the next "Saturday to stand upon the pillory at Ailsbury for the space of "two hours, from eleven o'clock to one, with a Paper upon your "head with this inscription, *For writing, printing and publishing* "*a schismatical book intitled, The Child's Instructor, or a new and* "*easy Primmer.* And the next Thursday to stand in the same "manner, and for the same time, in the market of Winslow; "and there your Book shall be openly burnt before your face "by the common hangman, in disgrace of you and your doctrine. "And you shall forfeit to the King's Majesty the sum of £20 "and shall remain in gaol until you find sureties for your good "behaviour and appearance at the next assizes, there to renounce "your doctrine, and make such public submission as shall be "enjoined you."

According to this sentence he was kept close prisoner till the Saturday following, and then about eleven o'clock was carried to the pillory at Aylesbury, where he stood full two hours to a minute, was denied the liberty of speaking to the spectators, and "had his hands as well as his head carefully kept in the pillory "the whole time. On the Thursday following he stood in the "same manner and for the same time at Winslow, the town "where he lived, and had his book burnt before him. After this,

1. Commons' Journals, Vol. 8, p. 467.

"upon paying his fine, and giving sufficient security for his good "behaviour, he was set at liberty; but was never brought to "make a recantation.[1]

Among the State Papers of the period is preserved the following letter from Thomas Disney, apparently minister of Stoke Hamond, Bucks:—

"Honoured Sir,

And loving Brother this Primer owned by Benjamin Keach as the Author and bought by my man George Chilton for five pence of Henry Keach of Stableford Mill neare me, a miller; who then sayd that his brother Benjamin Keach is author of it, and that there are fiveteene hundred of them printed. This Benjamin Keach is a Tayler, and one that is a teacher in this new fangled way, and lives at Winslow a market towne in Buckinghamshire. Pray take some speedie course to acquaint my Lord Archbishop his grace with it, whereby his authoritie may issue forth that ye impression may be seized upon before they be much more dispersed to ye poysoining of people; they contayning (as I conceive) factious, schismaticall, and hereticall matter. Some are scattered in my parish, and perchance in noe place sooner, because he hath a sister here and some others of his gang, two whereof I have bought up. Pray let me have your speedie account of it. I doubt not but it will be taken as acceptable service to God's Church, and beleeve it a very thankefull obligement to

Stoke hamond in   Honoured Sir
Bucks —64   Your truely loving Brother
May 26th   Thomas Disney.

(Addressed)

These for his honoured friend Luke Wilkes esqre. at Whitehall with speed pray present.

226.

A book entitled "That neither temporalities, nor tythes, is due to the bishops, prelates, nor clergy, by any gospel rule, and that kings, princes, and lords

1.   Howell's State Trials, Vol. 6, p. 702.
2.   Domestic State Papers, Charles II, Vol, 98, No, 116,

PART IV.]   [TO BE CONTINUED.

INDEX

EXPURGATORIUS

ANGLICANUS:

OR

A DESCRIPTIVE CATALOGUE OF THE PRINCIPAL BOOKS

PRINTED OR PUBLISHED IN ENGLAND,

WHICH HAVE BEEN SUPPRESSED,

OR BURNT BY THE COMMON HANGMAN,

OR CENSURED,

OR FOR WHICH THE AUTHORS, PRINTERS, OR PUBLISHERS

HAVE BEEN PROSECUTED.

BY W. H. HART, F.S.A.

PRICE ONE SHILLING AND SIXPENCE.

LONDON:

JOHN RUSSELL SMITH, 36, SOHO SQUARE.

1877.

HART AND SON, PRINTERS,]   [SAFFRON WALDEN.

NOTICE.

———◆———

THE progress of this Publication has been un-avoidably delayed through illness, domestic affliction, and other causes; but the Editor now hopes to bring the entire work to a speedy conclusion; health and other things permitting.

W. H. HART, F.S.A.

Campbell Lodge,
    Burch Road,
        Rosherville, Kent.
May, 1877.

temporal may justly take the temporalities and tythes from them, and dispose of them for the defence and benefit of the kingdom, and the relief of the poor, proved by the laws and practices of twenty kings of England, Judah, and France, and also by 120 authors besides, dedicated to the king's most excellent Majesty. About 1671.

The author of this book is unknown; but the printer, Mr. Francis Smith, before the book was finished was taken into custody under a general warrant, and carried to Lambeth House to appear before the then Bishop, but eventually all proceedings against him dropped.[1]

227.

England's Appeal from the Private Caballe at Whitehall to the great Council of the Nation, the Lords and Commons in Parliament assembled. By a true lover of his country. 1673.

A quarto pamphlet of 52 pages, a copy of which is in the editor's possession. For publishing the same, Francis Smith the bookseller was committed into the custody of five of the King's messengers by the Council Board, to about £50 charges and damages.[2]

228.

The Quaker and his maid. 1675.

On June 26th, 1675, a warrant was issued by the Secretary of State to search for this pamphlet. The editor has not as yet been able to discover a copy. It was reprinted in the year 1739 under this title, "A merry conversation which lately passed between a "very noted Quaker and his maid, upon a very merry occasion. "To which is added, The Members to their Sovereign, By Hil—d "Ja—bs, Esqre. Third edition." It is a grossly indecent production. A copy of this reprint is in the editor's possession, purchased from the library of the late George Daniel, Esq., Canonbury Square. It is in octavo, and contains 18 pages.

1. Howell's State Trials, Vol, 7, p. 950,
2. Howell's State Trials, Vol, 7, p. 950,

229.

Verses on the Death of Edward Coleman, who was executed for high treason on December 3. 1678.[1]

These verses were published by Henry Nevill, otherwise Henry Payne, of Medborne in Leicestershire, on January 10th, 16$\frac{78}{79}$, for which the following information was filed against him by the Attorney General.

"Middlesexia scilicet. Memorandum quod Willielmus Jones "miles attornatus domini regis nunc generalis qui pro eodem "domino rege in hac parte sequitur in propria persona sua venit "hic in curiam dicti domini regis coram ipso rege apud West- "monasterium die Jovis proximo post octabas Sancti Hillarii "isto eodem termino et pro eodem domino rege dat curiæ hic "intelligi et informari quod Termino Sancti Michaelis anno regni " domini nostri Caroli Secundi Dei gratia Angliæ Scotiæ Franciæ " et Hiberniæ Regis fidei defensoris &c. tricesimo, in curia dicti " domini regis coram ipso rege apud Westmonasterium in "comitatu Middlesexiæ (eadem curia apud Westmonasterium " in comitatu Middlesexiæ tunc tenta existente) quidam Edwardus

---

1. For a full account of Coleman's trial see Howell's State Trials, Vol. 7, p. 1. Burnet, in his history of his own time, Vol. 1, p. 393, speaks thus of Coleman: " The Duchess of York had one put about her to be her Secretary, "Coleman; who became so active in the affairs of the party, and ended his "life'so unfortunately, that since I had much conversation with him, his "circumstances may deserve that his character should be given, though his " person did not. I.was told he was a clergyman's son: but he was early "catched by the Jesuits, and bred many years among them. He understood "the art of managing controversies, chiefly that great one of the authority of "the church, better than any of their priests. He was a bold man, resolved "to raise himself, which he did by dedicating himself wholly to the Jesuits: "and so he was raised by them. He had a great easiness in writing in several "languages; and writ many long letters, and was the chief correspondent the "party had in England. He lived at a vast expence. And talked in so pos- "itive a manner, that it looked like one who knew he was well supported. I " soon saw into his temper; and I warned the Duke of it. For 1 looked on "him as a man much liker to spoil business than to carry it on dexterously. "He got into the confidence of P. Ferrier the king of France's confessor; "and tried to get into the same pitch of confidence with P. de la Chaise, who "succeeded him in that post. He went about everywhere, even to the jails "among the criminals, to make proselytes. He dealt much both in the giving "and taking of bribes."

"Coleman nuper de parochia Sancti Martini in Campis in com-
"itatu Middlesexiæ generosus debito modo per sacramentum
"duodecim juratorum proborum et legalium hominum comitatus
"Middlesexiæ prædicti indictatus fuit pro diversis altis proditio-
"nibus in falso malitiose subdole et proditorie proposicon'
"compassacon' imaginacon' et intenden' seditionis et rebellionis
"infra hoc regnum Angliæ et dictum dominum regem nunc de
"regali statu titulo potestate et regimine regni sui penitus
"deprivandum deponendum dejiciendum et exhæretandum ac
"ipsum dominum regem ad mortem et finalem destructionem
"adducendum et ponendum et gubernationem ejusdem regni et
"sinceram Dei religionem in eodem regno recte et legibus ejus-
"dem regni stabilitas pro voluntate et libito ejus mutandas et
"alterandas et statuta totius hujus regni Angliæ per universas
"ejus partes bene instituta et ordinata totaliter subvertenda et
"distruenda et guerram contra dictum dominum regem nunc
"infra hoc regnum Angliæ levandam et procurandam. Et quod
"prædictus Edwardus Coleman postea scilicet prædicto termino
"Sancti Michaelis anno regni dicti domini regis nunc tricesimo
"supradicto in curia dicti domini regis coram ipso rege apud
"Westmonasterium prædictum in dicto comitatu 'Middlesexiæ
"debito modo per sacramentum duodecim juratorum patriæ pro
"alta proditione prædicta convictus fuit et postea attinctus post-
"eaque tractus suspensus et exartuatus fuit. Et quod quidam
"Henricus Nevill de Medborne in Comitatu Leicestriæ generosus
"alias dictus Henricus Payne de Medborne prædicta in dicto
"comitatu Leicestriæ generosus præmissa prædicta bene sciens
"sed existens homo perniciosus et seditiosus et machinans et
"malitiose intendens prædicta crimen et offensam altæ proditio-
"nis minuere necnon veredictum et judicium prædicta versus
"præfatum Edwardum Coleman pro prædicta alta proditione ut
"præfertur legittimo modo obtenta habita et reddita in odium et
"vilipendium cum omnibus ligeis et subditis dicti domini regis
"inducere et inferre ac ad prædictum Edwardum Coleman qui
"pro proditione prædicta per ipsum ut præfertur commissa in
"forma prædicta rite et juste punitus fuit gloriosissimum Dei
"martyrem per pravos et superstitiosos homines Romanæ
"Religionis infra hoc regnum Angliæ reputandum et colendum
"procurare et causare decimo die Januarii anno regni domini
"Caroli Secundi nunc Regis Angliæ &c. tricesimo apud paroch-

"iam Sanctæ Margarettæ Westmonasterii in comitatu Middle-
"sexiæ falso illicite injuste nequiter malitiose scandalose et
"seditiose fecit composuit et scripsit et fieri componi et scribi
"causavit quoddam falsum malitiosum scandalosum libellosum
"et seditiosum libellum intitulatum *To the Glorious Martyr*
"*E. C.* per quas duas literas E. C. prædictus Henricus inuit et
"intelligi designavit præfatum Edwardum Coleman qui pro alta
"proditione ut præfertur legittimo modo convictus attinctus
"posteaque tractus suspensus et exartuatus fuit cujus quidem
"falsi malitiosi scandalosi libellosi et seditiosi libelli tenor
"sequitur.

"To the Glorious Martyr E. C.

"Haile Glorious soul! to whome the Crown is given;
"All hail thou mighty Favourite of Heaven!
"Triumphant Martyr from that endless Throne
"Where Thou must Raigne with Christ, disturb'd by none,
"Looke down a while, and view upon his Knee
"An undeserved Friend to Truth and Thee.
"Pardon that boasted Title, since that Love
"Which gave it here, must needs confirm't above:
"For 'twas a flaming Charity, which sure
"Since boundless here must endless there endure.
"But ah, alasse great Saint, I owne with Shame,
"That ill, I then, worse now, deserve the Name;
"Whilst here on Earth, my troubles kept me still,
"From Friendship's Laws, as now my Senses will;
"But what you pardon'd once on Fortune's score,
"Be pleas'd on Patience now to pity more;
"And for that good which you did here designe,
"Without Reward or least Desert of mine,
"Obtain me now from Our Great Lord and Thine;
"Not that I hope to equall you in Place,
"Tho' I would wish it with the like Disgrace;
"I only hope to view that holy Ring,
"Where Crowned Saints doe Hallelujahs sing.
"Prepare mee some low Place in that bright Quire,
"Where tho' I may not Sing I may admire.

"Et ulterius idem attornatus dicti domini regis nunc
"generalis pro eodem domino rege dat curiæ hic intelligi et
"informari quod Henricus Nevill alias dictus Henricus Payne

"postea scilicet dicto decimo die Januarii anno regni dicti domini
"regis nunc tricesimo supradicto apud parochiam Sanctæ
"Margarettæ Westmonasterii prædictum in dicto comitatu
"Middlesexiæ sciens prædictam falsum fictum malitiosum scan-
"dalosum libellosum et seditiosum libellum fore falsum malitio-
"sum scandalosum et seditiosum libellum adtunc et ibidem falso
"illicite injuste nequiter malitiose scandalose et seditiose diversis
"ligeis subditis dicti domini regis publicavit et publicari caus-
"avit in contemptum legum hujus regni Angliæ manifestum
"In malum et pernitiosissimum exemplum omnium aliorum in
"tali casu delinquentium ac contra pacem dicti domini regis
"nunc coronam et dignitatem suas &c.[1]

A manuscript copy of these verses is preserved in the British
Museum Library, written on the back of a printed paper, entitled
"The answer of Coleman's Ghost to H. N.'s Poetick Offering."
Nevill is there called a Priest, but in the preceding information
he is merely styled "Gentleman."

230.

An account of the growth of popery aud arbitrary
Government in England; more particularly from the
long prorogation of November, 1675, ending the 15th
of February, 1676, till the last meeting of Parliament
the 16th of July, 1677. By Andrew Marvell. Amsterdam. 1677.

This pamplet which traces the intrigues of the Court of
England with that of France, made a great impression on the
nation. A reward was offered in the Gazette for the discovery
of the author.

231.

A seasonable argument to persuade all the Grand
juries in England, to petition for a New Parliament;
Or, a List of the Principal Labourers in the Great
Design of Popery and Arbitrary Power, who have
betrayed their Country to the Conspirators, and bar-
gained with them to maintain a standing army in

1. Kings's Bench Judgment Roll, Easter, 31 Car. 2, rot. 68.

England, under the Command of the Bigotted Popish Duke; who, by the assistance of the Lord Lauderdale's Scotch Army, the Forces in Ireland, and those in France, hopes to bring all back to Rome. By Andrew Marvell. Amsterdam. 1677.

A reward was offered by Proclamation to such as would discover the author of this book. It is printed at length in Marvell's Works (ed. Thompson, 1776, Vol. 2, p. 555), also in Cobbett's Parliamentary History, Vol. 4, Appendix, p. xxii.

232.

To all the Royalists that suffered for His Majesty : and to all the rest of the good people of England, the Humble Apologie of the English Catholicks.

On November 28th, 1666, an order in Council was made for the Secretaries of State to cause the suppression of this " scandalous pamphlet," and to make strict enquiry after the author and printer.[1]

The following are copies of informations and other documents preserved among the Domestic State Papers concerning the publication of this book. It appears to have been written by Lord Castlemaine. A copy is preserved in the British Museum Library.

"An account concerning the English Catholics Apology."

December 5th, 1666.

"*Elizabeth Bud* (a Hawker) sayes That John Brereton (a Haw-" ker) was the onely disposer of it; but shee knowes not perfectly " his lodging.

" One *Radcliffe* (a Hawker) sayes as much and directed to his " lodging.

"*John Brereton* sayes that hee had 200 coppyes on Munday " last was sevenight from Two Gentlemen at the Bell and 3 Cranes-" Tavern by the Savoy in a Room one pair of Staires next the " street, but denyes to know the Persons, yet confesses to have " seen one of them severall times since.

" Hee sayes further that Hee was brought to them by One Fox " (a Hawker) and disposed of the coppyes as follows :—

1. Domestic State Papers, Charles 2, Vol. 179, No. 114.

"Two Quire to Anne Brache at the Parlt Stairs Foot
"One Quire to One Miller at Westminst'-Hall door.
"A Dozen to One Michel in Westminst'-Hall.
"The Residue Hee sold in the streets.

"The Examinate further sayes, That on Tuesday (the day
"following) Hee had 100 more of a Gentleman in a house by
"Charing-Cross which Gentleman hee hath since seen and knows
"again upon sight.

"Brache ⎫
"Miller ⎬ acknowledge according to Brereton's confession.
"Michel ⎭

"*Francis Fox* (a Hawker) sayes, That on Munday Nov: 26th
"a Porter called him to the Bell and 3 Cranes-Tavern in the
"Strand to Two Gentlemen, who sayd, They had a Parcell of
"Bookes to be disposed of. The Examinate demanded, what they
"were. They replyed, That they were *A Vindicacion of the*
"*Catholics that had suffer'd in his Majesty's Service.* The Exami-
"nate told them that Hee durst not meddle with them and soe
"went his way. After which acquainting Brereton with the
"business, Zwounds, sayes Brereton, why did you not take them?
"shew them me and I'l take them. Soe They went together and
"in Fox his presence, Brereton receaved 200 Bookes, as the
"Gentlemen sayd that delivered them in the Chamber one pair
"of stairs towards the Street.

"*William Galhampton* (Drawer in the Bell and 3 Cranes-Tavern)
"sayes, That Mathias Gateley in Company with another Gentle-
"man came thither, upon a Munday Morning and tooke up a
"Chamber one pair of Stairs toward the Street, and that they
"were the first Company that came into that Room.

"And Hee further sayes That Mr Gateley coming into the
"House, demanded if the news-bookes were out and that soon
"after This Examinate saw Fox and Brereton goe into Mr Gateley's
"Chamber and That Hee saw there upon the Table a large Deal-
"box; and that Mr Gateley called to the Drawer for a Hammer.
"Hee sayes moreover, that Mr Gateley and his Friend went out
"about 12 of the Clock, leaving a Waterman in the Chamber to
"looke to some Luggage and that Mr Gateley enquired of this
"Examinate for a backway to the Water-side.

"*John Joyce* (a Drawer in the Tavern above said) sayes That
"Mr Gateley with another Gentleman came upon Munday was

"sevenight in the morning into that House and took up the
"Chamber one pair of Stairs towards the Street, and kept it for
"themselves and a Waterman which They had to looke to some
"Goods from morning till 7 at night : about which hour This
"Examinate sayes that Hee lighted Mr Gateley a backway to the
"Water-side : a Waterman carrying his Luggage. This Ex-
"aminate sayes also that Hee saw Brereton (a Hawker) goe into
"Mr Gateley's Chamber in the morning.

"*Mrs. Layton* (Mistress of the s^d Tavern) sayes that Mr Gateley
"was there in the morning upon that day, when a Water-man
"was left in charge of some Goods in his Chamber and that Hee
"was in the Room, up One pair of Stairs next the street.

"*Mathias Gateley* sayes that Hee came not into that Tavern till
"about 4 of the Clock afternoon : but acknowledges that there he
"was and in the Chamber toward the Street in Company with
"one Mr Billingsley.

"Hee denyes the having any Box upon the Table ; The calling
"for a Hammer ; The having seen any of the Hawkers there ;
"And upon the whole matter, The having had anything to doe
"with the Catholicks Apology.

"The Mistress of the Tavern, Two Drawers, and the Two
"Hawkers doe all agree upon the same person."

(Indorsed).

Dec. 66.

Mr Lestranges
report of his enquiry
after the Ro. Cath.
Apology.

"The Examination of [   ] Gately taken before [   ]
"Sayth

"That he was not at the Bell Taverne on Monday Fortnight
"in the morning.

"That Friday month Mr Billingsley invited him to that Taverne,
"he being ready to goe to Roehampton to the E. of Aylesbury
"whom he serves, He had certaine Bundles of Cloathes, &c.
"which he called a Waterman to carry for him, denying to have
"been there on Monday.

"That he was there only once in a morning, but went not up
"Staires, and that was Friday fortnight.

"That on the day in question (Monday fortnight), He dranke
"his morning's draught with the page in a woman's house in
"St. John's Close about 10 where he parted not till about 11,
"then he dressed himselfe at home and dined at home, after that
"desiring leave to goe abroad 2 or 3 houres, in the afternoone he
"mett M[r] Billingsley towards Charing Crosse, with whom he
"dranke 2 glasses of wine at the King's head Taverne at Charing
"Crosse. Then to Billingsley's House who showed him the
"Cath[cke] Apology.

"That a Porter came and enquired for him by his name when
"he was drinking his morning's draught from Gately and com-
"pany. He came and found the Gentlemen in a forooome and
"under the Table was a parcell of Bookes, which they called to
"him to sell, which he declined, and so left them, and having
"told A. B. another Hawker of Books, they both went up
"together and A. B. tooke 200 of them to sell, and believes
"Gately from all Relacions and understands to have been one
"of the two.

"He demanded no money for the coppyes, but gave them
"freely. That those 200 were all he then saw.

"To the Right Hono[ble] the Lord Arlington,
    "The humble Peticion of Mathias Gateley now a Servant to
    "the Earle of Alisbury
"Sheweth
    "That whereas your Peticioner was comitted by your Lord-
"shipp's Order into custody for the Distributing of the Bookes
"called the *Apologie of the English Catholiques*, although your
"Peticioner is innocent of any such fact comitted by him.
    "That in regard your Peticioner is still in custody, and thereby
"at a great charge, and for that hee maketh no question but to
"cleere himselfe of the said Accusation.
        "Your Peticioner therefore humbly praies your Lord-
        "shipp to graunt him Liberty upon Baile whereby he
        "may bee in a capacity to bring his witnesses togeather

"for the cleereing of himselfe; And to that end your
"Lordshipp wil be alsoe pleased to appoint a speedy
"Day for hearing.

　　"And your Peticioner shall pray.

　"&c.

December 20th, 1666.

"The Examin" of Thomas Osborn, of Westminster.

"The Examinant saith

　　"he thinkes it to bee near a monith agoe
"since he was at the Printer's house : (whose name is
"Milborne) with my Lord Castlemain on the Saturday
"he went up Staires and at my Ld. Castlemain's intreaty
"helped him to compare a written Paper with one halfe
"printed which hee supposes was the Roman Catholiqs
"Apology, but never read the whole piece.

"Q.—What part hee had in the dispersing of them.

"Sayes, hee had none but saw severall copies of them afterwards
　　"in My Lord Castlemain's hands.

"Asked who was the Authour.

"Sayes he supposes my Lord Castlemain the Authour and hee
　　"thinkes hee heard him say soe.　Sayes moreover the
　　"written copy was in My Lord Castlemain's hand.

"If he knowes who dispersed them.

　　"Supposes dispersed by his Lordshipp's order for hee
　　"heard him say soe and saw him deliver some of them.

"Askt if hee bee a Roman Catholique.

"Sayes, Noe.

"The Examination of Tho : Milburn and his Wife.

"These Examinates agree upon the sight of M͏ʳ Tho : Osborn
"that Hee is the Person who came in company with Another
"Gentleman low of Stature and appearing to be a Person of
"Quality to the Printing-house and that the lesser of the Two
"went up stairs leaving M͏ʳ Osborn below.

"Milburn's wife sayes, that Mr Osborn stayd in the Room
"where shee was, while the other was above. That at last
"offering to goe up, The little Gentleman sayd to him Çozen,
"stay below, I'l come to you. That Mr Osborn spake nothing
"to her of anything to print; And that the Other coming
"down, They went away together. Shee says further, that they
"came a Second Time, upon a Saturday morning; and a third
"time in the Afternoon; at which time they stayd 3 or 4 houres
"and as she believes for a Proof. And being demanded who
"managed the business, shee sayes, that the little Gentleman
"seem'd to her to doe all, and that the Other appear'd to her,
"onely to come for company.

"Thomas Milburn sayes, That the little Gentleman appear'd
"first to him with One Scroop (or Pugh) in his company at the
"Crown Tavern in Smythfield, aud the 2nd time with the same
"Person at the Star in Holborn. He sayes further, That after-
"ward the little Gentleman came to his house with Mr Osborn.
"And that the little Gentleman gave him the coppy of the
"English Catholics Apology; Order'd the printing of it and
"pay'd for the Impression, and that Mr Osborn sayd nothing to
"him concerning the business, onely, at last, this Examinate saw
"them reading over the Proof together. But who was the
"Author of it, Hee knowes not.

233.

Sighs for the Pitchers: breathed out in a personal
Contribution to the National Humiliation the last of
May, 1666, in the cities of London and Westminster,
upon the near approaching engagement then expected
between the English and Dutch Navies. Wherewith
are Complicated such musings as were occasioned by a
Report of their actual engagement; and by observing
the Publike Rejoycing whilst this was preparing by the
Author, George Wither. Imprinted in the sad year
expressed in this seasonable Chronogram.

LorD haVe MerCIe Vpon Vs.
MDCLXVI.

On July 23rd, 1666, a warrant was issued by the Secretary of State to Lewis Dormay to apprehend George Wither, Henry Eversden, Sarah Anderton, Elizabeth Goslin, and Margaret Hicks for dispersing this "seditious pamphlet."[1] A copy of it is preserved in the British Museum Library.

234.

Nehushtan: or, a sober and peaceable discourse concerning the abolishing of things abused to Superstition and Idolatry; which may serve as one intire, and sufficient argument to evince that the Liturgy, Ceremonies, and other things used at this Day in the Church of England ought neither to be imposed, nor retained, but utterly extirpated and laid aside: and to vindicate the Nonconformists in their refusal to close with them. London. 1668.

This book was written by John Wilson, a Nonconformist, of Chester. Elizabeth Calvert was imprisoned for helping the author to print it, as appears from a petition presented by her to the Secretary of State wherein she states that she was wholly ignorant of the sedition contained therein, and she promised never to be concerned in such books for the future.[2]

235.

An appeal from the Country to the City for the preservation of his Majestie's Person, Liberty, Property, and the Protestant Religion. London. 1679.

This book was published by Benjamin Harris, Bookseller of Cornhill, and for so doing he was tried at the Guildhall, London, in 1680, and found guilty. He afterwards received sentence in the Court of King's Bench to pay a fine of £500; to stand on the Pillory an hour, and find sureties for his good behaviour for three years; and had it not been for Mr. Justice Pemberton, the

1. Domestic State Papers, Charles 2.
2. Domestic State Papers, Charles 2, Vol. 113, No. 128.

Chief Justice would have added that he should be publicly whipped.[1] On December 21, 1680, the House of Commons ordered an address for the remission of this fine to be presented to the King. The indictment is as follows :—

London. Memorandum quod Creswell Levins miles attornatus domini regis nunc generalis qui pro eodem domino rege in hac parte sequitur in propria persona sua venit hic in curia dicti domini regis coram ipso rege apud Westmonasterium die Jovis proxima post tres septimanas Sancti Michaelis isto eodem termino et pro eodem domino rege dat curiæ hic intelligi et informari quod Benjaminus Harris de parochia Sancti Michaelis Cornehill London Bookeseller machinans et malitiose intendens dominum nostrum Carolum Secundum nunc regem Angliæ &c. et gubernationem suam hujus regni Angliæ scandalizare et in contemptum ducere vicesimo secundo die Octobris anno regni dicti domini regis nunc Angliæ &c. tricesimo primo apud parochiam Sancti Michaelis Cornehill London prædictam quoddam scandalosum et seditiosum librum intitulatum *An Appeal from the Country to the City for the preservation of his Majestie's Person, Liberty, Property, and the Protestant Religion* publicavit et venditioni exposuit in quoquidem libro inter alia continetur prout sequitur in hæc verba *We in the Country have done our parts, in choosing for the generality good members to serve in Parliament; but if (as our two last Parliaments were) they must be dissolv'd or prorogu'd, when ever they come to redress the Grievances of the Subject, we may be pitied, but not blam'd. If the Plot takes effect, (as in all probability it will) our Parliaments are not then to be condemn'd, for that their not being suffer'd to sit occasion'd it.* in magnum scandalum et contemptum dicti domini regis et gubernationis suæ hujus regni Angliæ in malum exemplum omnium aliorum in tali casu delinquentium ac contra pacem dicti domini regis nunc coronam et dignitatem suas &c.

A copy of this book is in the Editor's possession. It is in small qnarto, and contains twenty-nine pages, but is without printer's name. Although printed anonymously, it is known to be the production of Charles Blount, and was reprinted in the year 1695, with other of his writings in a little volume entitled "The Miscellaneous Works of Charles Blount, Esq." The Editor

I. Howell's State Trials, Vol. 7, p. 926. Indictments, London and Middlesex. Mich. 31 Car. 2, No. 42.

of this collection was Charles Gildon, who ushers it into the world by a preface in defence of self-murder, Blount, having, as it appears destroyed himself. This unhappy man was son of Sir Henry Blount.

236.

A Letter from a person of quality to his friend in the Country, giving an account of the debates and resolutions in the House of Lords, in April and May, 1675, concerning a Bill entitled "A Bill to prevent the dangers which may arise from persons disaffected to the government." By John Locke.

It was ordered by the Privy Council to be burnt. "Our author" say the Editors of the Biographia Britannica " drew up this letter " at the desire of the Earl of Shaftesbury, and under his Lord- " ship's inspection, only committing to writing what the Earl did " in a manner dictate to him ; and this indeed is evident with " regard to that part which contains remarks upon the characters " and conduct of several of the nobility, since these could be " known only to his Lordship." It is printed at length in Cobbett's Parliamentary History, Vol. 4, Appendix, No. V.

237.

The Grand question Concerning the Judicature of the House of Peers stated and argued. And the case of Thomas Skinner, Merchant, Complaining of the East India Company, with the Proceedings thereupon, which gave occasion to that question, faithfully related. By a true well wisher to the Peace and good govern- ment of the Kingdom, and to the Dignity and Authority of Parliaments. London. 1669.

. On October 22nd, 1669, Richard Chiswell, Bookseller, was sent for by the House of Commons to give an account of the printing and publishing of this book, and upon examination he confessed that he caused the book to be printed, and that he had no formal licence for it, but it was sent to him by a Privy Councillor, the Lord Hollis, with direction and order to print it, and that he had no hire or reward in money, but only the benefit of the copy for doing it. It was then ordered that the Attorney General should draw up an indictment in the King's Bench against Chiswell for his offence in causing the book to be printed and published without licence. The House being afterwards informed that the said book was printed by one John Darby, a printer, it was ordered that Darby should be summoned to attend the House to give an account of his printing the book.[1] A copy of the book is preserved in the British Museum Library.

238.
Speech of the Lord Cavendish. 1679.

On April 25th, 1679, the House of Commons ordered that enquiry should be made as to the authors and publishers of this "false and scandalous pamphlet."[2]

239.
Sir Francis Winnington's speech. 1679.

On April 1st, 1679, the House of Commons ordered that a Committee should be appointed to enquire as to the authors and publishers of this "false and scandalous pamphlet."[3]

240.
Two letters from Mr. Mountagu, to the Lord Treasurer; one of the eleventh, the other of the eighteenth of January, 167⅞, which were read in the House of Commons. Together with the Lord Treasurer's speech in the House of Peers, upon an impeachment of High treason, &c., brought up against his Lordship by the House of Commons, December 23, 1678. London. 1679.

For the condemnation of this book see next article. A copy exists in the British Museum Library. It is in quarto and contains 15 pages.

1. Commons' Journals, Vol. 9, p. 100.
2. Commons' Journals, Vol. 9, p. 602.
3. Commons' Journals, Vol. 9, p. 579.

241.

A Letter from a Jesuit in Paris to his correspondent in London showing the most effectual way to ruin the government and the Protestant Religion. 1679.

On March 21st, 167⅜, it was ordered by the House of Commons that Jonathan Edwyn, living at the Three Roses, in Redcross Street, be immediately sent for to give the House an account by what authority he published this and the preceding pamphlet. The next day, on Mr. Hills being called in, he informed the House that he printed them by order of the Lord Treasurer; and a Committee was appointed to consider of these two pamphlets, and to report their opinions to the House. On the 26th, the House was informed that Doctor John Nelson was the author of the Letter from a Jesuit in Paris; he was therefore ordered to be sent for.

242.

The long Parliament dissolved.

For publishing this book, one J. Brown was brought to trial, and sentenced to pay a fine of 1000 marks, bound to good behaviour for seven years, and his name struck out of the roll of attorneys, without any offence alleged in his said vocation. Not being able to pay this fine, he lay in prison for three years till he was pardoned and restored to his place of attorney by royal warrant dated 15th December, 1679. The information does not appear to be entered on the Judgment Rolls, but Howell[2] extracts from the book the following words upon which the prosecution was founded:—

Nor let any man think it strange, that we account it treason for you to sit and act contrary to our laws; for if in the first parliament of Richard II, Grimes and Weston, for lack of courage only were adjudged guilty of high treason for surrendering the places committed to their trust; how much more you, if you turn renegadoes to the people that entrusted you, and as much as in you lie surrender not a little pitiful castle or two, but all the legal defence the people of England have for their lives, liberties, a properties at once! Neither let the

1.   Commons' Journals, Vol. 9, pp. 572, 574, 576.
2.   State Trials, Vol. 8, p. 188.

vain persuasion delude you, that no precedent can be found, that one English Parliament hath hanged up another; though peradventure even that may be proved a mistake; for an unprecedented crime calls for an unprecedented punishment; and if you shall be so wicked to do the one, or rather endeavour to do, (for now you are no longer a parliament) what ground of confidence you can have that none will be found so worthy to do the other, we cannot understand: and do faithfully promise if your unworthines provoke us to it, that we will use our honest and utmost endeavours (whenever a new parliament shall be called) to chuse such as may convince you of your mistake: The old and infallible observation, That Parliaments are the Pulse of the People, shall lose its esteem; or you will find, that this your presumption was over-fond; however, it argues but a bad mind to sin, because it is believed it shall not be punished.

243.

The Compendium; or, a short view of the late Tryals, in relation to the present plot against his Majesty and Government: with the speeches of those that have been executed. As also an humble address (at the close) to all the worthy Patriots of this once Flourishing and happy Kingdom. London. 1679.

For publishing this book an information was filed by the Attorney General against Matthew Turner, a Stationer, of the parish of St. Andrew, Holborn. Turner was tried in the summer of 1680, and was sentenced to pay a fine of 100 marks.[1]

The information is as follows :—[2]

Middlesexia. Memorandum quod Samuelis Astry Armiger, Coronator et Attornatus domini regis, in curia ipsius regis coram ipso rege qui pro eodem domino rege in hac parte sequitur in propria persona sua venit hic in curia dicti domini regis coram ipso rege apud Westmonasterium die Sabbati proximo post Crastinum Purificationis Beatæ Mariæ Virginis isto eodem Termino, et pro eodem domino rege dat curiæ hic intelligi et informari, quod cum quidam Edwardus Coleman et diversi alii proditores pro diversis separalibus proditionibus per debitam legis

---

1. Howell's State Trials, Vol. 8, p. 189.
2. Indictments, London and Midd., Hilary 31 and 32 Car. 2, No. 9. King's Bench Judgment Roll, Easter 32 Car. 2, rot. 88 a.

formam super testimonium diversorum credibilium testium
convicti et attincti fuerunt, quidam tamen Matheus Turner de
parochia Sancti Andreæ Holborne in Comitatu Middlesexiæ,
Stationer, machinans et malitiose intendens gubernationem
domini regis nunc hujus regni sui Angliæ et administrationem
justitiæ in eodem regno et testes productos ex parte domini regis
super triationem proditorum prædictorum scandalizare, et in
odium et contemptum ducere, vicesimo primo die Januarii anno
regni domini nostri Caroli Secundi, Dei gratia Angliæ, Scotiæ,
Franciæ, et Hiberniæ Regis, Fidei Defensoris &c., tricesimo
primo, apud parochiam Sancti Andreæ Holborne prædictam
in comitatu prædicto, quoddam falsum, scandalosum, seditiosum
et malitiosum librum, intitulatum *The Compendium, or a
short view of the late Trialls in relation to the present plott
against his Majestie and Government with the speeches of those that
have beene executed, as alsoe an humble addresse at the close to all the
worthie patriots of this once flourishing and happy Kingdome.*
maliciose et seditiose publicavit et venditioni exposuit; in quoquidem libro continetur relatio evidentiarum datarum super
triationem proditorum prædictorum, et post talem relationem in
eodem libro inter alia continetur prout sequitur *An humble address
to all worthy patriots, of what Rank soever they be. Having (my Lords
and Gentlemen) given you this exact and short account of the late
Judicial Proceedings; for when should I have ended, had I not (in
spight of the continual follies that occurr'd) forc'd my self to Bounds?
I say, having given you this short account, I know not whether you are
now more surpris'd (for surpris'd I am sure you are) at the strange
Incohèrencies, nay, Impossibilities, in the charge all along, or at the
mighty weight of the defence, though the accusers themselves had bin
men of repute and probity. For, after a sober and close consideration
(to which nothing can more conduce than an Abstract, or Compendium)
what have they lay'd at the dores of Catholicks, that, by its monstrous
and disagreeing parts, shows not it self to be wholly vain and chimerical?*
Et in alio loco ejusdem libri continetur prout sequitur, *There is
not one Witness against us, who has not either bin a most Profligated
Wretch, by the unanimous Consent of all that knew him, or given at least
Prognosticks by his Poverty or Temper, that the first Opportunity would
infallibly make him so.* In magnum vilipendium scandalum et
contemptum testium dicti domini regis versus proditores prædictos
in contemptum dicti domini regis et gubernationis suæ ac legum

suarum, in malum exemplum omnium aliorum in tali casu
delinquentium, ac contra pacem dicti domini regis nunc, coronam
et dignitatem suas &c.

244.

The Weekly Packet of Advice from Rome, or the History of Popery. August 1, 1679.

For publishing this periodical Henry Carr was tried at the
Guildhall, London, in 1680, and found guilty.

The following is a copy of the information against him :—

Londonia Scilicet—Memorandum quod Samuelis Astry armiger coronator et attornatus domini regis in curia ipsius domini
regis coram ipso rege qui pro eodem domino rege in hac parte
sequitur in propria persona sua venit hic in curiam dicti domini
regis coram ipso apud Westmonasterium die Mercurii proximo
post octabas Purificationis Beatæ Mariæ Virginis isto eodem
termino et pro eodem domino rege dat curiæ hic intelligi et
informari quod cum quædam designatio anglice *a plott* proditoriæ
conspirationis nuper habita fuit infra hoc regnum Angliæ inter
diversos falsos proditores hujus regni Angliæ ad interficiendum
et murdrandum dominum nostrum Carolum Secundum supremum
dominum suum et gubernationem hujus regni Angliæ et sinceram
Dei religionem infra hoc regnum Angliæ bene et pie stabilitatam
subvertere et distruere et Romanam religionem infra hoc regnum
Angliæ inducere cumque etiam diversi proditores pro alta
proditione prædicta legittimo modo convicti et attincti fuerunt et
aliæ personæ pro alta proditione prædicta per debitam legis
formam triati et acquetati fuerunt quidam tamen Henricus Carre
de parochia Sancti Sepulchri Londoniæ generosus præmissorum
non ignarus sed machinans et malitiose intendens gubernationem
dicti domini regis hujus regni sui Angliæ et administrationem
justitiæ in eodem regno scandalizare et in odium et contemptum
ducere primo die Augusti anno regni dicti domini regis nunc
tricesimo primo apud parochiam Sancti Sepulchri Londoniæ
prædictæ quoddam falsum scandalosum et malitiosum librum
intitulatum *The weekly Pacquet of Advice from Rome or the History*
of Popery malitiose et illicite imprimi causavit et publicavit in
quoquidem libro continetur inter alia prout sequitur *There is lately*
found out by an Experienc'd Physician, an Incomparable Medicament

called, The Wonder-working Plaister, truely Catholick in Operation, somewhat of Kin to the Jesuites Powder, but more effectual. The Vertues of it are strange and various; it will make Justice deaf as well as blinde, take out spots of deepest Treasons more cleverly than Castle-soap does common Stains: It alters a man's Constitution in two or three days, more than the Virtuosi's Transfusion of Blood in seven years. 'Tis a great Alexipharmick, and helps Poysons, and those that use them. It miraculously exalts and purifies the Eye sight, and makes people behold nothing but Innocence in the blackest Malefactors. 'Tis a mighty Cordial for a declining Cause, and stifles a Plot as certainly as the Itch is destroy'd by Butter and Brimstone. In a word, it makes Fools wise men, and wise men Fools; and both of them Knaves. The colour of this precious Balm is bright and dazling; and being applied privately to the Fist in decent manner, and a competent Dose, infallibly performs all the said Cures, and many others, not fit here to be mentioned. In magnum contemptum dicti domini regis nunc et legum suorum in magnum scandalum gubernationis dicti domini regis hujus regni Angliæ et administrationis justitiæ in eodem in malum exemplum omnium aliorum in tali casu delinquentium ac contra pacem dicti domini regis nunc coronam et dignitatem suas &c.[1]

245.

New year's gift for the Lord Chief Justice Scroggs, being some remarks on his speech made the first day of Michaelmas, 1679.

For the publication of this paper a prosecution was instituted against Francis Smith, but the result does not appear. The following is a copy of the Indictment.

Londonia. Memorandum quod Samuel Astry armiger coronator et attornatus domini regis in curia ipsius regis coram ipso rege, qui pro eodem domino rege in hac parte sequitur, in propria persona sua venit hic in curiam dicti domini regis coram ipso rege apud Westmonasterium, die Veneris proxima post Octabas Sancti Hillarii isto eodem termino, et pro eodem domino rege dat cùriæ hic intelligi et informari, quod Franciscus Smyth, junior, de parochia Sancti Stephani Wallbrooke, Londonia, Stationer, machinans et malitiose

---

1. Indictments, London and Middlesex, Hil 31 and 32 Charles 2, No. 10.

intendens Willielmum Scroggs militem, Capitalem Justiciarium
domini regis ad placita coram ipso rege tenenda assignatum
(quantum in eo est) scandalizare, et depravare, in hüs
quæ officium suum judiciale tangunt et ipsum Capitalem
Justiciarium in odium et contemptum ducere, sexto die
Januarii anno regni domini nostri Caroli Secundi Dei
gratia Angliæ, Scotiæ, Franciæ, et Hiberniæ Regis, Fidei
Defensoris &c., tricesimo primo, apud parochiam Sancti
Michaelis in Cornhill Londonia, quoddam falsum scandalosum,
malitiosum, et odiosum libellum, intitulatum *A New year's guift
for the Lord Chief in Justice Scgs beinge some remarkes on his
speech made the first day of Michaelmas Terme* 1679 falso, malitiose,
et seditiose publicavit et publicari causavit, in quoquidem falso
et scandaloso libello (inter alia) continetur prout sequitur,
in hæc verba, *When I heard his lordshipp* (dictum Capitalem
Justiciarium innuendo) *after one so greate an aduenture of acquit-
ting Sir George Wakeman* (quendam Georgium Wakeman
Barronettum, qui pro alta proditione nuper indictatus fuit, et
superinde per quandam juratam patriæ inter dominum regem
et præfatum Georgium captam debito modo acquietatus fuit,
innuendo) *in soe capital a crime as beinge hired and receivinge part
of the money to poysen his sacred Majesty* (dominum Carolum
Secundum nunc Regem Angliæ innuendo) *should make an other
adventure of a Speech to Justifie it I stood amazed at his confidence,
instead of admiring his Justice, and was apt to conclude that he
vainely thought, wee never should have another Session of Parliament,
as alsoe that his lordshipp forgott, or never read of Empson and
Dudley.* Et in alio loco ejusdum falsi et scandalosi libelli
continetur prout sequitur in hæc verba. *He* (prædictum
Capitalem Justiciarium innuendo) *sayes moreover that Justice
should flow like a mighty Streame, we see he* (prædictum Capitalem
Justiciarium innuendo) *can speake some truth though hee acte but
little, but let him tell us whether* 10000 *guinnyes will it make a
mighty Dam to stopp this mighty streame, sometimes with some
persons in some cases.* Et in alio loco ejusdum falsi et scandalosi
libelli, (post mentionem factam de triatione cujusdam Edwardi
Colman pro alta proditione) continetur prout sequitur, videlicet,
*and if you doe but observe his lordshipps carriage in summing upp
the evidence both at the one triall and the other* (triationem prædicti
Edwardi Coleman et triationem prædicti Georgii Wakeman

innuendo) *you will assuredly find it as different and contrary as white is to black, or as the lord chiefe Justice is sometymes, to Sir William at others.* In magnum scandalum et contemptum dicti Capitalis Justiciarii, et authoritatis suæ depravationem, ad grave dampnum dicti Capitalis Justiciarii, in malum et pernitiosum exemplum omnium aliorum in tali casu delinquentium, ac contra pacem dicti domini regis nunc; coronam et dignitatem suas, &c."[1]

A copy of this paper is preserved among the Nicholl's Collection of Newspapers, at the Bodleian Library, Oxford.

246.

A Satire against In-justice: or, Scroggs upon Scroggs. 1679. A folio broadside containing 16 three line stanzas.

Jane Curtis was prosecuted by direction of Chief Justice Scroggs, for selling this broadside—" Which his Lordship called " a libel against him : and her friends tendering sufficient bail, " and desiring him to have mercy upon her poverty and condition " he swore by the name of God she should go to prison, and he " would show her no more mercy than they could expect from a " wolf that came to devour them ; and she might bring her " Habeas Corpus, and come out so ; which she was forced to do ; " and after informed against and prosecuted to her utter ruin, " four or five terms after."[2]

A copy is preserved in the Guildhall Library. The entire production is as follows :—

A
SATYR
AGAINST
IN-JUSTICE:
OR,
Sc — — gs upon Sc — — gs.

---

1. A Butcher's Son (Judge) Capital,
    Poor Protestants for to enthral,
    And *England* to enslave, Sirs.

---

1. Indictments, London and Middlesex, Hilary, 31 and 32 Chas. 2, No 1. King's Bench Judgment Roll, Easter 32 Car. 2, rot. 77.
2. Howell's State Trials. Vol. 8, p. 191.

2. Lose but our *Laws* and *Lives* (we must)
    When to do Justice, we intrust
        So known and errand Knaves, Sirs.

3. Some hungry Priests he once did fell
    With mighty Stroaks, and them to Hell
        Sent furiously away, Sirs.

4. Would you know why? The reason's plain;
    They had no English nor French Coyn
        To purchase longer Stay, Sirs.

5. The Pope, to Purgatory sends
    Who neither Money have (nor Friends ;)
        In this he's not alone, Sirs.

6. Our Judge to Mercy's not inclin'd,
    Unless Gold change Conscience and Mind,
        You are infallibly gone, Sirs.

7. His Father once exempted was
    Out of all Juries ; Why? Because
        He was a man of Blood, Sirs.

8. And why the Butcherly Son, forsooth,
    Should now be Judge and Jury both
        Can't well be understood, Sirs.

9. The good old man, with Knife and Knocks,
    Made harmless Sheep and stubborn Ox
        Stoop to him in his fury.

10. But the Brib'd Son, like greedy Auff,
    Kneels down and worships Golden Calf,
        And so did all the Jury.

11. Better hadst been at Father's Trade,
    An honest Livelihood t'have made,
        In hampering Bulls with Collers.

12. Than to thy Country prove unjust ;
    First sell, and then betray thy Trust
        For so many hard Rix-dollers.

13. Priest and Physician thou didst save
    From Gallows, Fire, and the Grave
        For which we can't endure thee.

14.   The one can ne'er absolve thy Sins,
        And th'other, though he now begins,
        Of Knavery ne're can cure thee.

15.   But lest we all should end thy Life,
        And with a keen-whet Chopping-knife,
        In a thousand pieces cleave thee.

16.   Let th' Parliament first him undertake,
        They'll make the Rascal stink at Stake ;
        And so like a Knave let's leave thee.

                    FINIS.

The following is a copy of the information against the
publisher.

Londonia. Memorandum quod Creswell Levins miles attornatus domini regis nunc generalis qui pro eodem domino rege in
hac parte sequitur, in propria persona sua venit hic in curiam
dicti domini regis coram ipso rege apud Westmonasterium, die,
Jovis proxima post tres septimanas Sancti Michaelis isto eodem
termino, et pro eodem domino rege dat curiæ hic intelligi et
informari quod Jana Curtice uxor Langley Curtice de parochia
Sancti Martini Ludgate Londonia Stationer, machinans et malitiose
intendens Willielmum Scroggs militem Capitalem Justiciarium
domini regis ad placita coram ipso rege tenenda assignatum
scandalizare et ipsum Capitalem Justiciarium in hüs quæ ipsum
Capitalem Justiciarium et officium suum judicialem tangunt et
authoritatem dicti domini regis in odium et contemptum ducere,
vicesimo die Octobris anno regni domini nostri Caroli Secundi,
Dei gratia Angliæ Scotiæ Franciæ et Hiberniæ Regis Fidei
Defensoris &c. tricesimo primo, apud parochiam Sancti Martini
Ludgate prædictam in Warda de Farringdon extra Londoniam,
quoddam falsum malitiosum infamosum scandalosum et odiosum
libellum intitulatum *A Satyr against In-justice : or Sc—gs upon
Sc—gs.* in manibus suis obtinuit in quoquidem libello (inter alia)
continetur prout sequitur in hac verba *Some hungry Priests he*
(prædictum Capitalem Justiciarium innuendo) *once did fell With
mighty Stroaks, and them to Hell Sent furiously away, Sirs. Would
you know why ? The reason's plain ; They had no English nor French
Coyn To purchase longer Stay, Sirs. The Pope, to Purgatory sends
Who neither Money have (nor Friends ;) In this he's not alone, Sirs.*

Our Judge (prædictum Capitalem Justiciarium innuendo) *to Mercy's not inclin'd, Unless Gold change Conscience and Mind, You are infallibly gone, Sirs.* Et prædicta Jana Curtice sciens libellum prædictum fore scandalosum et infamosum libellum postea scilicet dicto vicesimo die Octobris anno supradicto apud Londoniam prædictam in parochia et warda prædictis idem libellum publicavit et venditioni exposuit in magnum scandalum et vilependium et contemptum dicti Capitalis Justiciarii et authoritatis dicti domini Regis, in malum exemplum omnium aliorum in tali casu delinquentium ac contra pacem dicti domini regis nunc coronam et dignitatem suas &c.[1]

247.

Some observations upon the late Trials of Sir George Wakeman, Corker, & Marshal, &c. By Tom Ticklefoot, the Tabourer, late Clerk to Justice Clodpate. 1679.

For publishing this book, Edward Berry, Stationer, of Gray's Inn, was committed by Chief Justice Scroggs; and though he tendered £1000 bail, yet the Chief Justice said he would take no bail; he should go to prison, and come out according to law. And after he, with much trouble and charge got out by a Habeas Corpus, he was forced by himself or his attorney to attend five terms before he could be discharged, though no information was exhibited against him in all that time.

Francis Smith was also prosecuted for publishing this book. He was tried at the Guildhall, in 1680, and a small fine imposed on him. Jane Curtis was also tried for the same offence.[2] The book itself is printed at length in Howell's State Trials, Vol. 7, p. 687.

248.

The Serious Queries against the Conventicle Act, proving it to be against the laws of God, of Nature, and of Magna Charta. 1680.

1. Indictments, London and Middlesex, Mich. 31 Car. 2, No. 43.
2. Howell's State Trials, Vol. 7, p. 931 ; Vol. 8, p. 191.

For the publication of this book, Francis Smith was committed into the custody of five of the King's messengers, by the Council-board to about £50 charge and damage.[1]

249.

The Protestant Domestic Intelligence, or News both from City and Country. No. 57. Tuesday, January 20, 1679.

For publishing this newspaper, a prosecution was instituted against Benjamin Harris. The information is as follows :—

Memorandum quod Samuel Astry Armiger Coronator et Attornatus domini regis in curia ipsius regis coram ipso rege qui pro eodem domino rege in hac parte sequitur in propria persona sua venit hic in curiam dicti domini regis coram ipso rege apud Westmonasterium die veneris post Octabas Sancti Hillarii isto eodem termino, et pro eodem domino rege dat curiæ hic intelligi et informari quod cum Willielmus Scroggs miles vicesimo die Januarii anno regni dicti domini regis nunc tricesimo primo, et diu antea et continue abinde hucusqne fuit et adhuc est Capitalis Justiciarius domini regis ad placita coram ipso rege tenenda assignatus et officium illud capitalis Justiciarii bene et fideliter exercuit absque aliqua oppressione injuria sive malegestura quidam tamen Benjaminus Harris de parochia Sancti Michaelis in Cornhill Londonia Stationer machinans et malitiose intendens prædictum Willielmum Scroggs militem Capitalem Justiciarium domini regis ad placita coram ipso rege tenenda assignatum scandalizare ac in odium et contemptum ducere prædicto vicesimo die Januarii anno regni domini nostri Caroli Secundi Dei gratia Angliæ Scotiæ Franciæ et Hiberniæ Regis Fidei Defensoris &c. tricesimo primo, apud parochiam Sancti Michaelis Cornhill Londonia prædictam quoddam falsum malitiosum scandalosum et odiosum libellum intitulatum *The Protestant Domestick Intelligence or News both from City and Country. Published to prevent false reports,* falso malitiose et scandalose imprimi causavit et publicavit in quo quidem falso malitioso et scandaloso libello (inter alia) continetur prout sequitur *On Friday last, the 16 instant, Articles of high Misdemeanor were offered by way of Complaint to the Kings most Excellent Majestie, and the Right Honourable the Lords and others of His*

---

1.   Howell's State Trials, Vol. 7, p. 950.

Majesties most Honorable Privie Council by Dr. Oates and Captain William Bedlow, against the Lord Chief Justice Scroggs, (prædictum Capitalem Justiciarium innuendo) *therefore if any have been oppressed or injured by the said Lord Chief Justice, they will be speedilie Heard, if they in time come in; the Cause will its thought be heard the beginning of February.* In magnum scandalum ignominium et contemptum dicti Capitalis Justiciarii et authoritatis suæ in malum et pernitiosum exemplum omnium aliorum in tali casu delinquentium ac contra pacem dicti domini regis nunc coronam et dignitatem suas &c.[1]

The result of the prosecution does not appear.

A copy of this newspaper is preserved in the Library of the British Museum.

250.

A speech lately made by a noble Peer of the Realm. London. Printed for F.S. at the Elephant and Castle near the Royal Exchange in Cornhill. 1681.

This was published by Francis Smith, the bookseller, and for so doing, a prosecution was instituted against him. He was tried and convicted, but his sentence does not appear.

The information is as follows :—

Memorandum quod Cresswell Levinz miles attornatus Domini Regis nunc generalis qui pro eodem domino rege in hac parte sequitur in propria persona sua venit hic in curiam dicti domini regis coram ipso rege apud Westmonasterium die Sabbati proxima post crastinum Purificationis Beatæ Mariæ Virginis isto eodem termino et pro eodem domino rege dat curiæ hic intelligi et informari quod Franciscus Smith nuper de parochia Sancti Michaelis Cornhill · Londonia Bibliopola vicesimo quarto die Decembris anno regni domini nostri Caroli Secundi nunc Regis Angliæ &c. tricesimo secundo apud parochiam prædictam infra civitatem Londoniæ prædictam vi et armis &c. falso et malitiose scripsit et publicavit et scribi imprimi et publicari causavit quendam fictum falsum seditiosum et scandalosum libellum intitulatum *A Speech lately made by a Noble Peere of the Realme* in quo quidem libello continetur hæc falsa ficta et scandalosa verba sequentia *My lords 'tis a very hard thing to say that we cannot trust*

1. Indictments, London and Middlesex, Hil. 31 and 32 Car. 2, No. 2.

the King, and that wee have beene already deceived so often that wee see plainely the apprehensions of discontent in the people is no argument at Court And though our Prince be in himselfe an excellent person that the people have the greatest inclinations imaginable to love; yet we must say he is such an one as no story affords us a paralell of; howe plaine and how many are the profes of the designe to murder him, how little is he apprehensive of it. Et in altera parte ejusdem libelli continetur hæc falsa ficta et scandalosa verba sequentia scilicet *My lords I here of a bargaine in the house of Commons and an addresse made to the King, but this I know and must boldly say it, and plainely, that the nation is betrayed if upon any termes we part with our money till wee are sure the King is ours, have what lawes you will, and what condicions you will they will be of no use but wast paper before Easter if the Court have money to set up for popery and arbitrary designe in the meane while on the other hand give me leave to tell you my lords the King hath no reason to distrust his people no man can goe home and say that If the King comply with his people they will doe nothing for him but teare all up from him we want a government and we want a Prince that we may trust even with the spending of half our annuall revenues for some time for the preservation of the Kingdome.* In malum et pernitiosum exemplum omnium aliorum in tali casu delinquentium ac contra pacem dicti domini regis nunc coronam et dignitatem suas &c.[1]

This speech was never spoken; and was, by order of the Lords, burnt by the hands of the hangman. A copy is preserved among the Chetham Collection of Broadsides, Manchester, No. 2628; and it is also printed in Cobbett's Parliamentary History, Vol. 4, App. No. X.

251.

An Act of Common Councill of the City of London, (made in the first and second years of the reign of Philip and Mary) for retrenching of the expenses of the Lord Mayor and Sheriffs, etc. Published, with additional reasons for putting the said Act in present execution, and now offered to the consideration of

---

[1]. Indictments, London and Middlesex, Hil. 32 and 33 Car. 2, No. 28.

all good Citizens by some Well-Wishers of the present
and future prosperity of the said City. Presented to
my Lord Mayor, Aldermen, and Sheriffs. London:
Printed for F. Smith, at the Elephant and Castle in
Cornhill, near the Royal Exchange. 1680.

For this book, an indictment was preferred against Francis
Smith, the publisher, at the Guildhall, London, on September
16, 1680, but it was thrown out by the grand jury. The best
account of this book, and the prosecution thereupon, will be
found in a tract published by Smith, at the time, and entitled, "An
"Account of the injurious proceedings of Sir George Jeffreys,
"Knight, late Recorder of London, against Francis Smith,
"Bookseller, with his arbitrary carriage towards the grand jury
"at Guildhall, Sept. 16, 1680, upon an indictment exhibited
"against the said Francis Smith, for publishing a pretended libel;
"entitled, 'An Act of Common Council.'"

The following is a copy of the indictment against Smith :—

London, ss. The Jurors for our Lord the King upon their
oaths present that Francis Smith, late of London, Bookseller,
being a man seditious and pernicious, plotting and intending the
peace and common tranquillity of this kingdom to disturb, and
discord, differences and ill will, amongst the citizens and inhabitants of the city of London, to stir up, provoke and procure;
also the Mayor, Aldermen, and Sheriffs of the City of London,
now in being, and the Mayor, Aldermen, and Sheriffs of the City
of London, for the time past in great odium, contempt, and base
accompt to bring; the same Francis Smith, the 17th day of
August, in the reign of our Sovereign Lord Charles the Second,
by the grace of God, of England, Scotland, France and Ireland,
King, Defender of the Faith, &c. the two and thirtieth at London,
viz. in the parish of St. Michael Cornhill in the ward of Cornhill
London, aforesaid, with force and arms &c. unlawfully, wickedly,
maliciously, scandalously, and seditiously printed, and caused to be
printed, a certain malicious, scandalous, and seditious book, of and
concerning the expences of the Lord Mayors, Aldermen, and
Sheriffs of the City aforesaid, in their houses, in the time of their
several offices; entituled *An Act of Common Council of the City*

of London, (made in the first and second years of the reign of Philip and Mary) for retrenching of the expences of the Lord Mayor and Sheriffs &c. Published with additional Reasons for putting the said Act in present Execution, and now offered to the Consideration of all good Citizens by some Well-wishers of the present and future prosperity of the said City. Presented to my Lord Mayor, Aldermen, and Sheriffs. In which book by the said Francis Smith then so as aforesaid published, printed and caused to be printed, the same Francis Smith then and there, viz. the day and year before mentioned, at the parish and ward aforesaid, mischievously, unlawfully, wickedly, maliciously, scandalously, and seditiously printed, made known openly, and published, mischievously, malicious, scandalous, and seditious sentences, in these English words following, viz. :—

Reader,

   As by this Act you may observe, that our Predecessors taking notice, that the extravagancies of Mayors and Sheriffs caused (as they say) almost all good citizens to flie and refuse the service; so to prevent that mischief in the future, they limited them in their living to the method directed by this Act. And if when little was spent besides the growth of our own Country, Beer and Ale being then their drink, they thought it their wisdom to set bounds to Luxurious Profuseness, there is much more reason for it now, when Debauchery is come to that height, that the fifth part of the charge of a Shrievalty is in in Wine, the growth of another Country. And when Feasts, hardly heard of in former times, are risen to that Excess, as would be scandalous to mention, as those called the Chequer and Spittle Feasts; the first costing in Wine betwixt Seventy and Eighty Pounds; and the latter. after the pretended Service of God in hearing a Sermon, costs above Three Hundred Pounds to each Sheriff. And though much after this rate is the rest of the year spent, yet when the Example of this Act is urged for laying aside these sinful Feasts, and reducing the rest unto this Pattern, which is a wholsom Law; some who should see to the putting it in execution, will not hear of it; and possibly, because they would have others be as profuse as themselves have been, though there are these Reasons for a Reformation herein.

And these mischievous, malicious, and seditious sentences, in these English words following, viz. :—

Because nothing can tend more to the Advancement of any City or Country than the having wise and good Magistrates; and that so long as the great expence of Shrievalties continue, the City must (as this Act suggests) have an Eye to Wealth, more than Parts or Vertue, in the choice of their Sheriffs; and that such as their Sheriffs are, such will the Court of Aldermen be: and therefore as necessary for the good Government of this great City, the charge of Shrievalties ought to be reduced to such an Order and Method, as may be an Encouragement to Men of more Honesty than Riches to serve the Place.

And these mischievous, malicious, scandalous, and seditious sentences, in these English words following, viz.

No man hath reason to be expensive in his Shrievalty; because though the Court of Aldermen hath a rule for supplying, as any die their vacant places out of those that have served Sheriffs, yet they make their Election to depend upon the uncertain humour of their Court, thereby frustrating when they please all Compensation for the Expence and Drudgery of a Shrievalty, as lately appeared in their Choice of Sir Simon Lewis, one of their present Sheriffs, rejecting Sir Thomas Stamp, who had served the Place several years before with good approbation, and was presented to them by the Ward he lives in as a deserving Person. And whereas each Ward when they want an Alderman, do present two Commoners to the Court, for them to chuse one; the Ward of Bassishaw, to the end that Sir Thomas might unavoidably be chosen, joyned the younger (and not the elder) Sheriff with him, not thinking that an old Sheriff would be baulked, to chuse one that had not served his year; and yet notwithstanding, the Court by their Prerogative passed by Sir Thomas, to the disappointing of the Ward that sent him. And this Example is, I suppose a good reason for Sheriffs in the future not to spend more in their Shrievalties, than is necessary, when their Reward is so uncertain.

And these mischievous, malicious, scandalous, and seditious sentences, in these English words following, viz.

Debauchery in this Expence is a Sin before God, and were it known, would be a scandal in the sight of Man; as appears in that of Three thousand Pounds Expence in all manner of ways, above Five hundred Pounds is in Wine; when a Lord, or Gentleman that formerly lived at the rate of Ten or Twelve thousand Pounds per annum, did not, as is well known (but thirty years ago) spend an hundred Pounds in Wine.

To the great Scandal and Contempt of our said Lord the King, to the great Reproach and Scandal of the Authority of the Mayor, Aldermen, and Sheriffs, of the City aforesaid; to the great Disturbance of the Peace of our said Lord the King, to the Evil Example of others in the like case offending, and against the Peace of the said Lord the King, his Crown and Dynasty, &c.

A copy of this pamphlet is preserved in the Guildhall Library, London.

252.

Malice defeated : or a brief relation of the accusation and deliverance of Elizabeth Cellier, wherein her proceedings, both before and during her confinement, are particularly related, and the mystery of the Meal Tub fully discovered. 1680.

For writing, printing, and publishing this book, Mrs. Elizabeth Cellier, was tried at the Old Bailey, in September, 1680, and found guilty. She was sentenced to a fine of £1000, and to be imprisoned until payment; and also to stand on the pillory three times, the first time at the Maypole, in the Strand, the second time in Covent Garden, and the third time at Charing Cross; and her books were to be burnt by the Common Hangman.

The indictment against her is as follows :—

Juratores pro domino rege super sacramentum suum præsentant quod Elizabetha Cellier uxor ———— Cellier de parochia Sancti Clementis Dacorum in comitatu Middlesexiæ generosi, eadem Elizabetha existente religionis papalis, Deum præ oculis suis non habens sed instigatione diabolica mota et seductà et falso et malitiose machinans et intendens serenissimum Dominum nostrum Carolum Secundum Dei gratia Angliæ, Scotiæ, Franciæ et Hiberniæ Regem et gubernationem suam hujus regni Angliæ necnon veram religionem protestantem infra hoc regnum Angliæ lege stabilitatam, in odium, infamiam et contemptum inducere et inferre, et scandalum et infamiam imponere super quibusdam personis qui producti fuissent testes et testimonium dedissent ex parte dicti domini regis contra prædictam Elizabetham Cellier et alias personas de alta proditione indictatas primo die Augusti anno regni dicti domini regis tricesimo secundo apud prædictam parochiam Sancti Clementis Dacorum in Comitatu Middlesexiæ prædicto falso malitiose et seditiose scripsit et publicavit et scribi imprimi publicari causavit quendam fictum falsum et scandalosum libellum intitulatum *Malice defeated: or a brief relation of the accusation and deliverance of Elizabeth Cellier, wherein her proceedings both before and during her confinement are particularly related, and the mystery of the Meal-Tub fully discovered. Together with an abstract of her arraignment and tryal, written by herself, for the satisfaction of all lovers of undisguized truth.* In quo quidem libello continentur hæc falsa ficta et scandalosa verba et figuræ sequentia, scilicet. *I hope it will not seem strange to any honest and loyal person, of what way or religion soever, that I being born and bred up under Protestant Parents, should now openly profess myself of another Church.* (Ecclesiam Romanam innuendo). *For my education being in those times, when my own Parents and Relations, for their constant and faithful affection to the King and Royal Family, were Persecuted, the King himself Murthered, the Bishops and Church destroy'd, the whole Loyal party merely for being so, opprest and ruin'd; And all as was pretended by the Authors of these villanies, for their being Papists and Idolaters, the constant Character given by them, to the King and his friend, to make them odious, they assuming to themselves, only the Name of Protestants, making that the Glorious title by which they pretended right to all things. These sort of Proceedings, as I grew in understanding, produc'd in me more and more Horror of the party that committed them, and put me on Inquiry into that Religion, to which they pretended the greatest Antipathy, wherein I thank God, I found my Innate Loyalty, not only Confirm'd, but Incourag'd, and let Callumny say what it will; I never heard from any Papist as they call them, Priests nor lay-man, but that they and I, and all true Catholicks, owe our lives to the defence of our Lawful King, which our Present Soveraign, Charles the Second is, whom God long and happily preserve so. These sorts of Doctrines agreeing to my Publick Morralls, and no way as ever I was taught, contradicting my Private ones, Commending at the same time to me, Charity and Devotion, I without any scruple, have hitherto followed Glorying to myself to be in Communion with those* (papistas innuendo) *who were the humble Instruments of his Majesties happy Preservation, from the fatall Battel at Worcester, and whom though poor, no Temptation could invite, to betray him to those, who, by a pretended Protestant principle, sought his Innocent blood. These truths I hope may satisfy any indifferent person in my first*

*Change, nor can they wonder at my continuance therein, notwith-
standing the Horrid Crimes of Treason and Murther laid to the charge
of some persons considerable, for their quallity and fortunes in that
party. For when I reflected who were the witnesses, and what unlikely
things they deposed, and observ'd, that many of the chiefest Sticklers
for the Plot, were those, or the Sons of those, that acted the principal
parts in the last Tragedy, which History told me too, had the Prologue
of a pretended Popish Plot. I say, these things made me doubtful of
the whole; and the more I search'd for Truth, the more I doubted that
the old Enemies of the Crown were again at work for its destruction.
I being fully confirm'd in this, thought it my duty, through all sorts of
hazards, to relieve the Poor Imprison'd Catholicks, who in great numbers
were locked up in Gaoles, starving for want of bread, and this I did
some months before I ever saw the Countess of Powis or any of those
Honourable persons that were accused, or receiving one penny of their
mony directly or indirectly, till about the latter end of January, (78)
the Prisoners increasing very much.* Et in alia parte ejusdem libelli
(inter alia) continentur hæc falsa ficta et scandalosa verba scilicet
*About this time I went daily to the prisons to perform those offices of
Charity I was oblig'd to, And on Thursday, January the 9th, (78)
I Din'd in Newgate in the Room called the Castle on the Master's side
Debtors, and about four in the afternoon, I came down into the Lodge
with five Women, of which three were Protestants, and we all heard
Terrible Grones and Squeeks which came out of the Dungeon, called
the Condemned Hole. I asked Harris the Turnkey, what Dole-full cry
it was, he said, it was a Woman in Labour. I bid him put us into
the Room to her, and we would help her, but he drove us away very
rudely, both out of the Lodge, and from the door; we went behind the
Gate, and there lissened, and soon found that it was the voice of a strong
man in Torture, and heard, as we thought, between his grones, the
winding up of some Engine: these cries stop'd the passengers under the
Gate, and we six went to the Turner's shop without the Gate, and stood
there amaized with the Horror, and dread of what we heard; when one
of the officers of the Prison came out in great hast, seeming to run from
the Noise. One of us catcht hold of him, saying, Oh! What are they
doing in the Prison?* Officer. *I dare not tell you.* Mistres. *It's
a Man upon the Rack, I'le lay my life on't.* Officer. *It is something
like it.* Cellier. *Who is it Prance?* Officer. *Pray Madam do not
ask me, for I dare not tell ye, but it is that I am not able to heare any
longer: Pray let me go, with that he run away toward Holborn as fast*

*as he could. We heard these grones perfectly to the end of the Old
Bayly, they continued till near seven of the Clock, and then a person in
the habit of a Minister, of middle stature, Gray hair'd, accompanied
with two other Men, went into the Lodge, the Prisoners were locked up,
and the outward door of the Lodge also, at which I set a person to
stand, and observe what she could ; and a Prisoner loaded with Irons,
was brought into the Lodge, and examin'd a long time, and the Prisoners
that came down as low as they could, heard the person Examin'd with
great vehemency, say often, I know nothing of it, I'me innocent : he
forc'd me to bely myself, What would you have me say ? Will you
murther me because I will not bely myself and others ? Several other
such like expressions they heard spoken as by one in great Agony.
About four of the clock the next morning, the Prisoners that lay in a
Place above the hole, heard the same cry again two houres, and on
Saturday Morning again, and about Eight a Clock that morning a
person I employ'd to spy out the truth of that affair, did see the
Turn keys carrying a Bed into the hole, she asked whoe it was for, they
told her, it was for Prance, who was gone Mad, and had tore his bed
in pieces. That night the Examiners came again, and after an houres
Conference Prance was led away to the Prsss-yard : This, and many
things of the like nature, made me very Inquisitive to know what
pass'd in the Prison. Soon after this Francis Corral a Coachman, that
had been put into Newgate, upon suspicion of carrying away Sir
Edmond-Bury-Godfrey's body, and lay there 13 weeks and three days
in great missery, got out, I went to see him, and found him a sad
spectacle, having the flesh worn away, and great holes in both his legs,
by the weight of his Irons. And having been chain'd so long double,
that he could not stand upright ; he told me much of his hard and cruel
usage, as that he had been squeez'd and hasped into a thing like a
Trough, in a dungeon under ground ; which put him to inexpressible
torment, insomuch that he soonded, and that a Person in the habit of a
Minister stood by all the time. That a Duke beat him, Pull'd him by
the Hair, and set his drawn Sword to his breast three times, and
swore he would run him through ; and another great Lord, laid down a
heap of Gold, and told him it was five hundred Pounds, and that he
should have it all, and be taken into the aforesaid Duke's house, if he
would confess what they would have him ; and one F. a vintner,
that lives at the sign of the Half Moon in Ch—— St—— by whose
contrivance he was accused, took him aside, and bid him name some
person, and say, they Imploy'd him to take up the dead body in*

*Somerset-yard, and gave him mony for so doing; that if he would do
this, both F. and he, should have mony enough.   He also told me, that
he was kept from Thursday till Sunday without victualls or drink, having
his hands every Night Chain'd behind him, and being all this time
locked to a staple which was driven into the Floor, with a chain not
above a yard long, that in this great extremity, was forc'd to drink
his own water; and that the Jaylor beat his wife, because she brought
victuals, and prayed that he might have it, and threw Milk on the
ground, and bid her be gone, and not look at him.*   Et in altera parte
ejusdem libelli continentur (inter alia) hæc falsa ficta et scandalosa verba sequentia scilicet *My arraignment, which (in confidence
of my own innocence) I continually prest for.   Not but that I knew
the danger, as to this Life, of encountering the Devil in the worst
of his Instruments, which are PERJURERS INCOURAGED to
that degree as that profligated Wretch* quendam Thomam Dangerfield testem productum ex parte domini regis contra prædictam
Elizabetham Cellier pro alta proditione innuendo *was, and has
been since his being exposed to the World in his true colours both at
mine, and at another's Tryal.*   Et in altera parte ejusdem libelli
continentur hæc falsa ficta et scandalosa verba sequentia scilicet
*Nor have I since received anything towards my losses, or the least
civility from any of them.   Whilst Dangerfield* (prædictam Thomam
Dangerfield iterum innuendo) *(when made a Prisoner for apparent
Recorded Rogueries,) was visited by and from Persons of Considerable
Quality, with great Sums of Gold and Silver, to encourage him in the
new Villanies he had undertaken, not against Me alone, but Persons in
whose Safety all good Men (as well Protestants as others) in the three
kingdoms are concerned.*   Et in altera parte ejusdem libelli vocati
A Postscript to the impartial reader continente hæc falsa ficta et
scandalosa verba sequentia scilicet *And whensoever his Majesty
pleases to make it as safe and honourable to speak truth as it is
apparent it hath been gainful and meritorious to do the contrary, there
will not want witnesses to testify the truth of more than I have written
and persons that are above being made the hangman's hounds for
weekly pensions, or any other considerations whatsoever.*   In malum et
perniciosissimum exemplum omnium aliorum in tali casu delinquentium contra pacem dicti domini regis coronam et dignitatem
suas.   By a Treasury warrant, dated May 16th, 1687, Mrs. Cellier
was discharged from the judgment which had been pronounced
against her.[1]

1.   Treasury Records; King's Warrant Book, No. 5, p. 105.

253.

The two first books of Philostratus, concerning the life of Apollonius Tyaneus; written originally in Greek, and now published in English: together with philological notes upon each chapter; by Charles Blount. London. 1680. Folio.

According to Dr. Adam Clarke, "this piece was published with the design to invalidate the testimony of the evangelists concerning the miracles of our Blessed Lord." A few copies only were dispersed before the work was suppressed. Two copies exist in the British Museum Library.

254.

A Popish damnable Plot against our Religion and Liberties, fairly laid open and discovered in the Breviats of Threescore and Four Letters and Papers of Intelligence past betwixt the Pope, Duke of York, Cardinal Norfolk, Cardinal Cibo, Cardinal Barbarina, Nuncio and Internuncio for the Pope in Italy, France, and Flanders, and the Lord Arundel, Mr. Coleman, Mr. Cooke, Mr. Coune. And also the said Mr. Coleman, Albany, Sr. German, Lybourn, Sheldon, Throgmorton, and several others. As they were drawn up by the Secret Committee of the House of Commons, for the satisfaction of the House of Lords in the Bill against the Duke of York and expected Tryals of the Lords. Now published for the vindication of the House of Commons upon the said Bill, and for satisfaction of all the faithful subjects of His Majestie's Kingdom, with several animadversions and remarks made upon the said letters. London. 1680.

This was a pamphlet containing reflections upon Sir Edward Dering, a member of the House of Commons; and on November 15, 1680, upon a debate in that House, it was resolved that "all the reflective parts upon Sir Edward Dering were false, scandalous and libellous." Mr. Yarrington, who was summoned to the bar of the House with others, respecting the printing and publishing of this book, stated that all the animadversions contained therein were penned by Dr. Tonge, and that he received the abstract of the several letters therein mentioned, from a Scrivener in Essex Court, in the Temple. It was thereupon resolved that Dr. Tonge should have notice to attend the House the next day, and that Mr. Yarrington and the others concerned in the publication of the pamphlet, should be committed to the custody of the Serjeant at Arms for their breach of privilege; but they were all in a few days discharged from custody, after receiving the censure of the House.[1] A copy of this pamphlet is preserved in the British Museum Library. It is in folio, and contains 31 pages.

255.

A Dialogue betwixt the Devil and the Ignoramus Doctor.

A set of verses printed and published by Nathaniel Thomson, a printer, living in the parish of St. Dunstan in the West. For this publication he was prosecuted. The following is a copy of the indictment :—

Londonia. Juratores pro domino rege super sacramentum suum præsentant quod Nathaniel Thomson nuper de parochia Sancti Dunstani in Occidente in Warda de Farringdon exti Londoniam prædictam Typographus decimo die Octobris anno regni domini nostri Caroli Secundi Dei gratia Angliæ Scotiæ Franciæ et Hiberniæ regis Fidei Defensoris &c. tricesimo tertio illicite nequiter et malitiose machinans et intendens quietum statum et communem pacem et tranquillitatem ligeorum et subditorum dicti domini regis infra civitatem Londoniæ et alibi infra hoc regnum Angliæ inquietare et perturbare, et diversas differentias inter ligeos et subditos prædictos excitare movere et procurare, necnon quendam Titum Oates clericum unum divulgatorum anglice *discoverers* et testium proditoriæ conspirationis papistarum dictum dominum regem nunc ad murdrandum et veram protestantem religionem infra hoc regnum Angliæ stabilitatam et

---

1. Commons' Journals, vol. 9, pp. 649, 651, 652, 654, 656.

professam ad destruendam in maximum odium contemptum
infamiam et scandalum cum omnibus ligeis et subditis dicti
domini regis nunc eundem Titum Oates adtunc cognoscentibus
et tunc imposterum cognoscendis inducere, ac diversas lites et
differentias inter præfatum Titum Oates ac omnes prædictos
ligeos et subditos dicti domini regis eidem Tito Oates tunc
cognitos et cognoscendos excitare movere et procurare, necnon
bona nomen famam testimonium et reputationem ejusdem Titi
Oates pejorare et auferre postea scilicet dicto decimo die Octobris
anno supradicto apud Londoniam videlicet in parochiam et warda
prædictis ad nefandissimas et malitiosas machinationes et intentiones suas prædictas celerius efficienda et exequenda quoddam
falsum scandalosum et odiosum libellum de et concernentem
præfato Tito Oates et ad defamationem opprobium et scandalum
ejusdem Titi Oates intitulatum *A Dialogue betwixt the Devil and
the Ignoramus Doctor* illicite nequiter et malitiose devisatum
compositum et scriptum per quosdam homines quorum nomina
juratoribus prædictis adhuc ignota sunt ipse prædictus Nathaniel
Thomson adtunc et ibidem illicite nequiter libellose et malitiose
impressit et publicavit et imprimi et publicari causavit tenor
cujusdem libelli sequitur scilicet :—

A Dialogue betwixt the Devil and the Ignoramus [Salamanca][1] *Doctor.*

Devil.

Behold from the Infernal Lake I'm come,
To fright thy Soul to its Eternal Doom :
To tell thee, Villain, that thy Roign's expir'd,
And now be sure thou shalt no longer hir'd
Be by Me, nor any of the Damn'd,
To drench in Innocent Blood this mournful Land.
Hence then begone, and do no more pursue
Villanies Hell could ne'er act, but by you :
Now Heaven stops my Power and I thy Hand,
And now I tell thee, Doctor, Thou art damn'd.

Doctor.

O Spectre ! spare awhile my dreadful Doom !
Go back and tell the Damn'd, I come, I come ;
Only let me compleat the Ills I've begun,
Then Heaven farewel, and unto You I come.

1. This word is in the printed book, but is omitted in the indictment

Devil.

The Blood o' th' Innocent aloud does cry,
Revenge, Revenge, on cursed Dr. Ti——
No more o' th' Innocent shall bleed, nor die.

Doctor.

Well, the time's come, the fatal day's at hand,
That I for ever, ever must be damn'd :
O curs'd Revenge ! what Mischiefs have I done ?
Abjur'd the Father, and blasphem'd the Son.
The Sacred Spirit of Truth at once have I
Banish'd ; and that my vengeance I might buy,
I've caus'd the best of Innocents to dye.
See where their Ghosts appear in purple ray'd,
Victims, by Perjury above betray'd :
See how they shake their Heads, and bleed afresh ;
Their wounds gape wide in their new murder'd flesh ;
And these most frightful Visions come, 'cause I
Th' bloody villanous Murderer stand by.
'Tis true that I the cruel Murderer am,
And thousands more by Perjury to trepan.
I solemnly did vow, and often swear,
And none t' escape, from the Peasant to the Peer ;
Nay Sacred Prelates, Princes, Queens, and Kings.
Should have made up my Bloody Offerings.
Ten thousand more of Innocents had dy'd,
'Cause I King, Queen, and Duke had Sacrificed :
Cities and Towns I'd Fir'd, if not withstood,
And quench'd the flames with Innocent Blood.
Let me but live in this world three years more,
This Island then shall swim in Christian gore ;
I'le subvert Governments, and murder Kings,
Sow discord among friends : I'll do such things
Shall make the World believe there is not that
Villanous thing I have not power to act
I'le make the World believe (let me but stay)
That Light is Darkness, and that Night is Day ;
That I the Saviour of the Nation am,
And that CHRIST was of no avail to man ;
Then I the Sacred Gospels will destroy,

Swear they'r but fictious Stories, and a Lye,
Perswade them that the Bible's but a Farce,
No more to be esteemed than is my A——
So I'le improve the Art of Perjury,
That none who are not skill'd in Villany
Shall live; thus will I fit this Isle for Hell,
And then adieu the World, and Heaven farewel.
Thus I a Learned Doctor will commence,
And by the People be ador'd for Nonsence,
And with Sedition I their Souls will influence.

Devil.

Peace thou prophane wretch, hold, villain, hold,
For now with Heaven and Earth thou art too bold,
And I must tell thee, another Winter old
Thou shalt not be, thy life and soul are sold:
When flat on th' Altar Thou thyself didst lay,
Remember that thou gav'st thy Soul away
To me; and swor'st for ever thou'dst be mine,
Might'st thou but compass thy Hellish Design,
To imbrue thy Hands in Innocent Blood,
And murder all who had the face of good:
Devils and Hell thou hast in this outdone,
By thy damn'd Perjury ith' face oth' Sun.
Hence then begone to Hell, away, away,
For in this place thou shalt no longer stay.

[Spoken by an old Acquaintance.]

Why how now Doctor, vanish'd fled and gone,
What none but Monsieur Devil and You alone?
Are all you Papists come to this damn'd end,
Thus to be hamper'd and ridden by a Fiend?
Unpitied ly; blaspheme and groan thy last,
Belch forth thy unhallow'd Soul, and blast
Hell itself, with thy unsanctified Breath,
And groveling ith' shades of Eternal Death,
I leave thee. Ha, ha, ha, ha, poor Doctor,
Good Night little good Mr. Devil's Doctor.

In contemptum dicti domini regis nunc, legumque suarum, ad magnum opprobium scandalum defamationem et infamiam præfati Titi Oates, in magnam perturbationem pacis dicti domini

regis et populi sui inquietudinem, in malum exemplum omnium aliorum consimili casu delinquentium, ac contra pacem dicti domini regis nunc coronam et dignitatem suas &c.[1]
The result of the prosecution does not appear.

I have not been able to meet with a copy of the original verses, which, no doubt, would be printed in the form of a broadside; but they are reprinted in a little book entitled "A Collection of 86 Loyal Poems, all of them written upon the two late plots, viz., The Horrid Salamanca Plot in 1678, and the present fanatical conspiracy in 1683." Collected by N[athaniel] T[hompson.] 1685.

256.

The true Domestic Intelligence, or News both from City and Country. No. 83, From Friday, April 16, to Tuesday, April 20, 1680.

Ditto——No. 84, From Tuesday, April 20, to Friday, April 23, 1680.

These periodicals, copies of which are preserved in the British Museum Library, were printed and published by Nathaniel Thompson and William Badcock, and a prosecution was thereupon instituted against them. They were tried and found guilty, and a fine of £3 6s. 8d. set on each of them. The following is a copy of the information:—

Memorandum quod Creswell Levinz miles attornatus domini regis nunc generalis qui pro eodem domino rege in hac parte sequitur in propria persona sua venit hic in curiam dicti domini regis coram ipso rege apud Westmonasterium, die Mercurii proximo post quindenam Paschæ isto eodem termino, et pro eodem domino rege dat curiam hic intelligi et informari, quod Nathaniel Thompson de parochia Sancti Dunstani in occidente Londoniæ Printer, et Willielmus Badcocke de parochia Sanctæ Bridgettæ alias Brides Londoniæ Wiredrawer, machinantes et malitiose intendentes agitare et procurare seditionem, litem, et discordiam inter diversos fideles subditos dicti domini regis nunc infra hoc regnum Angliæ, et præcipue inter gubernatores, inhabitantes, et parochianos parochiæ Sanctæ Bridgettæ alias Brides Londoniæ, et gubernationem, necnon gubernatores

1. Indictments, London and Middlesex, Hil. 33 Charles 2, No. 22.

ejusdem parochiæ in contemptum, scandalum et infamiam cum
prædictis parochianis prædictæ parochiæ Sanctæ Bridgettæ
alias Brides inducere et inferre, decimo sexto die Aprilis,
anno regni dicti domini regis nunc tricesimo secundo, apud
parochiam Sancti Dunstani in occidente in wardà de Farringdon
extra Londoniam, quoddam odiosum, scandalosum, et diffamatorium libellum, intitulatum *The True Domestic Intelligence or
News both from City and Country* causaverunt, et uter eorum
causavit imprimi, publicari, et dispergi in, per, et trans totam
civitatem Londoniæ, et diversos alios comitatus et locos infra
hoc regnum Angliæ, in quoquidem libello (inter alia) continetur
quædam falsa, ficta, seditiosa, et scandalosa materia prout
sequitur in hiis Anglicanis verbis, videlicet, *Several persons,
Parishioners of St. Bride's, London, are going about in that Parish
to get Subscriptions for destroying the Antient ·Annual Elective
Vestry in that Parish, and to set up instead thereof a Rump Vestry
for life; wherefore all the said Parishioners that are Rumpishly
affected, may first consider the Act of Parliament, and his Majesties
late Proclamation about tumultuous and factious Petitions for alteration
of established Lawes and Customs, which will direct in this case.
And note, the different effect of the said Vestries is this, That if any
person of the Annual Elective Vestry do unlawfully, or against the
good of the Parish, he may be turned out at the next Election, but
the Rump Vestry are above that Interruption.* Et postea iidem
Nathaniel et Willielmus ulterius machinantes et malitiose
intendentes defamare et scandalizare prædictos gubernatores
prædictæ parochiæ Sanctæ Bridgettæ alias Brides et gubernationem ejusdem parochiæ et seminare litem et discordiam
inter prædictos gubernatores et parochianos ejusdem parochiæ
Sanctæ Bridgettæ et eosdem in contemptum et ignominiam
inferre et ducere postea scilicet vicesimo die Aprilis, anno regni
dicti domini regis tricesimo secundo supradicto, apud parochiam
Sancti Dunstani in occidente prædictam, in wardà de Farringdon
extra Londoniam prædicta, quoddam alium libellum scandalosum
diffamatorium intitulatum *The True Domestic Intelligence or News
both from City and Country* similiter causaverunt, et quilibet
eorum causavit imprimi, publicari, et dispergi, in, per, et trans
totam civitatem Londoniæ, et diversos alios comitatus et locos
infra hoc regnum Angliæ, in quoquidem libello ultimo
mencionato (inter alia) continetur hæc alia falsa, ficta, seditiosa,

et scandalosa materia, prout sequitur in hiis aliis Anglicanis verbis et figuris sequentibus videlicet *The great point now depending in St Bride's Parish, London, To advise how some persons may spend and waste the parish money and goods at pleasure, and how to secure the Officers from giving an honest account, and how some may lord it, and keep the rest of the parishioners in awe and incline them to give treats to be equally and lawfully dealt with. The opinion is summ'd up in short thus, That the crafty guilty ones should wheedle in the simple ones, about the eighth part of the Parishioners that do pay to the poor, and name themselves the majority, and subscribe their names for getting 15 or 20 persons composed into a Rump Vestry for life; And if 3 or 4 dissenting persons from the Church joyn with the rest 7 or 800, call them all such; and it will operate effectually, as 'tis conceived, or else be sure at the choice of Vestrymen to wheedle, wrangle, evade, shuffle, and hector the people, if possible, into a belief, that they are not themselves, and that a Negative Vote is senseless, and was never used in a free choice, but that 10 hands in the affirmative shall carry it against 2 or 300 that would be of the negative, else at the last shift allow onely the majority to be guess'd at without the distinction by Pole or Negative Vote with Hands. Note the Authority of St. Bride's Annual Elective Vestry is chiefly this, to honestly and prudently manage the Parish Moneys, Goods, Lands, and Tenements, and prevent the mis-applying, imbezeling, or wasting any of the same. Now, whether the antient Annual Elective Vestry, or an innovated select Rump Vestry for life, are the fittest for that purpose, it is referred to any indifferent honest man to judge.* In magnum scandalum et contemptum dicti domini regis, et magnum nocumentum ignominiam, litem, et discordiam prædictorum gubernatorum ac parochianorum, et inhabitantium parochiæ Sanctæ Bridgettæ, alias Bride's, prædictæ, in malum exemplum omnium aliorum in tali casu delinquentium, et contra pacem dicti domini regis nunc, coronam et dignitatem suas.[1]

257.

Directions to a Painter. 1680.

On February 20th, 1680, a Warrant was issued by His Majesty in Council, to the Stationers' Company, for the seizing

---

1. King's Bench Judgment Roll, Easter, 32 Charles 2, rot. 84.

of this "scandalous and dangerous pamphlet," which was accordingly done, and about 1,200 copies were found, and burnt, by His Majesty's Order, at Whitehall-gate.

258.
The Observator in Question and Answer, No. 27, Saturday, June 25, 1681.

This Periodical, a copy of which is preserved in the British Museum Library, was printed and published by Joan Broome, and a prosecution was therefore instituted against her. The indictment is as follows :—

Londonia, Juratores pro domino rege super sacramentum suum præsentant quod Johanna Broome, nuper de parochia Sancti Gregorii in warda de Castlebaynard Londoniæ prædicta vidua, Deum præ oculis suis non habens, sed instigatione diabolica mota et seducta, et falso, et malitiose machinans et intendens pacem et communem tranquillitatem hujus regni Angliæ perturbare, ac diversas dissensiones et differentias inter diversos ligeos et subditos dicti domini regis Religionis Protestantis suscitare et movere et proditorie conspirationes Papistarum contra dictum dominum regem nunc supprimere, necnon machinans et contrivans discordiam inter dictum dominum regem et ligeos et subditos suos infra hoc regnum Angliæ suscitare et movere, et dictum dominum regem in displicentiam et suspicionem erga Communes hujus regni Angliæ nuper in Parliamento assemblatos excitare, vicesimo quinto die Junii anno regni domini nostri Caroli Secundi Dei gratia Angliæ, Scotiæ, Franciæ, et Hiberniæ regis, Fidei Defensoris &c. In tricesimo tertio et diversis aliis diebus et vicibus tunc antea vi et armis, &c., apud Londoniam videlicet in parochia et warda prædictis falso, nequiter, libellose, et malitiose impressit et publicavit, et imprimi et publicari causavit quendam fictum falsum et scandalosum libellum de et concernentem præfatos ligeos et subditos, necnon Communes hujus regni Angliæ nuper in Parliamento assemblatos, intitulatum *The Observator in Question and Answer* devisatum scriptum et compositum per quosdam homines juratoribus prædictis adhuc ignotos, in quoquidem libello continentur hæc ficta, falsa, libellosa, et scandalosa verba sequentia : *Q. Why should not we Encounter those addresses now with Petitions ? A. I'le dictate a petition to ye, If you'le write it ; but do it faithfully, then and without Interruption ; (and upon my Soul) I'le speak the sense of the Party as near as I can. Q. I'le be Just to ye : And now begin when you will, I'm ready for you. A. Your Majestse's most humble and obedient Subjects, having suffer'd many Disappointments, by reason both of Short and of Long Parliaments, and the late executing of the Law, against Dissenters : The Pretences of Tyranny and Popery being grown Stale ; the Popish Plot drawn almost to the Dregs, and the Eyes of the People so far open'd, that they begin to see their Friends from their Enemies ; to the Disheartening of All True Protestants, and the Encouraging of the sons of the Church, We your Majestie's Dissenting Subjects, being thereby brought unto so low a state, That without a timely Relief, we the Godly People of the Land must Inevitably perish ; May it please your Majesty to grant the Right of Calling and Dissolving Parliaments, Entring into Associations, Leagues and Covenants ; The Power of the Militia ; War and Peace : Life and Death ; The Authority of Enacting, suspending, and Repealing Laws, to be in your Liege People, the Commons of England, And these things being granted, (whereof your Petitioners stand in Great need) If your Majesty wants either Men, or Moneys for the support of your Royall Dignity and Government, your Majesty shall see what we your Loyall Petitioners will do for you. Q. What a Rogue are you to make me write such a Petition ? A. And what a Fool were you to expect others ? for all the Rest is Cant and Gibbrish, But this is English.* Ad magnam disturbationem pacis dicti domini regis, in malum exemplum omnium aliorum in consimili casu delinquentium, ac contra pacem dicti domini regis nunc coronam et dignitatem suas &c.[1]

The result of the prosecution does not appear.

259.

The Impartial Protestant Mercury, April 28, 1681.

For publishing this periodical a prosecution was instituted against Henry Carr. The information is as follows :—

Memorandum quod Samuel Astry armiger coronator et attornatus domini regis in curia ipsius regis coram ipso rege qui pro eodem domino rege in hac parte sequitur in propria persona sua venit hic in curia dicti domini regis coram ipso rege

1. Indictments, London and Middlesex, Hilary 33 Charles II, No. 21.

apud Westmonasterium die Sabbati proximo post Crastinum Animarum isto eodem termino, et pro eodem domino rege dat curiæ hic intelligi et informari quod Henricus Carr de parochia Sancti Sepulchri Londoniæ generosus existens perniciosa persona et machinans et malitiose intendens discordiam et scandalum inter dominum regem et populum suum et magnates hujus regni Angliæ incitare et movere vicesimo octavo die Aprilis anno regni domini nostri Caroli Secundi Dei gratia Angliæ, Scotiæ, Franciæ, et Hiberniæ regis, Fidei Defensoris, &c., tricesimo tertio apud Londoniam quoddam falsum scandalosum et malitiosum libellum intitulatum *The Impartiall Protestant Mercury.* In quoquidem libello inter alia continetur prout sequitur. *Hicks's Hall, Aprill the twenty seventh. Our Sessions for Middlesex began some days since, which 'tis said gave occasion to an old drudge at speechmaking most elegantly to exercise his talents; wherein (not to baulk the Common theme) the Dissenters and Whiggs were thrasht to atoms, and some were so unjust as to interpret it an insinuation that their Fines and Forfeitures must make up the extraordinary charges of the Government; but since 'tis notorious that the Papists have generally the better* [word illegible], *and are (at least) as obnoxious as other dissenters, others think the party (being an undoubted protestant as far as the law requires) intended that the laws should be briskly put in execution against them, though possibly he might mistake innocent and most useful sheep for Swine that root up the Government* publicavit, et publicari causavit, ad incitandum et movendum discordiam et scandalum inter dominum regem et populum suum, et magnates hujus regni Angliæ manifesta : in malum et perniciosum exemplum omnium aliorum in tali casu delinquentium, ac contra pacem dicti domini regis nunc coronam et dignitatem suas &c.[1]

The result of this prosecution does not appear.

260.

English Liberties, or the Freeborn Subject's inheritance. 1682.

This was published by Henry Carr, for which a prosecution was instituted against him. The following is a copy of the information :—

1. Indictments, London and Middlesex, Mich. 34 Charles 2, No. 85.

Memorandum quod Samuel Astry Armiger, coronator et attornatus domini regis, in curia ipsius regis coram ipso Rege, qui pro eodem domino rege in hac parte sequitur in propria persona sua venit hic in Curia dicti domini regis coram ipso rege apud Westmonasterium, die Martis proximo post crastinum Sancti Martini isto eodem termino et pro eodem domino rege dat Curiæ hic intelligi et informari quod Henricus Care nuper de parochia Sancti Sepulchri London generosus, machinans et malitiose intendens agitare et procurare discordiam et scandalum inter dominum regem et populum suum, et magnates hujus regni Angliæ incitare, et movere, et gubernationem ejusdem domini regis, et administrationem justitiæ in eodem regno stabilitæ scandalizare, et in odium et contemptum ducere, decimo septimo die Octobris anno regni domini nostri Caroli Secundi, Dei gratia Angliæ, Scotiæ, Franciæ, et Hiberniæ, regis Fidei Defensoris, &c. tricesimo quarto, vi et armis, &c., apud parochiam prædictam infra Civitatem Londoniæ prædictam quoddam falsum, scandalosum, odiosum, et malitiosum libellum, intitulatem *English liberties or the Freeborne Subjectes Inheritance.* In quoquidam libello inter alia continetur prout sequitur. *Some directions concerning the choice of members to serve in Parliament, And the Quallifications that render a Gentleman fit or unfitt, worthy or undeserving of your voices for so great a trust. 1. Avoid all such as hold any office of considerable value during pleasure they beeing subject to be overawed.* Et in alio loco ejusdem falsi et scandalosi libelli continetur prout sequitur. 2. *Suspect all those (especially if they are men of ill repute) who in their profession are near relations have dependency upon the Court.* Et in alio loco ejusdem falsi et scandalosi libelli continetur prout sequitur in hæc verba. 3. *Meddle not with such as haue been or are like to prove pensioners or receive salaries for secret services* publicavit, et publicari causavit, prout per prædictum falsum scandalosum et malitiosum libellum inter alia plenius liquet et apparet. In magnum scandalum et contemptum dicti domini regis, et authoritatis suæ deprivationem, necnon in contemptum legum et gubernationem hujus regni Angliæ, et administrationis justitiæ in eodem regno stabilitæ, in malum et pernitiosum exemplum omnium aliorum in tali casu delinquentium, ac contra pacem dicti domini regis nunc coronam et dignitatem suas &c.[1]

The result of the prosecution does not appear.

1. Indictments, London and Middlesex, Mich. 34 Charles 2, No. 84.

PART V.]   [TO BE CONTINUED.

INDEX

EXPURGATORIUS

ANGLICANUS:

OR

A DESCRIPTIVE CATALOGUE OF THE PRINCIPAL BOOKS

PRINTED OR PUBLISHED IN ENGLAND,

WHICH HAVE BEEN SUPPRESSED,

OR BURNT BY THE COMMON HANGMAN,

OR CENSURED,

OR FOR WHICH THE AUTHORS, PRINTERS, OR PUBLISHERS

HAVE BEEN PROSECUTED.

BY W. H. HART, F.S.A.

PRICE ONE SHILLING AND SIXPENCE.

LONDON:

JOHN RUSSELL SMITH, 36, SOHO SQUARE.

1878.

HART AND SON, PRINTERS,]   [SAFFRON WALDEN.

261.

A letter to Mr. Miles Prance in relation to the murder of Sir Edmundbury Godfrey.

A copy of this publication is preserved in the British Museum Library. It is in folio, and contains three pages. For its condemnation see article 265.

262.

A second letter to Miles Prance in reply to the Ghost of Sir Edmundbury Godfrey.

A copy of this publication is preserved in the British Museum Library. It is in folio, and contains four pages. For its condemnation see article 265.

263.

The Loyal Protestant and True Domestic Intelligence, or News both from City and Country. No. 125, Tuesday, March 7, 1682.

A copy of this newspaper is preserved in the British Museum Library. For its condemnation see article 265.

264.

The Loyal Protestant and True Domestic Intelligence, or News both from City and Country. No. 127, Saturday, March 11, 1682.

A copy of this newspaper is preserved in the British Museum Library. For its condemnation see next article.

265.

The Loyal Protestant and True Domestic Intelligence, or News both from City and Country. No. 136, April 1, 1682.

For this, and the publications described in articles 261 to 264 importing that Sir Edmundbury Godfrey murdered himself, a prosecution was instituted against Nathaniel Thompson, William Pain, and John Farwell, and on Tuesday, June 20th, 1682,

they were tried at the Guildhall, London, and found guilty.
Thompson and Farwell were sentenced to stand on the pillory
in the Palace Yard, the last day of Term, between the hours
of Ten and One o'clock, for the space of an hour, and each
of them to pay a fine of £100, and to be imprisoned until
they paid it. Pain was only to pay a fine of £100. Accordingly,
on Wednesday, the 5th of July, 1682, Thompson and Farwell
stood in the pillory, in the Old Palace Yard, at Westminster,
with this writing over their heads—

" For libelling the Justice of the Nation, by making the
" world believe that Sir Edmundbury Godfrey murdered
" himself."

The following is a copy of the information :—

Memorandum quod Robertus Sawyer miles, Attornatus domini
Regis nunc Generalis, qui pro eodem domino Rege in hac parte
sequitur, in propria persona sua venit hic in curiam dicti domini
Regis, coram ipso Rege apud Westmonasterium, die Mercurii
proximo post quindenam Paschæ isto eodem termino, et pro
eodem domino Rege dat curiæ hic intelligi et informari, quod
die Martis proximo post crastinum Purificationis Beatæ Mariæ
Virginis, termino Sancti Hillarii annis regni domini Caroli Secundi
nunc Regis Angliæ &c. tricesimo et tricesimo primo, in curia dicti
domini Regis coram ipso Rege apud Westmonasterium, eadem
curia apud Westmonasterium in comitatu Middlesexiæ tunc tenta
existente, per sacramentum duodecim juratorum proborum et
legalium hominum comitatus Middlesexiæ prædictæ tunc et
ibidem juratorum et oneratorum ad inquirendum pro dicto domino
Rege et corpore comitatus prædicti, extitit præsentatum quod
Robertus Greene nuper de parochia Sanctæ Mariæ le Strond in
comitatu Middlesexiæ Laborer, [   ] Gerrald nuper de parochia
prædicta in comitatu prædicto clericus, Henricus Berry nuper
de parochia prædicta in comitatu prædicto Laborer, Laurencius
Hill nuper de parochia prædicta in comitatu prædicto Laborer,
Dominicus Kelly nuper de parochia prædicta in comitatu prædicto
clericus, et Philbert Vernat nuper de parochia prædicta in
comitatu prædicto Laborer, Deum præ oculis suis non habentes,
sed instigatione diabolica moti et seducti, duodecimo die Octobris
anno regni domini Caroli Secundi Dei gratia Angliæ Scotiæ
Franciæ et Hiberniæ Regis Fidei Defensoris &c. tricesimo, vi et

armis &c. apud parochiam Sanctæ Mariæ le Strond prædictæ in comitatu Middlesexiæ prædictæ in et super quendam Edmundum Berry Godfrey militem, in pace Dei et dicti Domini Regis nunc adtunc et ibidem existentem, felonice, voluntarie, et ex malitia sua præcogitata, insultum fecerunt. Et quod prædictus Robertus Greene quoddam sudarium panni lini *anglice a linen handkerchiffe*, valoris sex denariorum, circa collum ipsius Edmundi Berry Godfrey adtunc et ibidem felonice, voluntarie, et ex malitia sua præcogitata, plicavit, et fixavit *anglice did fold, and fasten*. Et quod prædictus Robertus Greene cum prædicto sudario sic per ipsum Robertum Greene plicato et fixato circa collum ipsius prædicti Edmundi Berry adtunc ipsum prædictum Edmundum Berry Godfrey felonice, voluntarie, et ex malitia sua præcogitata, suffocavit et strangulavit *anglice, choake and strangle*, de quibus-quidem suffocatione, et strangulatione ipsius Edmundi Berry Godfrey prædicti, per ipsum prædictum Robertum Greene in forma prædicta factis et perpetratis, ipse prædictus Edmundus Berry Godfrey adtunc et ibidem instanter obiit. Et quod prædicti [   ] Gerrald, Henricus Berry Laurentius Hill, Dominicus Kelly, et Philbert Vernat, adtunc et ibidem felonice, voluntarie, et ex malitia sua præcogitata fuerunt præsentes, auxiliantes, abettantes, comfortantes, assistentes, et manutenentes præfatum Robertum Greene ad prædictum Edmundum Berry Godfrey in forma prædicta felonice, voluntarie, et ex malitia sua præcogitata, interficiendum et murdrandum. Et sic juratores prædicti adtunc dixerunt super sacramentum suum prædictum quod prædictus Robertus Greene, [   ] Gerrald, Henricus Berry, Laurencius Hill, Dominicus Kelly, et Philbert Vernat, modo et forma prædictis, præfatum Edmundum Berry Godfrey felonice, voluntarie, et ex malitia sua præcogitata, interfecerunt et murdraverunt, contra pacem dicti domini Regis nunc, coronam et dignitatem suas &c., per quod præceptum fuit vicecomiti comitatus prædicti quod non omitteret &c. quin caperet eos si &c., ad respondendum &c. Quodque postea, scilicet die Mercurii proximo post crastinum Purificationis Beatæ Mariæ Virginis, termino Sancti Hillarii, anno regni domini Caroli Secundi nunc Regis Angliæ &c. trice-simo et tricesimo primo supradicto coram domino Rege apud Westmonasterium venerunt prædicti Robertus Greene, Henricus Berry, et Laurencius Hill sub custodia Willielmi Richardson generosi tunc custodis gaoli dicti domini Regis de Newgate virtute brevis dicti domini Regis de Habeas Corpus ad subjiciendum, recipiendum &c. in cujus custodia præantea ex causa predicta commissi fuerunt ad barram prædictæ curiæ dicti domini Regis tunc et ibidem ducti in propria persona sua, et adtunc et ibidem statim de præmissis prædictis eis superius impositis separatim allocuti qualiter se velint inde acquietari separatim, dixerunt quod ipsi in nullo fuerunt inde culpabiles et inde de bono et malo posuerunt se separatim super patriam. In quaquidem causa taliter processum fuit quod prædictus Robertus Greene, Henricus Berry, et Laurencius Hill postea scilicet die Lunæ proximo post octabas Purificationis Beatæ Mariæ Virginis termino Sancti Hillarii annis regni dicti domini Regis nunc tricesimo et tricesimo primo supradictis, in prædicta curia dicti domini Regis coram ipso Rege apud Westmonasterium prædictum in comitatu Middlesexiæ prædictæ, pro felonia et murdro prædictis in indictamento prædicto specificatis et contentis per quandam juratam patriæ debito modo triati fuerunt et adtunc et ibidem legitimo modo pro felonia et murdro prædictis convicti et attincti fuerunt, prout per recordum inde in prædicta curia dicti domini Regis coram ipso Rege apud Westmonasterium in comitatu Middlesexiæ prædictæ remanens filatum plenius liquet et apparet. Qui quidem Robertus Greene, Henricus Berry, et Laurencius Hill postea debito modo executi fuerunt, et pænam mortis subierunt juxta formam et effectum judicii et attincturæ prædictorum. Cumque etiam quidam Milo Prance, super triationem prædictum fuit testis productus et juratus ex parte dicti domini Regis nunc adtunc et ibidem legitimo modo dedisset materialem evidenciam versus prædictos Robertum Greene, Henricum Berry, et Laurencium Hill ad probandum ipsos fore culpabiles de felonia et murdro prædictis in indictamento prædicto specificatis. Et quidam Willielmus Bedlowe, Johannes Browne, Elizabetha Curtis, Zacharias Skillarne, et Nicholaus Cambridge super triationem prædictum fuerunt testes similiter producti et jurati ex parte dicti domini Regis, et diversas materiales evidentias versus prædictos Robertum Greene, Henricum Berry, Laurencium Hill, ad probandum ipsos fore culpabiles de felonia et murdro prædictis in eodem indictamento mentionatis dederunt. Cumque etiam prædicti [ ] Gerrald, Robertus Greene, Laurencius Hill, Dominicus Kelly et Philbert Vernat tempore feloniæ et murdri prædictorum fuerunt Papistæ et manutentores Romanæ super-

stitionis. Et prædicti [ ] Gerrald Dominicus Kelly, et Philbert
Vernat fugam fecerunt et ad indictamentum prædictum adhuc
non comparuerunt nec aliquis eorum comparuit. Cumque etiam
super visum corporis prædicti Edmundi Berry Godfrey mortui
jacentis quædam inquisitio debito modo capta fuit coram Johanne
Cooper generoso tunc uno coronatorum dicti domini Regis
comitatus Middlesexiæ prædictæ per sacramentum proborum et
legalium hominum comitatus Middlesexiæ ultra numerum
duodecim personarum per quamquidem inquisitionem compertum
fuit quod quidam malefactores ignoti felonice et ex malitia sua
præpensa ipsum Edmundum Berry Godfrey strangulaverunt et
suffocaverunt de qua obiit. Et quod quidam Nathaniel Thompson
nuper de parochia Sancti Dunstani in Occidente Londoniæ Typho-
graphus, Willielmus Payne nuper de parochia prædicta infra
civitatem Londoniæ generosus, et Johannes Farwell nuper de
Westmonasterio in comitatu Middlesexiæ generosus præmissa
prædicta satis scientes, et existentes personæ diabolice effecti ac
machinantes practicantes et totis viribus suis intendentes pacem
et communem tranquillitatem hujus regni Angliæ perturbare et
quantum in ipsis fuit debitum legis cursum corrumpere, subvertere, et evadere, et justitiam hujus regni Angliæ in ea parte
defamare et scandalizare et tam præfatos Milonem Prance,
Willielmum Bedlowe, Johannem Browne, Elizabetham Curtis,
Zachariam Skillarne, et Nicholaum Cambridge quam prædictos
Johannem Cooper et probos et legales homines super inquisitionem prædictam super visum corporis prædicti juratos in
maximum odium contemptum et vilipendium cum omnibus ligeis
subditis dicti domini Regis nunc inducere et inferre ac ad deter-
rendum subditos dicti domini Regis a comparendo detigendo
et probando machinationes Papistorum contra dominum Regem
nunc et veram religionem per legem nunc stabilitatam et impie
et nefarie machinantes et intendentes ipsos prædictos [ ]
Gerrald, Dominicum Kelly et prædictum Philbertum Vernat a
subeundo pænas et sententias per legem super ipsos infligendas
pro murdro prædicto ac ad auxiliandum et assistandum ipsos quam-
vis inde culpabiles fore compertos minime culpabiles ac ad
decipiendum et fallandum subditos dicti domini Regis de et in
præmissis cum falsis affirmantiis et agreamentis suis et causare et
procurare quod creditum foret et estimaretur quod prædicti
Robertus Greene, Henricus Berry, et Laurencius Hill personæ, sic

ut præfertur, pro felonia et murdro prædictis prædicti Edmundi
Berry convicti et executi minus rite convicti et executi fuissent,
quodque prædictus Edmundus Berry Godfrey fuit felo de se et
seipsum felonice murdrasset, ipsi prædicti Nathaniel Thompson,
Willielmus Payne, et Johannes Farwell ad nequissimas,
nefandissimas, et diabolicas intentiones suas prædictas
perimplendas et proficiendas postea scilicet vicesimo tertio
die Februarii anno regni domini Caroli Secundi nunc Regis
Angliæ &c. tricesimo quarto apud parochiam Sanctæ Mariæ le
Bow Londoniæ vi et armis &c. falso, illicite, injuste, nequiter,
malitiose, scandalose, et diabolice, fecerunt, composuerunt et
imprimi causaverunt quendam falsum, scandalosum, et defamatorium libellum intitulatum, *A Letter to Mr. Miles Prance, in
relation to the murther of Sir Edmondbury Godfrey*, in quoquidem
libello inter alia continetur prout sequitur. *And hearing that the
Coroner's Jury or Inquest were first of opinion, and accordingly
declared, he was felo de se ; and that there was much art and skill
used to procure their verdict to the contrary ; more particularly, the
refusing of the body, (at their instance and request) to be opened.*
Ac in alio loco ejusdem libelli ulterius continetur prout sequitur.
*They say, that if a man, or any other creature be strangled, or hanged,
and his body cold, and the blood settled in the veins (as he must needs
be, if your evidence be true)* (evidentiam prædicti Milonis Prance
innuendo) *run twenty swords through such a body, not one drop of
blood will come out ; but on the contrary, his body, when found, was
full of blood, in so much that (over and above the cakes or great gobbets
of congealed putrified blood found afterwards in his cloaths) the consta-
ble when he pulled the sword out of his body, it crashed against his
back bone, and gobbets of blood and water gushed or gubbled out of that
wound in abundance, not only in that very place where the sword was
pulled out but in all his passage to the Whitehouse ; especially there
where his body was lifted over two high stumps ; and also when he was
laid upon the table, the blood and water so issued out of that wound,
that it ran from off the table upon the floor, and from thence into
the cellar. So that they do aver, that that wound that he received
by that sword, must of necessity be the cause of his death.* Ac in
alia parte ejusdem libelli ulterius continetur prout sequitur,
*They observe, that Bedloe's, (before the Committee of Lords),
and your evidence in relation to this gentleman's death, are as
different as the East is from the West ; for you dog him out of St.*

Clement's; the other decoys him from Charing Cross; you swear he was strangled with a handkerchief near the stables going to the water-side; Bedloe, that he was smothered with a pillow in a room in the great Court in Somerset-house. You say, he took horse at Soho; *Bedlow says, he took Coach at Clarendon-house, with many more such like contradictions; and considering the old proverb, fore-warn'd, fore arm'd; a further and fuller account of the whole matter expect.* Quodque prædicti Nathaniel Thompson, Willielmus Payne et Johannes Farwell ad nequissimas nefandissimas et diabolicas intentiones suas prædictas perimplendas et proficiendas postea scilicet tertio die Marcii anno regni dicti domini Regis nunc tricesimo quarto [*word defaced*] apud parochiam Sanctæ Mariæ le Bow Londoniæ prædictæ vi et armis et falso, illicite, injuste, nequiter, malitiose, scandalose, et diabolice, fecerunt composuerunt et imprimi causaverunt quendam alium falsum scandalosum et defamatorium libellum intitulatum, *A Second Letter to Miles Prance, in reply to the Ghost of Sir Edmondbury Godfrey,* in quoquidem ultimo mencionato libello inter alia continetur prout sequitur. *Next, whereas my letter saith, (and that truly) that the Coroner's Jury were first of opinion and accordingly declared he was* felo de se; *and that much art and skill was used to procure their verdict to the contrary.* Ac in alio loco ejusdem ultimo mencionati libelli inter alia continetur prout sequitur. *And it would be very material, if the Coroner would declare, what he received for that job, and of whom, and what evidence he had to induce the Jury to find (as the inquisition imports) that he was strangled with a linen cloth, a matter of fact never so much as spoken of, until you came in with your evidence, which was not in some weeks after. And I do again aver, that the body was required by the jurors to be opened, and was refused; and if the body was in their and the Coroner's power (as the Ghost insinuates) such power was concealed from and denied the Jury.* Et in alio loco ejusdem ultimo mentionati libelli inter alia continetur prout sequitur, *He is to understand that Mr. Brown, the two surgeons* (prædictos Zachariam Skillarne, et Nicholam Cambridge innuendo) *and Mrs. Curtis are not competent (nor can be material) witnesses in this case.* Et in alio loco ejusdem ultimo mentionati libelli inter alia ulterius continetur prout sequitur, *But Mr. Prance, it will be fully proved, that the body was full of blood, and that there were cakes or gobbets of dry blood found in his cloaths, which (with his body) stunk extremely.* And it *will be also fully and effectually proved that his eyes, nostrils, and corners of his mouth were fly-blown.* Ac in alio loco ejusdem ultimo mentionati libelli inter alia continetur prout sequitur, *And as to the seventh and last paragraph, which relates only to the difference betwixt yours and Mr. Bedlow's evidence, I must take notice, that what you and he swear are very contradictory.* Et in alio loco ejusdem ultimo mentionati libelli inter alia ulterius continetur prout sequitur, *But I cannot omit to take further notice of Mrs. Curtis's affidavit in relation to the drops of wax found upon the cloaths, in which I cannot say but she may swear true : but this I do aver, that if it be so, those drops were put upon the cloaths long after he was found, and after the jury had sat on the body ; for there was no such thing then on the cloaths. And I suppose this was some artifice used by those, who, either out of interest or design, were desirous to confirm his being murthered at Somerset-House.* Ac ulterius idem Attornatus dicti domini Regis nunc Generalis pro eodem domino Rege dat curiam hic intelligi et informari quod prædicti Nathaniel Thompson, Willielmus Payne, et Johannes Farwell in ulteriorem prosecutionem prædictæ falsæ nequissimæ et malitiosæ machinationis et intentionis suarum prædictarum postea scilicet septimo die Martii anno regni dicti domini Regis nunc tricesimo quarto supradicto apud parochiam Sanctæ Mariæ le Bow Londoniæ prædictam vi et armis &c. falso, illicite, injuste, nequiter, malitiose, scandalose, et diabolice composuerunt, fecerunt, et imprimi causaverunt quendam alium falsum scandalosum et defamatorium libellum intitulatum, *The Loyal Protestant, and True Domestic Intelligence, or News both from City and Country,* in quoquidem ultimo mentionato libello continetur prout sequitur, *That there is not in the said letter* (prædictum falsum scandalosum et defamatorium libellum intitulatum A Letter to Mr. Miles Prance, in relation to the murder of Sir Edmundbury Godfrey præantea primo mencionatum innuendo) *the least item or circumstance, but what will be by undeniable evidence made out to be the truth : So the said Mr. Prance, having not as yet vouchsafed an answer to that letter, he will speedily receive a further letter relating to that murther ; wherein the further truth will not only be fully set forth, and other circumstances set out.* Et ulterius idem Attornatus dicti domini Regis nunc Generalis pro eodem domino Rege dat curiam hic intelligi et informari quod prædictus Nathaniel Thompson, Willielmus Payne, et Johannes Farwell in ulteriorem prosecutionem prædictæ falsæ nequissimæ et malitiosæ machinationis et intentionis suarum prædictarum postea scilicet undecimo die Marcii anno regni dicti domini Regis nunc tricesimo quarto supradicto apud parochiam Sanctæ Mariæ le Bow Londoniæ prædictam vi et armis, falso, illicite, injuste, nequiter, malitiose, scandalose, et diabolicə composuerunt, fecerunt, et imprimi causaverunt quendam alium falsum scandalosum et defamatorium libellum intitulatum, *The Loyal Protestant and True Domestick Intelligence, or News both from City and Country*, in quoquidem ultimo mentionato libello inter alia continetur prout sequitur, *Whereas Dick Janeway in this Day's Mercury, promises an answer to the late Letter to Mr: Prance, &c. This is to give him and all the world notice, that such an answer is impatiently expected by the author of that letter, who questions not but to prove every tittle of that letter to the satisfaction of all mankind: And besides he is very desirous that the Courantier (according to his last Pacquet of Advice from Rome) would go on, and use his interest, to procure the Lord Mayor, Court of Aldermen and Common Council of London, to inspect the Truth of that letter; whereby it will appear inevitably that there is not one Papist or popishly affected person concerned in that letter, or in the proof of the of the particulars thereof; but the same (with divers other material circumstances relating to the murther of Sir Edmundbury Godfrey, and the fraud and blind put upon the world in relation thereto) will be more fully, plainly and manifestly proved, without giving ill words, or scurrilous language, or reflections to any person that really are or supposed to be therein concerned in any circumstance whatsoever.* Et ulterius idem Attornatus dicti domini Regis nunc Generalis pro eodem domino Rege dat curiam hic intelligi et informari quod prædicti Nathaniel Thompson, Willielmus Payne et Johannes Farwell in ulteriorem prosecutionem prædictæ falsæ nequissimæ et malitiosæ machinationis et intentionis suarum prædictarum postea scilicet primo die Aprilis anno regni dicti domini Regis nunc tricesimo quarto supradicto vi et armis &c. apud parochiam Sanctæ Mariæ le Bow Londoniæ prædictam falso, illicite, injuste nequiter, malitiose, scandalose, et diabolice fecerunt composuerunt, et imprimi causaverunt quendam alium falsum, scandalosum et defamatorium libellum intitulatum, *The Loyal Protestant, and True Domestic Intelligence, or News both from City and Country*, in quoquidem ultimo mentionato libello inter alia continetur prout sequitur, *Last Wednesday, Nathaniel Thompson, (upon summons) appeared before the Lords of his Majesty's most Honourable Privy Council, about the letters to Mr. Miles Prance, concerning the death of Sir Edmundbury Godfrey where he justified the matter, and produced the authors, who are ready to prove (by undeniable and substantial witnesses, not in the least accused, or suspected of Popery, as the malicious party do suggest) that every tittle and iota of those letters are true.* Quodque in alia parte ejusdem ultimo mentionati libelli inter alia continetur prout sequitur, *Mr. Thompson and the gentlemen his friends, are to attend the next Wednesday at Council where they do not doubt but that Honourable Board will put them into a method to prove the whole, or any particular which their Honours in their great wisdom shall think convenient to be brought to the test or examination.* Et ulterius idem Attornatus dicti domini Regis nunc Generalis pro eodem domino Rege dat curiæ hic intelligi et informari quod prædicti Nathaniel Thompson, Willielmus Payne, et Johannes Farwell vicesimo tertio die Februarii anno regni dicti domini Regis nunc tricesimo quarto supradicto diversis aliis diebus et vicibus inter prædictum vicesimum tertium diem Februarii anno tricesimo quarto supradicto et diem exhibitionis hujus informationis apud parochiam Sanctæ Mariæ le Bow Londoniæ prædictam scienter, et quilibet eorum scienter prædictos separales libellos fore falsos malitiosos et scandalosos et seditiosos vi et armis &c. falso illicite injuste nequiter malitiose scandalose et diabolice prædictos falsos malitiosos scandalosos et seditiosos libellos utteraverunt, publicaverunt et quilibet eorum utteravit et publicavit, in contemptum legum hujus regni Angliæ manifestum, ac scandalum et defamationem publicæ justitiæ ejusdem, in malum exemplum omnium aliorum in tali casu delinquentium, ac contra pacem dicti domini Regis nunc coronam et dignitatem suas &c.

266.

The Memoirs of James Lord Audley Earl of Castlehaven, his engagement and carriage in the Wars of Ireland, from the year 1642 to the year 1651. Written by himself. London. 1680.

On August 3rd, 1682, Lord Castlehaven was summoned before the Council, the King being present, respecting the publication of this book, which he owned; and it was resolved that the

book was a libel against the government.[1] A copy of this
publication is preserved in the British Museum Library.

267.

The Loyal Protestant, and true Domestic Intelligence, or News both from City and Country, No. 166, Saturday, June 10th, 1682.

For publishing this periodical a prosecution was instituted
against Nathaniel Thomson and Mary his wife. The following
is a copy of the information :—

Londonia. Memorandum quod Samuel Astry armiger Coronator et Attornatus domini Regis in curia ipsius Regis coram
ipso Rege qui pro eodem domino Rege in hac parte sequitur in
propria persona sua venit hic in curiam dicti domini Regis
coram ipso Rege apud Westmonasterium die Lunæ proximo
post tres septimanas Sancti Michaelis isto eodem termino, et
pro eodem domino Rege dat curiæ hic intelligi et informari
quod Nathaniel Tompson nuper de parochia Sancti Dunstani
in Occidente Londoniæ Yeoman et Maria Tompson uxor
prædicti Nathanielis existentes personæ maledispositi ac machinantes practicantes et intendentes pacem et communem
tranquillitatem hujus regni Angliæ perturbare et diversas
personas infra hoc regnum Angliæ in odium et contemptum
dicti domini Regis et subditorum ipsius domini Regis inducere
et inferre, et ad nequissimas machinationes practicationes et
intentiones suas prædictas perimplenda et perficienda prædicti
Nathaniel Tompson et Maria Tompson decimo die Junii anno
regni domini Caroli Secundi nunc Regis Angliæ &c. tricesimo
quarto vi et armis &c. apud parochiam prædictam infra Civitatem
Londoniæ prædictam falso, illicite, injuste, nequiter, seditiose
et scandalose imprimi causaverunt et publicaverunt et uterque
eorum tunc et ibidem imprimi causavit et publicavit quoddam
falsum, malitiosum, scandalosum, et defamatorium libellum
intitulatum *The Loyal Protestant and True Domestick Intelligence,*
in quoquidem falso, scandaloso, et defamatorio libello inter
alia contenta fuerunt hæ falsæ, scandalosæ, et defamatoriæ
sententiæ in his Anglicanis verbis et figuris sequentibus
Windsor. June 7, 1682. This day the Court of Verge sate here,

1. See London Mercury, No. 36, Aug. 8, 1682.

where the 2 Portugal Cooks came to their tryals, and were (upon hearing the whole matter) found guilty of poysoning Mr. Benning the Turnbroach; the Foreman of the Jury was one Mr. White, the King's Plummer, near this place. We cannot hear of any sentence given against them as yet Benning excepted against a House-Jury, by reason he had formerly disobliged some of the Servants; wherefore he thought Justice would not be done him; they having had a prejudice against him ever since. Et ulterius idem Coronator et Attornatus dicti domini Regis pro eodem domino Rege dat curiæ hic intelligi et informari quod prædicti Nathaniel Tompson et Maria Tompson die et anno supradictis apud parochiam prædictam infra civitatem Londoniæ prædictam scientes prædictum falsum, scandalosum, et defamatorium libellum fore falsum et defamatorium libellum, falso, illicite, injuste, nequiter, malitiose, et seditiose vendiderunt, utteraverunt, et publicaverunt, et uterque eorum vendidit, utteravit, et publicavit, in malum exemplum omnium aliorum in tali casu delinquentium, ac contra pacem dicti domini Regis nunc coronam et dignitatem suas &c.[1]

The result of this prosecution does not appear. A copy of this publication is preserved in the British Museum Library.

268.

The True Protestant Mercury: or Occurrences Foreign and Domestic. No. 149. From Wednesday, June 7, to Saturday, June 10, 1682.

For publishing this periodical a prosecution was instituted against Thomas Snowden, printer, of the parish of St. Andrew by the Wardrobe, and Jane Curtis, wife of Langley Curtis, of the parish of St. Bride's, Fleet Street. The following is a copy of the information :—

Londonia. Memorandum quod Samuel Astry Armiger Coronator et Attornatus domini Regis in curia ipsius Regis coram ipso Rege qui pro eodem domino Rege in hac parte sequitur in propria persona sua venit hic in curia dicti domini Regis coram ipso Rege apud Westmonasterium die Lunæ proximo post tres septimanas Sancti Michaelis isto eodem termino et pro eodem domino Rege dat curiæ hic intelligi et informari quod Thomas Snowden de parochia Sancti Andreæ Wardrope

---

1. Indictments. Lond. and Midd., Mich. 34 Car. 2, No. 81.

Londoniæ Typographus et Jana Curtis uxor Langley Curtis
nuper de parochia Sanctæ Bridgettæ Londoniæ Yeoman existentes
personæ male dispositi ac machinantes practicantes et intendentes
pacem et communem tranquillitatem hujus regni Angliæ
perturbare et diversas personas infra hoc regnum Angliæ in
maximum odium contemptum et vilipendium non solum cum
dicto domino Rege, verum etiam cum aliis subditis ipsius
domini Regis inducere et inferre et ad nequissimas machinationes
practicationes et intentiones suas prædictas perimplenda et
perficienda prædicti Thomas Snowden et Jana Curtis vicesimo
die Junii anno regni domini Caroli Secundi nunc Regis Angliæ
&c. tricesimo quarto vi et armis &c. apud parochiam Sanctæ
Bridgettæ Londoniæ prædictam, falso, illicite, injuste, nequiter,
seditiose et scandalose, imprimi causaverunt et publicaverunt,
et uterque eorum adtunc et ibidem imprimi causavit et
publicavit quoddam falsum malitiosum scandalosum et defamatorium libellum intitulatum *The true Protestant Mercury or
occurrences foreign and domestic*, in quoquidem libello inter
alia contenta fuerunt hæ falsæ, fictæ, et scandalosæ sententiæ
in hiis Anglicanis verbis, *The two Portugal Cooks mentioned in
our last had their tryals on Wednesday last at Windsor, and were
found guilty of poysening Benning the Turnbroach. The foreman of
the jury was Mr. W. the King's Plummer, who lives near Windsor,
but we do not hear of any sentence given as yet against them. But
we hear that his Majesty declared before the trial, that whosoever
was found in the fault, should have no favour showed him. The
reason that he had excepted against the Jury of the King's servants,
was because he had formerly some quarrel with some of them, and
had discovered something against them, and therefore thought they
would not do him justice.* Et ulterius idem Coronator et Attornatus
dicti domini Regis pro eodem domino Rege dicit quod prædicti
Thomas Snowden et Jana Curtis dicto vicesimo die Junii anno
supradicto apud parochiam Sanctæ Bridgettæ Londoniæ prædictam falsum et scandalosum libellum falso, illicite, injuste,
nequiter et malitiose vendiderunt utteraverunt et publicaverunt
et uterque eorum vendidit utteravit et publicavit, in malum
exemplum omnium aliorum in tali casu delinquentium, ac
contra pacem dicti domini Regis nunc coronam et dignitatem
suas &c.[1]

A copy of this publication is preserved in the British Museum
Library.

---

1. Indictments. London and Midd., Mich. 34 Charles 2, No. 80.

269.

A second letter from a person of quality to his friend about abhorrers and addressors, &c. 1682.

This was written by Thomas Stringer, who appears to have been Secretary or Steward to the Earl of Shaftesbury; and for writing the same, a prosecution was instituted against him. The following is a copy of the indictment :—

Londonia. Juratores pro domino rege super sacramentum suum præsentant quod Thomas Stringer nuper de Londonia generosus machinans et intendens serenissimum dominum nostrum Carolum Secundum Dei gratia Angliæ Scotiæ Franciæ et Hiberniæ Regem Fidei Defensorem &c., et regimen suum in odium et infamiam inter subditos suas inferre, et pacem et communem tranquillitatem hujus regni Angliæ molestare et perturbare, et diversas differentias inter eosdem subditos excitare et procurare vicesimo die Junii anno regni dicti domini Regis nunc tricesimo quarto apud Londoniam videlicet in parochia Sancti Botulphi extra Aldersgate in Warda de Aldersgate Londoniæ prædicta vi et armis &c. falso seditiose et malitiose scripsit et publicavit et scribi imprimi et publicari causavit quendam scandalosum libellum intitulatum, *A Second letter from a person of quality to his friend about abhorrers and addressors, &c.* in quoquidem libello continentur hæc falsa ficta et scandalosa verba sequentia videlicet *Tis plain these men* (ligeos et subditos dicti domini regis nunc innuendo) *mean and intend by this abhorrence* (quandam detestationem versus associationem in papiris scriptam prætensam fore inventam inter quosdam papiros Anthonii Comitis Shaftesbury innuendo) *and under this notion to create an association for all the Tories to maintain a Popish Successor and to introduce arbitrary power. And whosoever joins with or doth not vigorously oppose such practices is guilty of these designs.* Et in altera parte ejusdem libelli continentur hæc falsa et scandalosa verba sequentia videlicet, *That which concerns the mercenary forces is no more than every man's duty as much as in him lies (which means as lawfully he may) to endeavour entirely to disband all such mercenary forces as we have reason to believe are raised to advance arbitrary power.* In malum et perniciosissimum exemplum omnium aliorum in consimili casu delinquentium ac contra pacem dicti domini regis nunc coronam et dignitatem suas &c.[1]

270.

The Addresses importing an abhorrence of an Association pretended to have been seized in the Earl of Shaftesbury's closet, laid open and detected. In a letter to a friend. 1682.

This was the production of Mr. Robert Ferguson, and for writing, printing, and publishing the same he was prosecuted.

The following is a copy of the indictment:

Juratores pro domino Rege super sacramentum suum præsentant quod Robertus Ferguson nuper de Londonia generosus, Deum præ oculis suis non habens sed instigatione diabolica motus et seductus, machinansque et intendens serenissimum dominum nostrum Carolum Secundum Dei gratia Angliæ Scotiæ Franciæ et Hiberniæ Regem Fidei Defensorem, et regimen suum in odium et infamiam inter subditos suos inferre ac pacem et communem tranquillitatem hujus regni Angliæ perturbare et diversas differentias inter eosdem subditos procurare vicesimo die Junii anno regni dicti domini regis nunc tricesimo quarto apud Londoniam videlicet in parochia Sancti Martini Ludgate in warda de Farringdon extra Londoniam prædicta vi et armis &c. falso seditiose et malitiose scripsit, impressit, et publicavit et scribi, imprimi et publicari causavit quendam scandalosum libellum intitulatum, *The Addresses importing an abhorrence of an association pretended to have been seized in the Earl of Shaftesbury's closet, laid open and detected. In a letter to a friend.* In quoquidem libello continentur hæc falsa ficta et scandalosa verba sequentia, *And as all Addresses of this nature tend to render the King, who ought to reign in the hearts of all his people, the Head meerly of one party and that a very inconsiderable one if compared with the bulk of the Nation; so they only serve to publish to all the world the distractions of the Kingdom, and to proclaim in the face of the Sun the weakness of the Government. What do the foreigners say upon the perusal of our Gazets, but that either things are not managed in England according to the Laws of the Constitution, or that his Majesty of*

1. Indictments. Lond. and Midd., Hilary 34 and 35 Charles 2, No. 22.

Great Britain reigns precariously, seeing his Ministers seek to support the Transactions of State, by courting the applause of a few little folk here and there through the Kingdom? In malum et pernicio-sissimum exemplum omnium aliorum in consimili casu delinquentium ac contra pacem dicti domini regis nunc coronam et dignitatem suas &c.[1]

A copy of this publication is in the British Museum Library. It is in folio and occupies four pages.

271.

An Historical and Political Discourse of the Laws and Government of England, from the first times to the end of the reign of Queen Elizabeth. With a vindication of the ancient way of Parliaments in England. Collected from some manuscript notes of John Selden, Esq.; by Nathaniel Bacon, of Gray's Inn, Esquire. London. 1682.

This is one of the reprints of the original edition of 1651. For publishing this reprint, a prosecution was instituted against John Starkey. The following is a copy of the indictment against him :—

Londonia.   Juratores pro domino Rege super sacramentum suum præsentant quod Johannes Starkey nuper de Londonia Stationer machinans et intendens Serenissimum Dominum nostrum Carolum Secundum Dei gratia Angliæ Scotiæ Franciæ et Hiberniæ Regem Fidei Defensorem &c. supremum et naturalem Dominum suum et regimen suum in odium infamiam et contemptum inter subditos suos inducere et inferre ac pacem et communem tranquillitatem hujus regni Angliæ perturbare vicesimo die Junii anno regni dicti domini Regis nunc tricesimo quarto apud Londoniam videlicet in parochia Sancti Dunstani in Occidente in Warda de Farringdon extra London prædicta vi et armis &c. falso seditiose et malitiose impressit et publicavit et imprimi et publicari causavit quendam librum scandalosum intitulatum *The continuation of the Historicall and Politicall Discourse of the Laws and Government of England until the end of the Reign of Queen Elizabeth with a vindication of the antient*

1. Indictments. Lond. and Midd., Hilary 34 and 35 Charles 2, No. 23.

way of Parliaments in England. In quo quidem libro de et concernente præfato domino Rege nunc continentur hæc falsa ficta et scandalosa verba sequentia videlicet, *I do easily grant that Kings have many Occasions and Opportunities to beguile their People, yet can they do nothing as Kings, but what of right they ought to doe: They may call Parliaments, but neither as often or seldome as they please, if the Statute-Laws of this Realme might take place.* Et in altera parte ejusdem libri continentur hæc falsa et scandalosa verba sequentia videlicet, *And though Kings may be chiefe Commanders, yet they are not the chiefe Rulers.* In malum et pernitiosissimum exemplum omnium aliorum in consimili casu delinquentium ac contra pacem dicti domini regis nunc coronam et dignitatem suas &c.[1]

Upon this indictment Starkey was outlawed, but in the first year of Will. and Mary he brought a writ of error and the outlawry was reversed.

272.

Mr. Hunt's postscript for rectifying some mistakes in some of the inferiour clergy, mischievous to our government and religion. With two Discourses about the Succession, and Bill of Exclusion. In answer to two Books affirming the unalterable right of Succession, and the unlawfulness of the Bill of Exclusion. London. 1682.

Thomas Hunt, Esq., of London, was prosecuted for publishing this. The information charges that Thomas Hunt, late of London, esquire, being a pernicious and seditious man, and contriving and maliciously intending to disturb the peace of England, and to create false opinions and suspicions among the king's subjects concerning the king and his government, and to cause them to think that the king was an abettor of Papists and most pernicious men conspiring to procure the subversion of the government of the kingdom and also the Protestant religion established by law, called *plotters*, and to excite rebellious seditions and discords between the king and his subjects, and to bring the king's government into contempt and hatred, did in

1. Indictments. Lond. and Midd., Hil. 34 and 35 Charles 2, No. 24.

order to carry out his most wicked and diabolical intentions, on the twentieth day of January in the thirty fourth year of the reign of King Charles the Second, at the parish of St. Michael Cornhill in London, unlawfully, wickedly, maliciously, scandalously, and seditiously make, compose and write, and cause to be printed, published and sold a certain false, scandalous, libellous, seditious, and defamatory book intituled *Mr Hunt's Postscript*, in which book in writing of and concerning the Papists and the *plots* in the same book mentioned to have been perpetrated, among other things is contained as follows —*Nay, as if they* [meaning Papists] *did not fear or care to loose the favour of their most indulgent Prince, which they have possest since he used Papists in making his Escape at Worcester; they have contrived these two last Plots with such Art, as to bring them under his Majesties Observation, and represented them as things fit for his encouragement. Sure if they were not urged with the fears of a real guilt, and a restless Conscience of the Plot, they would never have adventured thus to have interested the honor of the King, and to tempt him to abandon them to the publick Justice of the Nation: which begins to grow impatient by the delays of it against this hellish Plot. For we have had four Parliaments dissolved since the discovery of it, one a darling to the Crown. The bringing into question the Dissolution of that Parliament in the House of Peers, upon the reason of an unnatural Prorogation, was not long before censured, and some great Lords imprisoned therefore; proceedings so unwarrantable, that it was after thought fit by that House to obliterate the Memory of them; soe necessary was that Parliament then thought to the service of the Crown. The Dissolution of that Parliament, gave us reason to fear that the King had no more business for Parliaments. By these Dissolutions, no publick ends that are intelligible are served, no Interest but that of the Plot is gratified; no persons of any sort receive their satisfaction but the Plotters, who are respited thereby from publick Justice, and gain time to bring their Plot to effect.*[1]

The result of this prosecution does not appear. A copy of the book is preserved in the British Museum Library.

273.
The Presbyterian Paternoster; Creed, and Ten Commandments. 1681.

1. Indictments, London and Midd., Hil. 34 and 35 Charles 2, No. 95.

This is a single sheet printed on both sides. A copy is preserved in the Library of the British Museum.

In a newspaper of the period, The True Protestant Mercury of February 23, 1680-1, we find the following account of this production:—"Feb. 18, 1680-1. Complaint being made to the "Bishop of London of a most vile and blasphemous pamphlet, "lately published by one Hindmarsh, a bookseller in Cornhill, "intituled *The Presbyterian's Paternoster, Creed, and Decalogue,* "wherein the sacred form of prayer taught by our Blessed "Saviour to his disciples, the Ten Commandments, written with "the finger of the Almighty, and delivered with dreadful "Majesty, together with that Brief Summary of our Holy "Faith, commonly called *The Apostle's Creed,* were most impu- "dently depraved and profaned, and to the horror of all pious "ears, the scandal of Christianity, and indelible shame of the "Nation, turned into ridicule and impiety ; his Lordship "detesting such abominations, presented the said pamphlet to "the consideration of His Majesty's most Honourable Privy "Council ; and 'tis said, the said Bookseller will at the Sessions "beginning to be holden this week for London be indicted (as "he most justly deserves) for blasphemy ; in the mean time all "sober men of the Church of England (for which every true "Protestant has a profound deference and respect, though dis- "senting from some superfluous ceremonies, so much perhaps "the more eagerly contended for by domineering spirits, by "how much the less necessary they are) will take notice what "kind of persons these are, who so studiously make it their "business to render Dissenters odious and suspected, with those "swarms of seditious libels, daily spawned by *Th. Too. S. M.* "this worthy gentleman in Cornhill, and others. And that the "authors of such pamphlets, whatever they scribble, are no real "sons of the Church of England, but a disparagement unto her, "by shrouding themselves under her mantle, being in truth, "either disguised Papists, or else mere Ruffians, debaucht rake- "hells and Atheists."

Very soon afterwards at the Sessions of Peace held at Guild- hall, the Grand Jury found a true bill against Hindmarsh, Thomson the printer and Parson Ashington the alleged writer of this "detestable blasphemous pamphlet." To quote the forcible words of the next number of The True Protestant

Mercury—"The Secretary of Hell that contrived this horrid "piece is confessed to be one Ashington, credibly reported to be "a beneficed parson in Northamptonshire, but non-resident; "and skulking here about town to practise more freely de- "bauchery and do mischief. There are warrants issued forth "against him; and some say, he was once seiz'd, and by "negligence suffered to escape; at present we cannot hear that "he is in custody."

Hindmarsh brought a certiorari to remove the indictment into the King's Bench, but Mr. Justice Dolben forthwith granted a procedendo to try it immediately; and the indictment being read, Hindmarsh pleaded guilty, and was immediately ordered to be taken into custody, and was afterwards bailed, "the Court "resenting so justly the heinousness of the offence, that they "deferred giving sentence till next term, resolving to do it in a "public manner at the King's Bench, all the Judges being "present."[1]

On the 24th June Hindmarsh appeared in the Court of King's Bench and moved to have his bail discharged; the Lord Chief Justice told him he deserved to be severely punished, and asked him what he had done to expect such a favour? His Counsel alleged, that he had discovered the author, who had already done penance for it. Notwithstanding which the Lord Chief Justice ordered him to prosecute the said author at common law by the first day of the next term, and then they would consider of discharging his bail."[2]

The following is a copy of this curious paper.

The Presbyterian PATERNOSTER; CREED, and TEN COMMANDMENTS.

Manent veteris vestigia fraudis. *Virg.*

The Pater Noster.

Our Father which art in Hell, magnify'd be thy name; thy Arbitrary Kingdom come, thy Tyranical will be done in *England* now, as it was in *Forty One;* Give us in this our Day

1. The True Protestant Mercury, No. 32, April 13 to April 16, 1681.
2.   Ditto   No. 49. June 22 to June 25, 1681.

a holy occasion of Rebellion; and forgive us our shew of Godliness for thy sake, as we forgive others their holy Hypocrisy
for our *good Cause;* and lead us not into an agreement of *King*
and *Parliament;* But Deliver us from *Monarchy* and *Hierarchy;*
and then thine shall be this Kingdom, its Power and Glory, for
ever and ever, *Amen.*

The CREED.

I Believe in *John Calvin,* the Father of our Religion, disposer
of *٭* Heaven and *٭* Earth; and in *Owen,* *٭* They the
Baxter and *Jenkins* &c. his dear Sons our Lords, only Saints
who were Conceived by the *Spirit* of *Fanaticism,* *٭* Dominion is
born of *Schism* and *Faction,* suffer'd under the founded in Gr
Act of Uniformity; were Silenced, Dead and Buried;
and had descended into Hell, but that they arose again in the
year of *Toleration;* ascended into *Tub-Pulpits,* and now sit at
the right hand of the Lord S—— from whence they are
coming to judge both the *Church* and the *State.* I Believe in
the Holy *Assembly of Divines,* the Holy *National Synod,* the
Seperate Meetings, the *Act of Oblivion,* the *Resurrection from
Dead Rites,* and *Toleration Everlasting.* Amen.

The Ten Commandments.

The same which *John Presbyter* hath spoken in 20 Chapters of
his *Works;* saying, *I am the Lord thy God, which brought thee out
of the Land of Antichrist, out of the House of Ceremonious Bondage.*

I.

Thou shalt have no other Gods but Me.

II.

Thou shalt not make any Image, or likeness of any *Saint* in
Heaven above, (except *S. Oliver &c.*) or bow down at the
Adorable name of *Jesus* here on Earth; nor use the Sign of the
Cross in the *Waters of Baptism;* For I the Lord thy God in my
Jealousie murder'd the Father, and will visit his *Superstitious
Iniquity* upon his Children, unto the third and fourth Generation
of them that hate me; but shew Mercy unto thousands in them
that love me, and keep my Damnable and Rebellious Com-
mandments.

III.

Thou shalt not make the *Solemn League* and *Covenant* vain, nor subscribe the *Declaration;* nor take the Oaths of *Allegiance* and *Supremacy,* unless (with a Jesuitical *salvo,*) to obtain places of Honour and Power.

IV.

Remember that thou keep holy the Remembrance of Forty One. Many years didst thou labour, yet could'st not do all that thou hadst to do; But in *Forty One* the Lord thy God sent thee a Sabbath of Deliverance; Thou shalt therefore now remember to do all manner of work that thou didst then, Thou, and thy Son, and thy Daughter, thy Man-Servant, and thy Maid-Servant, the Brutes and Proselytes that are within thy Conventicles; For in *Forty One* the Lord thy God made ENGLAND and SCOTLAND Rebellious; thou shalt therefore Bless the year Forty One; and hallow it.

V.

Honour *Fanaticism* thy Father, and *Schism* thy Mother, that thy Days may be long in the Land which the Lord thy God will once more give thee.

VI.

Thou shalt do no Murder, but upon *Majesty, Episcopacy* and *Loyalty.*

VII.

Thou shalt not commit Adultry, save with the *Holy Sisterhood,* to get Babes of Grace.

VIII.

Thou shalt not steal, unless by *Sequestration, Composition,* or *Publick Faith.*

IX.

Thou shalt not bear False witness against a *Brother,* but may'st swallow Perjury by a Popish Reservation for the good of Holy Cause.

X.

Thou shalt Covet nothing but *Crown-Lands, Bishops Lands,* and the Estates of *Malignants.*

POSTSCRIPT.

Thus is our New Religion
Model'd by that of Forty One ;
And we must root up Monarchy
To stop the growth of Popery ;
And undermining Church *and*
State,
Rome's *Practices we'll Ante-*
date ;
The better to prevent the PLOT,
Ourselves will do what they
cou'd not.
We'll cure all fear of French
Invasion,
By ruining at home the Nation.
And since Petitions *do no good,*
And all our Tricks are under-
stood :
Since He who never us'd to fail,
Doth now, our little Matchiavel;
We'll to the World Proclaim
aloud,

The King *and* Duke *thirst*
after Bloud.
Curtis, Harris, Smith and
Care,
Shall Thrice a Week the King-
dom scare,
As if the Devil, Turk, *or* Pope,
Were just arrived in the Hope,
We'll authorize Men to Rebel,
By Tales from Hatfield, *and*
from Hell :
And then perswade the silly
Nation,
That Treason *comes by* Reve-
lation :
And that Imaginary Ghosts
Are Envoys *from the Lord of*
Hosts.
Nor will We cease, till we pull
down
Episcopacy *and the* Crown.

Printed for *Tom Tell-troth* at the Sign of the *Old King's Head* in
Axe Yard in King Street, Westminster.

274.

An Apostrophe of the Loyal Party to his Majesty.
1681.

At the Sessions for the City of London held on June 1, 1681,
the Jury made a presentment against this "seditious pamphlet,
"contrived by Papists, and believed to be printed by the Popish
"Printer in Fetter Lane, the design of it being to overthrow
"the ancient constitution of this kingdom."[1] The Editor has
not been able to discover a copy.

275.

The Vindication of the English Roman Catholics.
1681.

1. The Impartial Protestant Mercury, From Tuesday May 31, to Friday
June 3. 1681. No. 12.

On Monday October 10. 1681 a complaint was made by Justice Warcup of this "popish invective libel" dated from Antwerp. The publisher was had before the Council, and was to answer the same before the King and Council, on the following Friday.[1] No further proceedings can be found, neither can the Editor discover a copy of the book.

276.

Smith's Protestant Intelligence; Domestic and Forein. Numb. 21. From Thursday April 7. to Monday April 11. 1681.

For publishing this newspaper, a copy of which is preserved in the British Museum Library, a prosecution was instituted against Francis Smith. The information charges that Francis Smith, the elder, late of the parish of St. Christopher, London, Yeoman, being a pernicious and seditious man, contriving and maliciously intending to disturb the peace and common tranquillity of this kingdom, and to make, excite and procure discord between the King and his subjects did, on the first day of October, in the thirty third year of the reign of King Charles the Second, in the parish aforesaid, falsely, unlawfully, unjustly, wickedly, seditiously and scandalously cause to be printed, sold, uttered and published a certain false, malicious, scandalous, and seditious libel intituled *Smith's Protestant Intelligence, Domestick and Forein* in which are contained these false, malicious, and scandalous sentences following, *April 9. Mr Everard having two Orders of Council sent him for to attend on his Majesty at the Board Yesterday, he there Appearing, constantly refused to give a Bond for to Prosecute Fitzharris; but, that the Reasons that made others (whose Office it was) to decline it, ought to make him much more shie to do it, It was thereupon granted to him that the King's Attorney General would prosecute. But it being insisted that he should give in his Evidence, as the law required (if what he had discovered were true). Everard, (as 'tis said) replied, that he would think of that, and return his Answer after some convenient time, if he were resolved as to some Difficulties and Quæries; viz.— Whether it was the*

1. The Impartial Protestant Mercury, No. 50, From Tuesday October 11 to Friday October 14, 1681.

Opinion of that Honourable Board, that Fitzharris could be tried elsewhere than in Parliament, and whether it were safe enough for Mr. Everard to give his Evidence elsewhere non obstante the Impeachment of the said Fitzharris by the Commons, especially after the Impeachment was lodged with the Lords, and entred in their Books, because the Lords might receive and reassume the Impeachment in another Parliament (as in case of the Lords of the Tower) and then the Commons might become Prosecutors themselves.[1]

277.

Del Teatro Brittanico o vero Historia dello Stato, Antico, e Presente, Corte, Governo Spirituale, e Temporale, Leggi, Massime, Religioni, et Euuenimenti della Grande Brettagna. By Gregorio Leti. London. 1683.

For writing this work the author was banished the kingdom, and seven hundred copies were seized. A copy exists in the British Museum Library. It is in two volumes, quarto size.

278.

The Impartial Protestant Mercury, N° 89. From Friday Feb. 24 to Tuesday February 28. 168½.

At the Easter Sessions for Bristol in the year 1682 the Grand Jury presented this and the four following publications as being "infamous, scandalous, and seditious"; and the Court thereupon ordered that at its rising these libels be publicly burnt by the Beadle or Common Executioner.[2] A copy is preserved in the British Museum Library.

279.

The Impartial Protestant Mercury, N° 96. From Tuesday March 21 to Friday, March 24. 168½.

A copy is preserved in the British Museum Library.

280.

The sad and lamentable cry of oppression and cruelty in the City of Bristol. 1682.

The editor has not met with a copy of this work.

1. King's Bench Judgment Roll, Trin. 35., Charles 2 rot., 81.
1. London Gazette. No. 1717. From May 1 to May 4. 1682.

281.

More sad and lamentable news from Bristol. 1682.

The editor has not met with a copy of this work.

282.

The devouring informers of Bristol &c. Being an additional account of some late proceedings of those ravenous beasts of prey, against Dissenting Protestants. Bristol. April 22. 1682.

A copy of this tract is preserved in the British Museum Library. It is in quarto, and contains four pages.

283.

Smith's Currant Intelligence, or an impartial account of transactions both forraign and domestick. Published from Tuesday, March 23 to Saturday March 27. [1680].

For publishing this newspaper, a copy of which is preserved in the Library of the British Museum, a prosecution was instituted against John Smith of Queen Street, in the County of Middlesex, Printer. The information charges that the defendant being a pernicious person, and contriving and maliciously intending to excite discord and scandal between the King and his people and the nobles of the kingdom, did on the twenty seventh day of March, in the thirty second year of the reign of King Charles the Second, in the parish of St. Giles in the Fields, Co : Midd :. publish and cause to be published a certain false, scandalous, and malicious libel intituled *Smith's Currant Intelligence, or an impartial account of transactions both forraign and domestick* containing among other things as follows :—*The Project for carrying and recarrying of Letters from place to place throughout all the Cities of London and Westminster, for a penny a Letter, so often mentioned in the Intelligences, is, as Dr. Oates says, a farther branch of the Popish Plot; for that he is credibly informed, it is the most dextrous Invention of Mr. Henry Nevill alias Pain, who is notoriously known to be a great asserter of the Catholick cause, and shrewdly suspected to be a promoter of this*

*way of Treasonable Correspondencies ; And it is to be feared, as that
good Invention of Pipes hath wholly destroyed the Trade of Tankard
Bearer, so this silly Invention will only serve to ruine the poor
Porters.*[1]

284.

England's Alarm : or, a most humble declaration,
address, and fervent petition to his most Excellent
Majesty Charles the Second, King of Great Britain
and Ireland; and to his most honourable and grand
Council the Parliament of England; as also to the
City of London, and the whole nation in general.
Concerning the great Overtures, Catastrophes, and
Grand Occurrences about to inundate and pour in
upon us, as the Judgments of Almighty God upon
Antichrist and his adherents, and the Pride, Nauseancy,
and Errour of Professors, in the years 1680 and 1681.
Written by a true lover of the true Protestant Religion,
and of his Tottering poor Native Country of England
Johannes Philangus.

London. Printed for Thomas Pasham, in Fleet
Lane. 1679.

This book is ascribed by the compilers of the Catalogue of the
Museum Library to William Petyt; and there are several
other productions of Johannes Philangus ; but it does not appear
upon what authority Petyt is considered the author. A copy is
preserved in the British Museum Library. It is in folio, and
contains six pages.

For printing this work a prosecution was instituted against
James Cottrell, a printer of the parish of St. Sepulchre.in
London. The information charges that he, being a pernicious
person, and contriving and maliciously intending to create
discord and scandal between the King and his people, and the
nobles of the kingdom, did on the twenty sixth day of March

1. King's Bench Judgment Roll, Easter 35, Charles 2. No. 310 rot. 23,
34 & 103.

in the thirty second year of the reign of King Charles the Second, at the parish of St. Sepulchre in the City of London publish and cause to be published a false scandalous and malicious libel intituled *England's Alarm, &c.* (as in title), containing among other things as follows : *Remember, England, if thou art not mad drunk with the Whores Charms how that thy preaching Ministers are turn'd into dumb Dogs and ravening Wolves. And they bear rule by thy means, and thou lovest to have it so.*

285.

The Neck of the Quakers broken ; or cut in sunder by the two-edged sword of the Spirit which is put into my Mouth. First, in a Letter to Edward Bourne a Quaker. Secondly, in answer to a letter to Samuel Hooton and W. S. Thirdly, in a letter to Richard Farnsworth, Quaker. Fourthly, in answer to a printed pamphlet of the said Richard Farnsworth, entituled, Truth Ascended : or, The Anointed and Sealed of the Lord defended, &c. Written by Lodowick Muggleton, one of the two last Prophets and Witnesses unto the High and Mighty God, the Man Christ Jesus in Glory. Amsterdam : Printed in the year of our Lord God, 1663. And are to be had in Great Trinity Lane, over against the Lyon and the Lamb.

The author of this book was founder of the sect called Muggletonians. He was born in 1609, and was bred up to be a tailor. Abandoning his trade in 1651, he set up himself and his companion John Reeves as the "two last witnesses" mentioned in the apocalypse as having power to prophesy, and to smite mankind with plagues. They began to fulfil their "commission" by denouncing all religious sects, and especially the Ranters and the Quakers. An exposition of their doctrines, was published in "The Divine Looking-Glass." In this work,

---

1.   King's Bench Judgment Roll, Trinity 35, Charles 2., part 2, m. 89.

among other wild vagaries, were propounded the views that the Trinity are merely the three different names, and not the three distinct persons, of one God; that God has a real human body; and that he left Elias as his vicegerent in heaven when he came down to the earth to die on the cross. These profane heresies provoked much opposition. They were attacked by William Penn, the Quaker, in a book entitled *The New Witnesses proved Old Hereticks*. 1672.

For writing this book Muggleton was prosecuted; and was tried at the Old Bailey on Wednesday, the 17th of January, 167$\frac{6}{7}$; he was found guilty, and sentenced by the Court to stand three days in the Pillory, one day in Cornhill near the Royal Exchange; the next day in Fleet Street near the end of Chancery Lane; and the third day in West Smithfield, from eleven to one o'clock each day, with a paper over his head describing his offence in large letters, and his books to be seized, and divided into three parts, to be burnt before his face near the Pillory by the Common Hangman; and besides, to be fined £500, and to continue in gaol till payment, and afterwards for his life, unless he procured good bail, "such as the Court should accept of, and not of his own gang, faction or sect," for being of good behaviour. Full particulars of his trial will be found in a little book, entituled, A true narrative of the Proceedings at the Sessions-house in the Old Baily, at a Sessions there held on Wednesday the 17th of January 167$\frac{6}{7}$, giving a full account of the true tryal and sentence of Lodowick Muggleton for blasphemous words and books. London. 167$\frac{6}{7}$.

The indictment charges that Lodowick Muggleton, late of London, labourer, being a pernicious, blasphemous and heretical man in his opinions, pretending and affirming that he was one of the two last prophets of the New Testament, designing and intending to disseminate his pernicious, blasphemous, seditious, heretical and monstrous opinions, and to disturb the common peace and tranquillity of this kingdom, and to deprave the true religion rightly established and exercised within this kingdom, also to move, make, and excite discords between the king and his subjects, and to bring into great hatred and contempt the king and his royal government in ecclesiastical causes, did on the thirtieth day of August in the twenty eighth year of the reign of King Charles the Second, at the parish of St. Giles without Cripplegate, London, with force and arms, falsely, unlawfully, wickedly, maliciously, scandalously, blasphemously, seditiously, schismatically, and heretically write, cause to be printed, sold, uttered and published a certain malicious, scandalous, blasphemous, seditious, and heretical book intituled *The neck of the Quakers broken, &c.* (setting out full title) in which book are contained these false, unlawful, blasphemous, seditious, schismatical, heretical, and scandalous sentences following, viz.:—*I write these lines unto you Edward Bourne, knowing you to be of the seed of the serpent, and appointed to eternal damnation before you were born, though you know it not, I do know it by your speaking evil of that Doctrine which is declared by us the Witnesses of the Spirit, by calling of it Deceit, Confusion, and Lies, with many more wicked speeches against the purest Truth that ever was declared by Prophet or Apostle, because this is the Commission of the Spirit, and the last Witness of God on earth. Therefore for these your hard sayings against the Doctrine of this Commission of the Spirit, in obedience unto my Commission, I do pronounce you cursed and damned soul and body from the presence of God, elect men and Angels, to eternity; neither shall that light within you, nor any God deliver you from this Curse, but according to my word it shall be upon you, because you shall know that God hath given power unto man to curse you to eternity, and that there is a Prophet of the Lord now in the Land. Written by Lodowick Muggleton, one of the two last Witnesses and Prophets unto the High and Mighty God the Man Christ Jesus in Glory. Vale.* And in another place of the same book are contained these false, feigned, malicious, scandalous, blasphemous, seditious and heretical sentences following, viz.:— *Now in this last age God hath given me power, and discerning to determine and give judgement upon men and women according as I do discern by their words, and I thereby also know what nature and seed they are of, and accordingly I give judgment upon them, for I do go by as certain a rule as the Judges of the Land do, when they give true Judgment according to the Law. For God hath ordained me the chief Judge in the world at this day to give sentence upon men and women's spiritual and eternal estate what will become of them after death. Full of this cursing I confess my mouth is, and I do rejoice in it too, I know that God is well pleased in the damnation of those that*

I have cursed, and I am wonderous well satisfied in giving judgement upon them, according to the tenor of my Commission; and this is that which you call swelling words. And in another place of the same book are contained these other false, feigned, malicious, scandalous, blasphemous, unlawful, seditious and heretical sentences following, viz.:—*Therefore I shall speak a few words unto you two in particular, because you two have committed that unpardonable sin that never will be forgiven in this world, nor in the world to come; for you have done despite unto the Spirit of Truth, in speaking evil of things you do not know, for you have called the Doctrine and Declaration of the Spirit, Blasphemy, Deceit, and Lies, with many other railing speeches, with high impudency, from a light within you, and from the dead letter without you, and hath presumptuously lifted up your selves with that light within you, to speak evil of the Commission of the Spirit, which we received from the true personal God without us, even the Man Christ Jesus in Glory. Therefore in obedience to my Commission, I do pronounce Samuel Hooton and W. S., for this their Blasphemy against the Holy Spirit that sent me, cursed and damned soules and bodies from the presence of God, elect men and Angels. to eternity. Your light within you, nor God without you shall deliver you from this Sentence which I have declared upon you, because you shall know that there is a true Prophet now in the last Age, as well as there hath been in former times. And this Sentence shall be the mark of your Reprobation in your foreheads to eternity, even as your great Grandfather had in his forehead, and all the Seed of Faith that shall read this Epistle and see you, shall see the mark of Reprobation in your foreheads, neither shall you scrape it out, but it will be seen by the Elect as long as you live. And when you dye, you shall pass through this first death into the second death, and in the Resurrection you shall never see the face of God, nor man, nor Angels, nor your own faces, to eternity: but you shall be in utter darkness, where is weeping, and gnashing of teeth for evermore.* To the great scandal and contempt of the King, his Crown and Dignity, also of the religion rightly established in this kingdom, to the bad and pernicious example of all others in like case offending, and against the peace of the King, his Crown and Dignity.

The indictment also further charges that—Nathaniel Powell late of the parish of St. Clement Danes, London, yeoman, being a pernicious, blasphemous, impious and profane person, and not having the fear of God in his heart, but moved and seduced by the instigation of the devil, and contriving and intending to deprave, scandalize and vilify the true Christian Religion rightly established and exercised within this kingdom ; also to blaspheme the wisdom, omnipotence and majesty of the Holy Trinity, and the incarnation of our Lord Jesus Christ, and to strengthen, confirm and ratify the aforesaid pernicious, seditious, heretical and monstrous opinions of the said Lodowick Muggleton within the kingdom of England, did, on the first day of April, in the thirty third year of the reign of King Charles the Second, at the parish of St. Clement Danes, aforesaid, say, pronounce, and publish falsely, scandalously, maliciously, profanely, blasphemously, and heretically these false, scandalous, profane, blasphemous, and heretical words in the presence and hearing of divers liege subjects of the said lord the King, viz.—*I rather believe in Mugggleton that stood on the Pillory, than in Jesus Christ, I have power to damn and to save, and if thou* (meaning a certain Gilbert Soper then and there present) *art not damned I never desire to see the face of God. I do believe in that Muggleton, that stood on the Pillory, next to God Almighty. That Muggleton had power to damn whom he pleased, whom he damned were damned to eternity, and whom he saved, were saved. I have power to damn and to save, I believe more in Muggleton than in Jesus Christ. I thank God, never offended God in my life, I have no sin to ask God pardon for, I say drunkenness is no sin, I have had the knowledge of my own salvation these twelve months, I have the power of damning and saving, I damn thee* (meaning a certain Richard Sharpe then and there present) *and God cannot save thy soul.* To the great scandal of the true profession of the Christian Religion, to the manifest contempt of the Holy Trinity, and blasphemy of the Deity of our Lord Jesus Christ, and to the bad and most pernicious example of all others in such case offending, and against the peace of the King his Crown and dignity.[1]

286.

No Protestant-Plot; or the present pretended

1. King's Bench Judgment Roll, Mich. 33, Car. 2, part 2, m. 137.

Conspiracy of Protestants against the King and Government discovered to be a conspiracy of the Papists against the King and his Protestant Subjects. London. 1681.

For printing this book, a prosecution was instituted against Richard Baldwin of the parish of St. Sepulchre in London. The information charges that the defendant, being a malicious and a seditious man, and contriving and maliciously intending to disturb the peace and common tranquillity of this kingdom, and to excite, move, and procure discord between the king and his subjects, and to bring into hatred and contempt the king's government and the due course of law of this kingdom, did, on the twentieth day of October in the thirty-third year of the reign of King Charles the Second, in the parish of St. Sepulchre aforesaid, falsely, unlawfully, wickedly, maliciously, seditiously, and scandalously cause to be printed, sold and published, a certain false, malicious, scandalous and seditious libel, intituled *No Protestant Plot*, containing among other things as follows :— *The King is of too much goodness, and a Prince of Greater Wisdom and more unstained justice, than that any of his subjects should apprehend or fear anything illegal from him while he acts free and unconstrained; but how far his Ministers, especially those who have been exasperated by the proceedings of Parliaments, may render his Authority a cloak to their malice, and make the pretence of his preservation and safety subservient to their revenge, is what we are jealous of. And tho' we would fain persuade ourselves that they are persons of more honour and integrity than to make reprisals upon the Lives of Peers for the injury which they suppose was done them; yet the imprisoning my Lord Shaftsbury upon the credit of Witnesses whose testimony they refused to believe in the case of my Lord Stafford, doth not a little surprize the thinking part of mankind. Now nothing can be more disservicable to his Majesty, or lessening to the honour of his Government, than to have his Authority abused to countenance a personal quarrel, and his Laws applied to revenge a private offence. And in another part as follows :—Nor can men persuade themselves to believe, but that the Imprisonment of my Lord Shaftsbury is built upon something which will not abide the Test, when they consider the way and method according to which he hath been all along treated. Before either*

Coleman or the Jesuits were sent to prison, they were allowed both to know and see the persons who had deposed against them. And it is generally believed, that every Englishman may demand it as his right. And therefore, the refusing it to my Lord Shaftsbury, does seem to intimate either that the Witnesses are not of a credit sufficient to support the confinement of so great a Peer, or else that it was not convenient to trust their carriage in this matter, as well as the general course of their lives, to an early and exact scrutiny. But as if this were not enough to create a suspition of some undue and indirect dealing in this affair, the refusing to administer an oath to those that were ready to swear to Indictments of Subornation against the Witnesses, doth exceedingly heighten all men's jealousies. For not to debate about the legality or illegality of this procedure, being obliged till this business do either before this or a higher judicature come under a review, to acquiesce silently in the Judgement of the Court; I shall only say: That as it is the first president of this kind, so the reducing it into common practice, would prove a general obstruction of the justice of the Law. And to make the receiving of Indictments depend upon the pleasure of the Attorney General were to settle on him a more Arbitrary Power than the Laws of England have placed in the King himself. And in another part as follows:—And we are the more inclined to believe this whole Conspiracy wherein the Earl of Shaftsbury and other Protestants are said to be engaged against the King and the Government, is only a malicious piece of revenge upon the zealous patriots of our Religion; by considering that Justice Warcup, and Mr. David Fitzgerald, are employed to conduct and manage the detection and discovery of it.[1]

A copy of the pamphlet is preserved in the British Museum Library. It is in quarto and contains 37 pages.

287.

A Satire, 1680.

This is a set of verses satirizing the Lord Chief Justice Scroggs, apparently very similar to those printed on p. 216, for which Jane Curtis was prosecuted.

For publishing them a prosecution was instituted against John Howe, of the parish of St. Michael, Cornhill, bookseller.

---

1. King's Bench Judgment Roll, Charles 2. No. 302, rot. 114.

The information charges that the defendant, contriving and maliciously intending to bring into hatred and contempt Sir William Scroggs, Lord Chief Justice, in those things which touch him and his judicial office and the King's authority, did, on the twenty-fourth day of May, in the thirty-second year of the reign of King Charles the Second, within the parish of St. Michael, Cornhill aforesaid, get into his hands a certain false, malicious, infamous, scandalous, and odious libel intituled *A Satire*, in which libel is contained among other things as follows :—*The Judge is a base butcher's sonne* (meaning the Lord Chief Justice.) *Most sly of nocent blood. But for ten thousand pound has done The Pope a deal of good. 'Twas he that villaine Wakeman cleared, Who was to have poysened the King, As plaine to all but twelve appeared, For which he deserves to swing.* (meaning again the Lord Chief Justice.) And that the said John Howe, knowing the aforesaid libel to be a scandalous and infamous libel, did on the said twenty-fourth day of May, publish and expose to sale the same libel, to the great scandal and contempt of the said Lord Chief Justice and the King's authority.[1]

There was also a prosecution against one Enoch Procer for publishing the same.[2]

288.

The Impartial Protestant Mercury. From Tuesday October 4 to Friday October 7, 1681. N° 48.

For publishing this newspaper, a copy of which is preserved in the British Museum Library, a prosecution was instituted against Janeway the printer.

The information charges that the defendant described as of London, yeoman, being a pernicious and seditious man, contriving and maliciously intending to disturb the peace and tranquillity of this kingdom, and to create, move, and excite discord between the king and his subjects, and to bring the king's government into contempt, did falsely, maliciously, and seditiously, with intent to persuade and induce the king's subjects to believe that this kingdom of England was governed by the

1. King's Bench Judgment Roll. Charles 2. No. 300, m. 88.
2. King's Bench Judgment Roll. Charles 2. No. 298, m. 109.

advice of the king of France, and that the secrets of the government of this kingdom were notified to the king of France, and that to fulfil his most wicked intentions, on the twentieth day of October in the thirty-third year of the reign of King Charles the Second, in the parish of St. Michael, Cornhill, London, falsely, unlawfully, wickedly, maliciously, scandalously, and seditiously cause to be printed, sold, and published a certain false, scandalous, and defamatory libel, intituled *The Impartial Protestant Mercury*, containing among other things as follows:—*There has been a fresh rumour of a Parliament like to be called to meet on the twenty-eighth of the next month, but we cannot find any foundation for that report, more than that a Person of Quality lately arrived from France relates, that he was told of such a thing at Paris.*[1]

On April 5, 1682, Janeway was called before the Council for printing and publishing false and seditious news, and he was thereupon ordered to give good security, to appear personally at the King's Bench Bar the first day of the next term, to answer such matters as should be exhibited against him on his majesty's behalf, and in the mean time to be of good behaviour; and he accordingly entered into recognizances for that purpose.[2]

289.

The Protestant Domestick Intelligence; or, News both from City and Country. Published to prevent false reports. Friday, March 12th, 16$\frac{79}{80}$. No. 72.

For publishing this newspaper, a copy of which is preserved in the British Museum Library, a prosecution was instituted against Nathaniel Crouch.

The information charges that the defendant, who is described as of the parish of St. Margaret, Lothbury, London, gentleman, being a pernicious person, and contriving and maliciously intending to incite and move discord and scandal between the king and his people, and the magnates of this kingdom, did on the twelfth day of March, in the thirty-second year of the reign of King Charles the Second, at the parish of St. Margaret,

1. King's Bench Judgment Roll. Charles 2. No. 302, rot. 113.
2. London Gazette. No. 1709. April 3 to April 6, 1682.

Lothbury, publish and cause to be published a certain false, scandalous, and malicious libel entituled *The Protestant Domestick Intelligence; or, News both from City and Country,* containing (among other things) as follows :—*Yesterday we are informed that Mrs. Le-Mair, alias Loveland, the mother of Philip Le-Mair was taken into custody, and that she has declared there is a Person of Honour, as well as one of the Lords in the Tower, concerned with her in the conspiracy against the Life of the Duke of Buckingham.*[1]

290.

Mercurius Civicus; or, a true account of affairs both foreign and domestick. Monday, 29 March, 1680. N° 3.

For publishing this newspaper, a copy of which is preserved in the British Museum Library, a prosecution was instituted against James Astwood, of the parish of St. Christopher, London, printer.

The information charges that the defendant, being a pernicious person, and contriving and maliciously intending to incite and move discord and scandal between the king and his people and the magnates of this kingdom, did on the thirtieth day of March, in the thirty-second year of the reign of King Charles the Second, at the parish of St. Christopher, London, print and cause to be printed, a certain false, scandalous, and malicious libel intituled *Mercurius Civicus: or, a True Account of affairs both foreign and Domestick,* containing (among other things) as follows : —*It is advised from the several places where the Lord Chief Justice North has been in circuit, that his Lordship hath been pleased to declare that the Act of Parliament for the Conviction of Popish Recusants ought to be put in force against none but Papists. And though several Protestants had been indicted hereon, he gave it as his Opinion. That the intention of that Act was purely to suppress Popery; and so directed the Jury not to find the Bill against Protestants as Popish Recusants but as Protestant Dissenters, which hath given a great deal of satisfaction to people, several protestants having been severely dealt withall by reason of that Act, which point the Parliament were in great consultation about rectifying.*[2]

1 King's Bench Judgment Roll. Charles 2. No. 298, rot. 106.
2. King's Bench Judgment Roll. Charles 2. No. 298, rot. 107.

291.

A Faithful relation of the most remarkable transactions which have happened at Tangier: since the
Moors have lately made their attacques upon the
Forts and Fortifications of that Famous Garrison,
likewise the strength and good posture of defence it
remains now in. With an account of the Trenches,
Lines and Works they have already drawn in order to
their besieging several of the said forts strongly
guarded by the English, and the advantageous success
the English have obtained over those infidels, in a
late fight between them; burning and demolishing
their works, beating them out of their trenches,
killing them, and pursuing them even to their Camp.

A pamphlet of four pages; a copy of which is preserved in
the British Museum Library. For its publication David
Mallett, of the parish of St. Martin, Ludgate, printer, was
prosecuted.

The information charges that the defendant published the
same with the intent to create discord and scandal between
the king and his people and the magnates of this kingdom;
but it does not set out any of the alleged objectionable passages
as is usually done.

292.

The Speech of the late Lord Russel to the Sheriffs;
together with the paper deliver'd by him to them, at
the Place of Execution, on July 21, 1683. London.
Printed by John Darby, by direction of the Lady
Russel. 1683.

A copy of this speech is preserved in the Library of the
British Museum. It is in folio and contains four pages.

For publishing the same, a prosecution was instituted against
John Darby, bookseller, of the parish of St. Bartholomew the
Great, London.

The information charges that the defendant being a pernicious and seditious man, and contriving and practising, and falsely, and maliciously, and wickedly and seditiously intending to disturb the peace of the king and the common tranquillity of this kingdom, and to weaken and bring into discredit and bad repute the laws and customs of this kingdom, and the ancient government and the common justice thereof, and to excite and procure discords and seditions between the king and his subjects, also to bring into discredit the trial and sentence of Lord William Russell, did, on the fourteenth day of August in the thirty-fifth year of the reign of King Charles the Second, at the parish of St. Bartholomew aforesaid, falsely, unlawfully, unjustly, wickedly, seditiously, maliciously, and scandalously, make, compose, and print and sell, utter, and publish a certain false, seditious, malicious, and scandalous libel intituled *The speech of the late Lord Russell to the Sheriffs, together with the paper delivered by him to them at the place of execution*, containing, among other things, these false, malicious, seditious and scandalous sentences, viz., *I wish with all my soul all our unhappy Differences were removed, and that all sincere Protestants would so far consider the danger of Popery, as to lay aside their Heats, and agree against the Common Enemy; and that the Churchmen would be less severe, and the Dissenters less scrupulous; For I think Bitterness and Persecution are at all times bad, but much more now. For Popery, I look on it as an Idolatrous and Bloody Religion, and therefore thought myself bound, in my Station, to do all I could against it. And by that, I foresaw I should procure such great Enemies to myself, and so powerful ones, that I have been now for some time expecting the worst. And blessed be God, I saw by the Axe, and not by the Fiery Tryal,* And in another part, these other false, seditious, scandalous and defamatory sentences, viz., *I did believe and do still, that Popery is breaking in upon the Nation; and that those who advance it, will stop at nothing, to carry on their Design: I am heartily sorry that so many Protestants give their helping hand to it.* And in another place are contained these other false, scandalous, seditious and defamatory sentences, following, *I cannot but give some touch about the Bill of Exclusion, and shew the Reasons of my appearing in that Business; which in short is this: That I thought the Nation was in such danger of Popery, and that the Expectation of a Popish Successor (as I have said in Parliament) put the King's life likewise in such danger, that I saw no way so effectual to secure both as such a Bill. As to the limitations which were proposed, if they were sincerely offered, and had pass'd into a Law, the Duke then would have been excluded from the Power of a King, and the Government quite altered, and little more than the Name of a King left. So I could not see either Sin or Fault in the one, when all People were willing to admit of t'other; but thought it better to have a King with his Prerogative, and the Nation easy and safe under him, than a King without it, which must have bred perpetual jealousies, and a Continual Struggle. All this I say, only to justify myself, and not to inflame others; Though I cannot but think my Earnestness in that matter has had no small Influence in my present Sufferings.* And in another place are contained these other false, scandalous, and seditious sentences following:—*I pray God lay not this to the charge, neither of the King's Counsel, nor Judges, nor Sheriffs, nor Jury: And for the Witnesses, I pity them, and wish them well. I shall not reckon up the Particulars wherein they did me wrong: I had rather their own Consciences should do that, to which, and the Mercies of God I leave them.* And in another place are contained these other false, malicious, scandalous and seditious sentences following:—*From the Time of chusing Sheriffs, I concluded the Heat in that Matter would produce something of this kind; and I am not much surprised to find it fall upon me. And I wish what is done to me, may put a stop, and satiate some Peoples' Revenge, and that no more innocent Blood be shed, for I must, and do still look upon mine as such, since I know I was guilty of no Treason; and therefore I would not betray my Innocence by Flight.*

On November 20th, 1683, Darby was tried, and found guilty, and on February 1, 168$\frac{3}{4}$ he was brought to the Court of King's Bench to receive judgment, which, he humbly submitting himself to the Court, and begging pardon, with a promise never to commit the like offence, the Court ordered to be, That he should pay 20 marks for a fine to the king, and find securities for good behaviour for twelve months, and that till this be paid and done, he should be committed to prison.[1]

293.
The Night Walker of Bloomsbury.

London Gazette, No. 1900. King's Bench Judgment Roll. Charles 2. No. 314, rot. 100.

A single sheet in folio printed on both sides. A copy is preserved in the British Museum Library.

Langley Curtis, the bookseller, was prosecuted for publishing this sheet. The indictment charges that the defendant, contriving and intending to disturb the peace and common tranquillity of this kingdom, and to bring the king into the greatest hatred, contempt, and infamy with all his subjects; and to cause, incite, and procure divers differences and false rumours concerning the pretended ghost of Lord William Russell, lately attainted and executed for high treason, did, on the twelfth day of October in the thirty-fifth year of the reign of King Charles the Second, at the parish of St. Bride aforesaid, unlawfully, seditiously, and maliciously print and publish, and cause to be printed and published, a certain feigned, false, seditious, and scandalous libel of and concerning the pretended ghost aforesaid, intituled *The Night Walker of Bloomsbury*, containing these false, feigned, and scandalous sentences following, viz., *Ralph : D'ye hear the newes. Will. What newes*, &c., &c., to *Caball of bigotted Papists*. And in another part as follows,—*Will. In this Meremaid's attire*, &c., &c., to *quickly changed the colour of his ghostly habit*.

Upon this indictment Curtis was tried on February 14, 168$\frac{3}{4}$, found guilty, and on April 21, 1684, sentenced to stand in and upon the Pillory in Bloomsbury Market between the hours of eleven and one o'clock, with a paper on his head denoting his offence in large letters, and at the same time the libel was to be burned by the Common Hangman. He was also sentenced to pay a fine of £500, to be committed to the Marshalsea until payment, and to find security for good behaviour during life.

The following is a complete copy of this publication :—[1]

THE NIGHT WALKER OF BLOOMSBURY :

Being the Result of several late Consultations between a Vintner, Judge Tallow-chandler, a Brace of Fishmongers, and a Printer, &c. In a Dialogue between *Ralph* and *Will*.

Entred according to Order.

1. King's Bench Judgment Roll. Charles 2. No. 316, rot. 88.

Ralph.   D'ye hear the News?

Will.   What News?

Ralph.   Why, they say my Lord *Russel* walks.

Will.   And do you believe it?

Ralph.   Why not? may not Lords walk as well as other people?

Will.   That's not the business—but I perceive you have heard but a piece of the Story—you have not heard how the Ghost came to be rais'd nor how he was laid.

Ralph.   Rais'd and Laid!—why then I warrant you take it to be nothing but a piece of Imposture.

Will.   Nothing more certain,—a meer silly, idle, foppish contrivance of a Cabal of bigotted *Papists.*

Ralph.   I must confess a Bigotted *Papist* is a very sottish sort of Animal.—But what did this deep design drive at?

Will.   Why, Sir, a certain *Vintner* not far from *Southampton Square*, a well-wisher, you may be sure, to any Religion he could get by, had a mind to draw custome to his empty House—For he had a vast prospect of gain from the success of the Action,—For, quo he to himself, the people will cry, whether shall we go? Go! says another, we'l go to the *Hobgoblin* that counterfeited the Lord *Russel's* Ghost—for, thought he, everybody will be glad to see a *Hobgoblin.*

Ralph.   Puh—this is some invention of yours to put a trick upon the poor *Papists.*

Will.   An Invention of mine! Tis all about the Town—and besides, there is nothing more common among the *Papists* than to counterfeit Spirits and Ghosts—I find you never read the Story of the four Monks of *Bearn* in *Switzerland*, that were hang'd for counterfeiting the *Virgin Mary*; nor of the Country Curate that lay with his Neece in the shape of *St. Barbara* But the Fryer had not so good luck: For he living in a young widow's House, would fain have frighted the young Widow into his Lascivious Embraces—and to that purpose haunted her chamber every Night in a Winding Sheet: But she, being a Woman of mettle, hid a Friend of hers privately in her chamber, that gave the Spirit such a severe Cudgel-correction, as made him quickly beg Quarter for his bruised Bones.

Ralph.   But all this while, where was the Profundity of the design?

Will. The profundity of the Design was to put the Lord Russels Speech upon Dr. Burnett—And of this they were resolv'd to have an acknowledgment out of the Lord Russel's own Mouth.

Ralph. That was hard to do, when his Head was cut off.

Will. Oh—but though the Head of his body was cut off, the Head of his Ghost was still on.—However, tho'. it be not to be deny'd, that a Spirit without a Head has a very brisk motion, yet the Committee were not so cunning as to know how to bring his Ghost out of *Buckinghamshire* into *Bloomsbury Square*—and therefore another expedient was to be found out.—The Committee was extreamly puzl'd to find out this Expedient, till the *Vintner*, inspir'd no doubt with his own *Pipes* and Tierces, had it presently in his Pate.—Quo he Ladies and Gentlemen, why may not I act a Ghost, as well as Matt. Medbourn ?

Ralph. Frolick for frolick now, it would be a very good humour to Indict this Vintner upon the Statute of 21 Jacob, 26, for endeavouring to personate the Lord *Russel's* Ghost, on purpose to procure an acknowledgment contrary to his will and consent.

Will. Faith, *Sir*, the very action itself procur'd him punishment enough, to be well drub'd, and two such lovely forehead marks of *Knave* and *Fool*, that Ten Fountains, with all the Soap in the City, will never wash off.

Ralph. Pardon me, *Sir*, I have a greater opinion of the *Vintner*, and that he acted what he did in the imitation of *Theseus* and *Eneas*, who both went to visit *Pluto's* Dominions; but this same *Vintner* undertook to be even a tormented Inhabitant of the Lower Shades himself, to advance the Popish Interest, which was much a more daring deed then that of *Theseus*. The *Vintner* had Listed himself in Hell, which *Theseus* never did.

Will. Ay—but *Theseus* was *Theseus*; Theseus kicked *Proserpina's* Dog before her Face, in her own Dining-Room : But this Bugbear of a *Vintner* suffer'd himself to be thrash'd like any mortal Coward, and yet the Fool had not the wit to *vanish*.— They say, had the Earth yielded never so little, the first blow the Beadle hit, had struck him down to the place from whence he pretended to come.

Ralph. But can you tell who hatched this Chicken of a Design ?

Will. Politick Heads, *Sir,* Politick Heads,—very Politick Heads—and of both Sexes too I assure ye.

Ralph. I must confess I admire neither of their ingenuities; and as for the Women, I find 'em much more famous for the crafty carrying on a Love intrigue, or concealing their private enjoyments, then in managing *Hobgoblin* Plots.

Will. Sir, I do tell ye, this Committee consisted of several Persons, Male and Female—*Imprimis,* The Man of the House, and his Wife, chief *Presidences* of the Council. In the next place, two *Fishmongers* in *Bloomsbury,* if you hunt after the name of the one, you may easily find it : the other a most rude and ungraceful acknowledger of the Lord *Russel's* former favours, as who had all along serv'd his Table from his own Shop; his Grandfather seems to have bin the Son of *Tomlins.*

Ralph. These *Fishmongers,* Sir, were notably drawn into this Conspiracy—twas emblematical—For as great undertakings require great silence, so none more likely then *Fishmongers* to bear the Proverb always in mind, *As mute as a Fish.*

Will. The next was a *Tallow-chandler,* who, tho' he live by the Night, takes his name from Noon-Day.

Ralph. Why that was it that spoil'd the whole Plot, to engage a *Tallow-chandler* in deeds of Darkness.

Will. Oh, Sir, but he was to have been a Witness—and none so fit to be witness as a man of Light—besides, Sir, he was to attend the *Hobgoblin,* and none so fit as a *Tallow Chandler* to hold a Candle to the Devil. But observe how the *Tallow Chandler* was match'd ; for the other witness was to be a *Papistical Printer* in the Neighbourhood.

Ralph. There y'are right again—for if the Truth should chance to slip out of the *Chandler's* memory, the *Printer* had always a *Register* ready to refresh it.

Will. By what I hear, theres no such need of rubbing up the *Tallow-chandler's* memory. A my word Sir, y'are got into pleasant company—Here's a *Vintner* acts the Devil—and a *Tallow-chandler* acts a Judge—and Judges, Sir, are no fools to have their memories rub'd.

Ralph. Who the Devil made the *Tallow-chandler* a Judge ?

Will. Wine and Fat Venson, Sir, at the *Crown-Tavern,* in *Bloomsbury;* For there it was that the *Tallow-chandler* a Witty, Jocose, Droll of a *Tallow-chandler,* finding there was something to be done to gratify the Company (for it was at a public Venson-Feast) took upon him the Dignity of the Coife, and causing Mr. *Hamden* to be arraign'd before him, Mercilesly condemn'd him to be hang'd.

Ralph. What had the *Tallow-chandler* to do with Mr. *Hamden.* —Surely he is to stand or fall by another sort of Judicature then six ith Pound.

Will. Oh, Sir, 'twas done to please a brace of Reverend Justices that were Stewards of the Feast—and such frolicks as these, Lord Sir, you cannot imagin how they digest Venson, Pasty Pudding Crust—There are some people so hot, that you would admire they do not melt their Grease, and get the Scratches with Galloping after such fancies as these.

Ralph. And yet when this *Tallow-chandler* serv'd Mr. *Hamden* with Candles, he did not scruple to take his Money, notwithstanding he might not then be of his severe Judges present opinion: And therefore there is some hope yet left, that Mr. *Hamden* may sweeten up his Judge into a Reprieve, upon a promise of laying in his *Winter* store out of *Bloomsbury.*

Will. There was an *Apothecary* too, whose spleen was extreamly tickl'd at the conceit of their design. Repute makes him a person of a bulky stature, famous for the beauty of his Wainscot Lady, and the wit of his Son, whom he teaches to curse the D. of M.

Ralph. Why truly, this *Pothecary* is highly to be applauded for his Loyalty : for to shew the Exquisiteness of his Allegiance, he sends his child to the Devil to confirm it.

Will. There were several others that met at two or three of these consults, that have open'd their Purses to save their Reputation.

Ralph. I am not apt to believe that people who concerned themselves with such a ridiculous Sham as this, had much Reputation to lose; and therefore their *Peter-Pence* were ill bestow'd. The Proverb is, *Discover, and shame the Devil.*

Will. That never could be better don then by the Dress with which they disguis'd him : For certainly all the *Fools* and *Zanies* in *Bartholomew-Fair* were never so quaintly rigg'd, as this same *Hob-thrush* of a *Vintner* was equipped to act his Tragick-Comedy.

Ralph. As how ?

Will. First they hung about his Neck a large *Night-Rail,* which the Gentlewoman of the House lent him out of her Zeal.

Ralph. Most Enigmatical, Problematical, Emphatical, and Emblematical—for a *Night-Rail* being a kind of a Cloak, was most proper to cover a piece of Knavery.

Will. To hide his lower parts, the *Fishmongers* lent him their *Aprons.*

Ralph. More Enigmatical still.—For *Fishmongers* being men of Lent and Fasting days—the *Fishmongers' Aprons* were to put the Ghost in mind of his sorrow, contrition, and repentance for owning a Speech that was none of own.

Will. By your favour, Sir, here's a Breach of an Act of Parliament discovered, to bring a Spirit out of his Grave in *Linnen,* whereas he ought to have appear'd in *Crape ;* and being a Lord in Lac't *Crape* too.

Ralph. Well! But what had the Goblin about his Head?

Will. His head was muffl'd up in a White Diaper Napkin— to shew that the Letter was drapered with the Inventions of several Writers, and not of one plain Woofe.

Ralph. Shame faw the Luggs on 'em for a Company of Dotards—as if the Devil were grown as fantastical as the *French,* to change his old fashions.—Now the old fashions of Ghosts, ever since I heard of Ghosts was always the same, a Winding-sheet with two Knots and a Taper in the Spirit's hands, with which the *Chandler* might easily have furnished the Devil. Or if the Spirit must needs rise in the same Cloaths he was burr'd, the Cabal had much better ha' club'd for a new *Crape* Funeral Suit—'Twould ha' serv'd the Goblin of a *Vintner* another time, when the juice of his own *Lime-Fats* had burnt up his Liver. I'le undertake there's ne're a Booth in *Pork Fair* but would have dressed up a Hobgoblin more artificially than such a consultation of Ninny Hammers—But when the Devil was thus betrumpery'd what did he do?

Will. In this Mere-maid's Attire, he went attended with the two *Fishmongers* for his Guard, and the *Chandler* and *Printer* were to be Witnesses they saw the Apparition.—At length when he came to his Posts, as the Contrivers had laid it, 'tis to be supposed, near the House where the Lord *Russel* liv'd, he fell a groaning like an Oxe at the first sticking; nay, he groan'd even like the Groaning-board itself; and after a short preamble of Lamentations lewdly uttered, He cried out, *Oh—I have no rest because of the Speech that I never made, but* Dr. Burnet.

Ralph. There's no fear on't, but he'l be taught to groan better when he comes to groan for himself. One would have thought he should have practised the. Art of Groaning more accurately before he went to groan upon such an Occasion as this—He should have groaned as if he had been groaning for his Life, that had taken such a part upon him—but it seems he rather fell a braying then a groaning, and so discover'd himself—for upon the noise, as some Report, or at least, as the Goblin deserv'd, one of the Watch coming up to him, and perceiving by his shoes, that he had no Cloven-Feet, *Can't ye be quiet,* quo he, *in your Grave? I'le make ye quiet;* and with that, gave him such a Palt o'th Pate and the Thigh, as quickly chang'd the colour of his Ghostly Habit.

Ralph. I' good faith, the Watchmen did more then all the Committee could do—for they only strove to make him a faigned Goblin, but the Watchman made him a real *Raw-Head and Bloody-Bones.*—A Catastrophe that such an enterprize justly deserv'd.—But what became of poor Raw-Head and Bloody-bones?

Will. The now real Goblin was forc'd to confess his name, and the names of his Associates, and to chear up the Watch with Drink and Money for the fright he had put 'em in, and so they let him go, to groan forth his own Lamentations to the Gulls that set him at Work.

Ralph. Well, I will say nothing of the Speech one way nor other, but sure it was an act neither generous nor christian-like; to raise up an Impostor to disturb the silence of a Gentleman's Grave that had paid his last debt to Justice.

Will. Barbarous and papistical, which is as much as needs be said of it.

Finis.

London: Printed by J. Grantham, MDCLXXXIII.

294.

The true Englishman speaking plain English. By Edward Fitzharris. 1681.

There does not appear to be a copy of this book preserved in the British Museum Library : but it is printed in extenso in the fourth volume of Cobbett's Parliamentary History. For writing the same, a prosecution was instituted against Fitzharris. The indictment charges first, that the defendant, described as late of the parish of St. Martin in the Fields, Middlesex, gentleman, did, on the twenty-second day of February, in the thirty-third year of the reign of King Charles the Second, compass treason with one Edmund Everard against the king ; and further, that the defendant as a false traitor did treasonably, maliciously and advisedly write and publish a certain most wicked and traitorous libel intituled *The true Englishman speaking plain English*, in which libel are expressed and declared the treasons and treasonable compassing, imaginations, and purposes of the defendant to excite and persuade the subjects of the King to rise up and rebel against the King and to deprive and depose the King from the style, honour, and royal name of the Imperial Crown of this kingdom, as follows : *If James* (meaning James, Duke of York) *be conscious and guilty, Charles* (meaning the King) *is so too, believe me, both these are brethren in iniquity, they are in confederacy with Pope and French to introduce Popery and Arbitrary Government as their actions demonstrate. The Parliament, Magna Charta, and liberty of the subject, are as heavy yokes they'd willingly cast off, for to make themselves as absolute as their Brother of France ; and if this can be proved to be their aim and main endeavour, why should not every true Briton be a Quaker thus far ? And let the English spirit be up and move all as one man to self defence, nay send if need be to open action and fling off those intolerable Riders.* (meaning the King and the Duke of York.) And in another part of the aforesaid most wicked and traitorous libel are contained among other things these false, seditious, and traitorous sentences following :—*J. and C.* (meaning James, Duke of York and the King) *both brethren in iniquity, corrupt both in root and branch as you have seen, they study but to enslave you to a Romish and French-like yoke. Is it not plain ? Have you not eyes, sense, or feeling ? Where is that old English noble spirit ? Are you become French asses to suffer any load to be laid upon you ? And if you can get no remedy from this next parliament, as certainly you will not, and that the K. repents not, complies not with their advice, then up, all as one man. O brave Englishmen, look to your*

(HERE ENDS THE ORIGINAL WORK)